Fact-Finding in International Arbitration

International Arbitration Law Library

VOLUME 67

Editors

Professor Julian D.M. Lew QC has been involved with international arbitration for more than forty years as counsel, as arbitrator and as an academic. He is the founder and has been the Head of the School of International Arbitration, Centre for Commercial Law Studies, Queen Mary University of London since its creation in 1985. He is now an independent international arbitrator at 20 Essex Street, London.

Stavros Brekoulakis is Professor at Queen Mary University of London and an associate member of 3 Verulam Buildings (Gray's Inn). He is a leading academic in international arbitration and has led, or been involved in, several projects with ICCA, ICC Commission and ILA. He also acts as an independent arbitrator and has been appointed as chairman, sole arbitrator, co-arbitrator and emergency arbitrator under the rules of all the major arbitration rules.

Introduction

Since its first volume published in 1993, this authoritative practitioner-oriented series has published in-depth and analytical works on niche aspects of international arbitration, authored by specialists in the field.

Objective

This authoritative and established series covering in-depth analyses of niche areas appeals to both practitioners and academics. The series includes specific monographs and PhD dissertations of high quality, which are practical and cover issues not fully explored in general texts.

Frequency

A volume is published whenever an interesting topic presents itself.

The titles published in this series are listed at the end of this volume.

Fact-Finding in International Arbitration

The Emergence of a Transnational *Lex Evidentiae*

Julian Bickmann

Wolters Kluwer

Published by:
Kluwer Law International B.V.
PO Box 316
2400 AH Alphen aan den Rijn
The Netherlands
E-mail: lrs-sales@wolterskluwer.com
Website: www.wolterskluwer.com/en/solutions/kluwerlawinternational

Sold and distributed by:
Wolters Kluwer Legal & Regulatory U.S.
7201 McKinney Circle
Frederick, MD 21704
United States of America
E-mail: customer.service@wolterskluwer.com

Printed on acid-free paper.

ISBN 978-94-035-1886-2

e-Book: ISBN 978-94-035-1986-9
web-PDF: ISBN 978-94-035-1996-8

Printed in the Netherlands.

Table of Contents

List of Abbreviations

&	and
a.M.	am Main
AAA	American Arbitration Association
ABGB	Allgemeines Bürgerliches Gesetzbuch (Austrian Civil Code)
ALI	American Law Institute
ALI/UNIDROIT Principles	American Law Institute/International Institute for the Unification of Private Law Principles of Transnational Civil Procedure
ALI/UNIDROIT Rules	American Law Institute/International Institute for the Unification of Private Law Rules of Transnational Civil Procedure
All ER	All England Law Reports
Am L Rep	American Law Reports
AnwBl	Anwaltsblatt (German periodical)
Art.	Article(s)
BeckRS	Beck online Rechtsprechung (German online law reports)
BGB	Bürgerliches Gesetzbuch (German Civil Code)
BGE	Entscheidungen des Schweizerischen Bundesgerichts (law reports of the Swiss Federal Tribunal)
BGH	Bundesgerichtshof (German Federal Court of Justice)
BGHZ	Sammlung der Entscheidungen des Bundesgerichtshofs in Zivilsachen (law reports of the German Federal Court of Justice)
BVerfG	Bundesverfassungsgericht (German Federal Constitutional Court)
CAFTA	Central American Free Trade Agreement
Camp	Campbell's Reports
CAS	Court of Arbitration for Sport

cf	confer
ch	chapter
CIArb	Chartered Institute of Arbitrators
CIArb Guidelines	Chartered Institute of Arbitrators Guidelines for Witness Conferencing in International Arbitration
CIETAC	China International Economic and Trade Arbitration Commission
Cir	United States Circuit Court
Comm	Commercial Court (England and Wales)
CSOH	Court of Session Outer House (Scotland)
D.C.	District of Columbia
D-G	European Commission's Directorate-General for Competition
DIS	Deutsche Institution für Schiedsgerichtsbarkeit (German Institution of Arbitration)
e.g.	*exempli gratia* (for example)
ECJ	Court of Justice of the European Union
ed(s)	editor(s)
edn	edition
et seq	*et sequens/et sequentes* (and the following one/and those that follow)
etc	*et cetera* (and so forth)
EU	European Union
EUR	Euro
EWHC (Comm)	High Court of England and Wales Decisions (Commercial Court)
EWHC (TCC)	High Court of England and Wales Decisions (Technology and Construction Court)
F.2d	Federal Reporter, Second Series (US law reports)
F.3d	Federal Reporter, Third Series (US law reports)
F.Supp.	Federal Supplement
F.Supp.2d	Federal Supplement, Second Series (US law reports)
FAA	US Federal Arbitration Act (Title 9 US Code)
Fordham Int'l L J	Fordham International Law Journal
GAR	Global Arbitration Review
GWE	Gesellschafts- und Wirtschaftsrecht (German periodical)
Hastings Int'l & Comp L Rev	Hastings International and Comparative Law Review
HKIAC	Hong Kong International Arbitration Centre
IBA	International Bar Association
IBA Rules	International Bar Association Rules on the Taking of Evidence
ibid	*ibidem* (in the same place)

ICANN	Internet Corporation for Assigned Names and Numbers
ICC	International Chamber of Commerce
ICCA	International Council for Commercial Arbitration
ICDR	International Centre for Dispute Resolution
ICJ	International Court of Justice
ICSID	International Centre for Settlement of Investment Disputes
IPRax	Praxis des Internationalen Privat- und Verfahrensrechts (German periodical)
IT	information technology
ITA	International Treaty Arbitration
IUSCT	Iran-United States Claims Tribunal
KB	King's Bench (England and Wales)
LCIA	London Court of International Arbitration
Lloyd's Rep	Lloyd's Law Reports
Model Law	United Nations Commission on International Trade Law Model Law on International Commercial Arbitration
n	(foot)note(s)
NCPC	Nouveau Code de procédure civile (French Civil Code)
NJOZ	Neue Juristische Online-Zeitschrift (German periodical)
NJW	Neue Juristische Wochenschrift (German periodical)
NLM	New Lex Marcatoria
No.	number(s)
NZV	Neue Zeitschrift für Verkehrsrecht (German periodical)
O.J.	Official Journal
OGH	Oberster Gerichtshof (Austrian Supreme Court of Justice)
OLG	Oberlandesgericht (German Higher Regional Court)
ONc	Docket number for procedures for the constitution of the arbitral tribunal (Austria)
ÖZPO	Österreichische Zivilprozessordnung (Autrian Code of Civil Procedure)
Pace Int'l L Rev	Pace International Law Review
para(s)	paragraph(s)
PCA	Permanent Court of Arbitration
PILA	Swiss Federal Statute on Private International Law
Prague Rules	Rules on the Efficient Conduct of Proceedings in International Arbitration
QB	Queen's Bench
QBD	Queen's Bench Division
s(s)	section(s)
SCAI	Swiss Chambers Arbitration Institution
SCC	Arbitration Institute of the Stockholm Chamber of Commerce

SchiedsVZ	Zeitschrift für Schiedsverfahren (German Arbitration Journal; periodical)
SFT	Swiss Federal Tribunal
SGHC	Singapore High Court
SIAC	Singapore International Arbitration Centre
Toolkit	Toolkit for Arbitrators on Corruption and Money Laundering in International Arbitration
UKHL	United Kingdom House of Lords
UKSC	United Kingdom Supreme Court
UN	United Nations
UNCITRAL	United Nations Commission on International Trade Law
UNIDROIT	International Institute for the Unification of Private Law
US	United States; United States Reports
USA	United States of America
USC	Code of Laws of the United States of America
USD	United States dollar(s)
v	versus
VAT	value-added tax
VIAC	Vienna International Arbitration Centre
Vienna Rules	Arbitration Rules of the Vienna International Arbitration Centre
VR	Victorian Reports (reports of judicial decisions in Victoria, Australia)
WIPO	World Intellectual Property Organization
WLR	Weekly Law Reports
WL	West Law
WTO	World Trade Organization
WVHB	Waren-Verein der Hamburger Börse
Ybk Comm Arb	ICCA Yearbook Commercial Arbitration (Kluwer 1976 – to date)
Young ICCA	ICCA group for young practitioners
ZPO	Zivilprozessordnung (German Code of Civil Procedure)

Acknowledgements

This book is based on my doctoral thesis entitled *Fact-Finding in International Arbitration: The Emergence of a Transnational Lex Evidentiae*, which was accepted by the Faculty of Law of the University of Cologne, Germany in the summer semester of 2022.

Special thanks go to my academic supervisors, Prof Dr Klaus Peter Berger and Prof Dr Heinz-Peter Mansel. Prof Dr Klaus Peter Berger as one of the leading experts in both Transnational Law and International Arbitration Law accompanied the work with great attention, interest and compassion from the beginning; the book owes crucial suggestions and impulses to him. Likewise, I would like to thank Prof Dr Heinz-Peter Mansel for his careful review and for his valuable remarks on the substance.

I am also deeply indebted to my colleagues, Dr Philipp K. Wagner, Dr Joseph Schwartz, Dr Florian Dupy and Katharina Meyer, who have always encouraged and supported me, and whose practical and analytical perspectives have been a great source of inspiration. The same applies to the many long conversations with Dr Ole Jensen, Tobias Strecker, Fabio Cavalcante and Niklas Andree, who accompanied me in collegial spirit and who were always there to help me with any questions or doubts.

Moreover, I would also like to thank Prof Julian Lew QC and Prof Stavros Brekoulakis for their kind acceptance of my work into the IALL series, as well as Eleanor Taylor and the entire publishing team for their attentiveness and helpful assistance.

The completion of the dissertation would not have been possible without the sympathy and constant support of my family. I would like to thank my parents, Dr Rosvita Bickmann and Dr Dietmar Goll-Bickmann, my brothers, Dr Marius Bickmann and Dr Nicolas Bickmann, my grandfather Werner Goll (†), my aunts, Prof Dr Claudia Bickmann (†) and Prof Dr Sigrun Goll as well as my uncle, Dr Dr Hans-Jürgen Bickmann for their great counsel and constant encouragement.

Finally, and especially, I would like to thank my wife, Larissa da Silva de Freitas, for her unconditional and loving support. This work is dedicated to her and our children, Antonio, Caetano and Cecilia.

Introduction

'Mr. Gantenbein,' she says – I wait. 'I won't tell anyone,' she says, 'that you aren't blind, you can count on that; and you won't tell anyone what you have seen.' This is a contract.[1] (Max Frisch, Gantenbein)

0.1 In law, just as in any other social environment, dealing with facts can be challenging. The present study strives to analyse the emergence of a transnational body of fact-finding rules in international arbitration, where the stakeholders encounter factual controversies in nearly every dispute. In a seemingly 'post-factual'[2] era, and in times of 'alternative facts',[3] it can be quite astonishing how diverse the parties' perception of the same relevant course of events can be. It is, therefore, an essential task of international arbitration procedures to define the disagreements between the parties and seek to determine the truth.[4] In order to resolve factual disputes in an orderly manner, the international arbitration community must thus be able to rely on a robust, consistent and predictable, albeit flexible and adaptive, set of rules.[5] Against this background, the present study shall both provide a stocktaking of the current practice and help to further consolidate the body of fact-finding rules, i.e., the *Lex Evidentiae*[6] in international arbitration.

0.2 On an international procedural level, the term 'fact-finding' bears different meanings. Especially in the contexts of international public law and international criminal law, it is frequently understood as a process of impartial investigation by commissions

---

1. Max Frisch, *Mein Name sei Gantenbein* (Fischer Taschenbuch Verlag 1964) 256: '»Herr Gantenbein«, sagt sie – Ich warte. »Ich werde niemand sagen«, sagt sie,»daß Sie nicht blind sind, verlassen Sie sich darauf, und auch Sie sagen niemand, was Sie gesehen haben.« Das ist ein Vertrag.' Translation by the author.
2. Vincent F Hendricks and Mads Vestergaard, *Reality Lost: Markets of Attention, Misinformation and Manipulation* (Springer International Publishing 2019) 103, 104.
3. *Ibid.*, 49–52.
4. *See* below, Chapter 2, B.II.2.
5. *See* below, Chapter 1, A.II.
6. *See* below, Chapter 1, B.

of international organizations.[7] The Permanent Court of Arbitration (PCA), for example, provides for Fact-Finding Commissions of Enquiry,[8] in particular for inter-state disputes, based on a specific set of rules and conventions. Likewise, the United Nations Fact-Finding Commissions, as well as the Office of the Prosecutor of the International Criminal Court, may engage in similar, commission-based proceedings to fulfil their mandates based on their specific sets of rules.[9]

0.3 The present study, conversely, deals with fact-finding in contexts where independent commissions are (largely) unavailable, such as in international commercial, investment or even sports arbitration. In these proceedings, fact-finding is carried out during the arbitration through the interplay and cooperation between the parties, the tribunal and, in particular, witnesses and experts.

0.4 The thus unfolding procedure is comprised of two relevant phases, namely first, the gathering of facts, i.e., the introduction of the parties' versions of the story into the proceeding,[10] and second, the determination of facts, i.e., the taking of evidence.[11] Accordingly, for the purposes of this study, fact-finding describes the entire fact-related proceeding, at the end of which the tribunal will have established the factual basis to which it will apply the law. Fact-finding thus includes the pleading of facts, the pre-hearing exchange of documents and other information, potential investigations by the tribunal, as well as the taking of evidence by hearing witnesses or experts or examining documents or other relevant material in the later stages. Particularly the first part of the procedure, the gathering of facts, is a frequently overlooked, albeit highly relevant, topic in international arbitration.

0.5 As the present analysis will show, the challenges of fact-finding in international arbitration are manifold (*A*). The purpose of this study is, therefore, to examine these challenges and underlying issues in order to contribute to the further development and stabilization of a transnational set of fact-finding rules (*B*). The analysis is accordingly based on the examination of arbitration laws and rules, legal commentary and awards. This will allow for the identification of commonalities and differences in their approaches, thereby consolidating the current practice (*C*); in particular with regard to the gathering of facts and the taking of evidence (*D*).

---

7. *See* for the historical development, Thomas M Franck and Laurence D Cherkis, 'The Problem of Fact-Finding in International Disputes' 18 Case Western Reserve Law Review 1483, 1493 et seqq.
8. The proceedings are governed by the Permanent Court of Arbitration Optional Rules for Fact-finding Commissions of Inquiry.
9. Mutoy Mubiala, 'The ICC's Interplay with UN Fact-Finding Commissions in Preliminary Examinations' in Morten Bergsmo and Carsten Stahn (eds), *Quality Control in Preliminary Examination: Volume 2* para. 26.3.1.
10. *See* below, Chapter 2.
11. *See* below, Chapter 3.

A CHALLENGES OF FACT-FINDING IN INTERNATIONAL ARBITRATION

0.6 The paramount task of international arbitration is to establish a factual record. To begin with, there is, of course, no independent definition of 'facts' in international arbitration law. For the purposes of this study, the term 'facts' shall describe all occurrences whose objective reality can be proven. This formula, which can be traced back to *Kant*,[12] aims at the delimitation of facts and opinions. Accordingly, opinions are those matters which are not provable but subject to personal contemplation.[13]

0.7 Although there are no statistics available, it is estimated that in 60%–70% of proceedings, factual issues are more relevant than legal issues.[14] In order to apply the law, the tribunal must clarify the factual basis by, for example, establishing the course of contractual negotiations, details of the parties' performances or technical specifications and (in) adequacies of delivered goods or services provided. The more disputed and complex the issues are the more demanding the fact-finding procedures turn out to be. The challenges faced by tribunals, parties and other stakeholders are manifold and occur on different levels.

0.8 Truth[15] versus Efficiency: Just like domestic courts, international arbitration tribunals face the fundamental challenge of striking the right balance between the aim to serve justice by finding the truth and the necessity of conducting the proceedings efficiently. The need for efficiency requires limiting the rounds of submissions, the exchange of documents, as well as the examination of witnesses and experts, at times, even at the risk of overlooking relevant points. Likewise, cut-off dates may render factual submissions and evidence inadmissible even if these may bear on the outcome of the dispute, i.e., even where these seem relevant and material. It follows that, in many cases, the tribunal must be satisfied with the truth in a procedural sense, in the hope that it is sufficiently close to the actual course of events.

0.9 Too much versus too little law: The tribunal's broad discretion combined with the variety of legal traditions leaves the arbitration community with both 'too much'[16] and 'too little law'.[17] Particularly in cases where the body of international arbitration law

---

12. Immanuel Kant, *Kritik Der Urtheilskraft, Akademieausgabe Band 5* (1781) 468; English translation: Immanuel Kant, *Critique of Judgement* (Nicholas Walker tr, Oxford University Press 2007) 297: 'The objects that answer to concepts whose objective reality can be proved are matters of fact (res facti). Such proof may be afforded by pure reason or by experience, and in the former case may derive from theoretical or practical data of reason, but in all cases it must be effected by means of an intuition corresponding to the relevant concepts.'
13. Kant, *Kritik Der Urtheilskraft, Akademieausgabe Band 5* (n. 12) 467: 'Meinungssache'; English translation: Kant, *Critique of Judgement* (n. 12) 296: 'matters of opinion'.
14. Nigel Blackaby and others, *Redfern and Hunter on International Arbitration* (6th edn, Oxford University Press 2015) para. 6.75; Jan Paulsson and Georgios Petrochilos, *UNCITRAL Arbitration* (Wolters Kluwer 2018) 235, 236.
15. *See* particularly on the term 'truth' below, Chapter 2, B.II.2.
16. Joshua Karton, 'International Arbitration as Comparative Law in Action' (2020) 2020 Journal of Dispute Resolution 293, 295–307.
17. *Ibid.*, 307–314.

does not provide any specific rule, clashes may arise if stakeholders from different jurisdictions come together, each convinced of the approach prevalent in their jurisdiction.[18] In practice, each international tribunal may adopt a (slightly) different approach to fact-finding, resulting in different requirements for the submission of pleadings or evidence or the examination thereof. As a matter of course, more uniformization is to be welcomed to meet the need for legal certainty and reliability.

0.10 Substance versus procedure: The underlying challenge is, therefore, to determine which rules to apply. This is particularly challenging as frequently, the distinction between procedural and substantive provisions is not clear-cut in international arbitration. Rather, many issues – such as the burden of proof, standard of proof or even pleading requirements – lie in the 'grey-zone'[19] between procedural and substantive law, as they affect both the investigation of the truth[20] and matters surrounding the organization of the proceedings. In many international proceedings, one can encounter issues that illustrate the difficulties, e.g., where counsel seek to rely on domestic pleading requirements,[21] where tribunals find it adequate to consider the burden of proof when ordering document production,[22] or where a party invokes privilege based on the requirements set out in its jurisdiction.[23]

0.11 Fact-finding and balance of powers: Fact-finding requires a fine balance between party autonomy and the tribunal's mandate and powers to conduct proceedings. In the traditional understanding, it is the parties' right and burden to plead facts[24] and submit evidence,[25] subsequent to which the tribunal resolves their factual disagreements by taking evidence. Ultimately, this concept has been challenged, since the powers and responsibilities of the tribunal and the parties seem to be gradually shifting. Rather than being a silent recipient of pleadings and evidence, the modern law of international arbitration promotes firm case-management and pro-activity of the tribunal.[26] Many modern arbitration rules expect the tribunal to closely follow the submissions from the beginning of the proceedings, to define relevant issues and notify parties thereof, and at times even to investigate facts and evidence on its own motion.[27] Against the backdrop of the traditional understanding, one may therefore say a paradigm shift is underway that could have a lasting impact on future proceedings.

---

18. *See, e.g.*, in case of the burden of proof (Chapter 3, A.II) or the standard of proof (Chapter 3, D).
19. Chrysoula Mavromati, 'The Laws Applicable to the Taking and Evaluation of Evidence in International Arbitration' in Franco Ferrari, Stefan Kröll and Chrysoula Mavromati (eds), *Conflict of Laws in International Arbitration* (2019) 195; Saar A Pauker, 'Substance and Procedure in International Arbitration' (2020) 36 Arbitration International 1, 19.
20. *See* below, Chapter 2, B.II.2.
21. *See* below, Chapter 2, A.II.2.
22. *See* below, Chapter 2, B.III.1.v.(c).
23. *See* below, Chapter 2, B.III.1.v.(a).
24. *See* below, Chapter 2, A.
25. *See* below, Chapter 3, A.
26. One consequence of this is that the tribunal is more closely involved in the fact-finding process and has, for example, the power to address certain issues and, under different sets of rules, demand further information and evidence. This naturally leads to a shift in the distribution of duties and powers, with a lasting impact on fact-finding procedures.
27. *See* below, Chapter 2, C and Chapter 3, A.III.

0.12 Fact-finding from a transnational perspective: As pointed out, there are plenty, probably too many, different solutions for each individual issue which can be identified in a seemingly infinite number of jurisdictions. The consideration of issues in isolation, however – rather than putting these into the overall procedural context of international arbitration – adds to the uncertainty. Similar to domestic proceedings and their codes, arbitration proceedings are based on a highly complex and interconnected system of individual steps and structures, which is why, '[any] alteration of one structure inevitably affects the functioning of the others, which, in turn, affects the entire process'.[28] In other words, the individual issues surrounding fact-finding cannot be satisfactorily addressed without considering the further steps of the arbitral procedure. When analysing the necessary level of detail to be pleaded, for example, other forms of information exchange must always be taken into account.[29] If parties are subject to broad discovery duties, the pleadings may be more vague. If, however, the parties do not exchange any further information in a formalized disclosure procedure, there is more weight on the pleadings to establish the facts.[30] In most cases, the aim must therefore be to find a genuinely arbitral solution, rather than adopting individual approaches from domestic litigation out of their respective context. Accordingly, as will be detailed below, the present study follows a holistic arbitral approach in order to put these issues into the overall procedural context to pave the way for suitable solutions.

0.13 Analysing these issues from a genuinely arbitral perspective ultimately means approaching them from a non-domestic and a-national, i.e., transnational angle. This poses a further challenge, since the analytical tools of traditional legal positivist theories are insufficient to fully capture and describe the process of transnationalization. Nonetheless, as this study will show, the current body of fact-finding rules has largely emerged from and is continuously developing through, its practical application, rather than being sanctioned by domestic legislators.[31]

B LEGAL FRAMEWORK

0.14 Transnational law is 'law in action'.[32] Transnational rules emerge, evolve, and stabilize through their practical application and as a consequence of the density of similar or equal provisions on a specific issue.[33] Accordingly, a study that aims to analyse transnational law must necessarily consider and examine the practice.

28. Arthur R Miller, 'Confidentiality, Protective Orders, and Public Access to the Courts' (1991) Vol. 105 Harvard Law Review 427, 446.
29. *See* below, Chapter 2, A.II.2.
30. *See* below, Chapter 2, A.II.2.
31. *See* below, Chapter 1, A.II.
32. *See* Karton (n. 16), who recently declared international arbitration to be 'comparative law in action'. *See* further the reference to Roscoe Pound, 'Law in Books and Law in Action' (1910) 44 American Law Review 12, who presumably coined the phrase in his famous article.
33. *See* below, Chapter 1, A.II.1.

0.15 While some approaches to research on transnational law primarily review and compare legal solutions within different national jurisdictions,[34] this study shifts the focus from domestic legislation to the very global arbitration law. To that end, rather than comparing the relevant issues and their solutions under domestic laws, the study strives to analyse (a portion of) the multitude of sets of ad hoc and arbitration rules, best practices, awards, and legal commentary, i.e., all bases that reflect the current (but fluid) transnational practice.[35]

0.16 Nonetheless, despite its spontaneous nature, the transnationalization of arbitration law continues to take place primarily within the framework of the (largely) dispositive arbitration laws. It follows that the analysis of transnational fact-finding rules and principles necessarily requires mapping the legal framework within which arbitral *Lex Evidentiae*[36] unfolds, or alternatively, with which transnational arbitration law may clash.[37]

0.17 For this purpose, the present study first reviews the general framework of fact-finding issues as provided for under the arbitration acts of England and Wales, the USA, Germany, Brazil, Spain, Switzerland, Austria and Italy as well as the Model Law. Based on this, the study then examines the respective applicable stipulations under UNCITRAL Arbitration Rules as well as various institutional rules (in particular, ICC, DIS, LCIA, SCC, VIAC, ICDR, HKIAC, SCAI, PCA, AAA and ICSID).

0.18 In most cases, however, both the arbitration laws and rules remain relatively vague, leaving the detailed application of the rules to the tribunal's discretion and/or the parties' agreements. It is therefore indispensable to further consider the practical implementation of the law, in particular (i) the partly codified soft law (such as the IBA Rules, Prague Rules or ALI/UNIDROIT Principles of Transnational Civil Procedure) as well as (ii) uncodified best practices, as captured by legal commentary and arbitral awards. One recurring problem, however, is that legal research in arbitration is regularly impaired by the issue of confidentiality. Despite growing trends towards more transparency, this is especially true in the field of commercial arbitration, where most awards are still not published, which complicates both the academic debate and the further development of the law.

0.19 The situation is different in investment arbitration, where different initiatives push towards more transparency and many awards and other decisions are nowadays publicly available.[38] The practice of investment arbitration is, therefore, a driving force in the development of an arbitral *Lex Evidentiae*, as many arbitral decisions, even outside of investment disputes, are oriented towards it. Similar tendencies can be

34. *See, e.g.*, Emmanuel Gaillard, *Legal Theory of International Arbitration* (Martinus Nijhoff Publishers 2010) 50–52; E Gaillard, 'Transnational Law: A Legal System or a Method of Decision Making?' (2001) 17 Arbitration International 59, 63 with a suggestion on a comparative approach in particular regarding substantive issues.
35. *See* below, Chapter 1, B.I.
36. *See* below, Chapter 1, B.
37. *See* below, Chapter 1, A.III.2.
38. *See, e.g.*, UNCITRAL Rules on Transparency in Treaty-based Investor-State Arbitration.

observed in legal commentary and essays on the law of evidence in international arbitration, which likewise helps to contribute to the uniformization and stabilization of the application of fact-finding rules.

C SCOPE AND STRUCTURE

0.20 Subsequent to this introduction, the analysis of fact-finding in international arbitration is divided into two main parts.

0.21 Chapter 1 provides the theoretical basis and is dedicated to outlining the conceptual foundations of transnational law.[39] It begins with a brief account of the current state of international arbitration law, which is mainly shaped by arbitration rules, guidelines, soft law, case law and legal commentary. Accordingly, it is largely (albeit not entirely) detached from the practices in civil litigation and, importantly, from the interference of domestic laws. This observation triggers the question of whether the current conduct of and body of rules in international arbitration can still be readily described by traditional, positivist legal theory, which centres on the power and authority of national states and their legislators. The answer shall be sought within the different theories of transnational law. In this context, positivist and pluralist theories of transnational law will be briefly contrasted by means of examples (Chapter 1, A). In particular, the pluralist theories of transnational law shift the focus away from state sanctions and control but describe spontaneous and decentralized law-making, independent of municipal legislators. This theoretical premise helps to conceptualize the emergence of a transnational *Lex Evidentiae* in international arbitration *(Chapter 1, B)*.

0.22 Accordingly, based on this theoretical underpinning, in the second and main part of this study, a stocktaking exercise shall provide an account of the current state of fact-finding in international arbitration, by analysing different arbitration acts, institutional and non-institutional arbitration rules and soft law, as well as case law and legal commentary. In accordance with the above definition of fact-finding, this part is divided into two main chapters. Chapter 2 is dedicated to the examination of fact-gathering. Starting with pleading requirements (Chapter 2, A), it proceeds to scrutinize the parties' burdens of disclosure (including document production, depositions and interrogatories and substantive information claims, Chapter 2, B). As a last measure of fact-gathering, this section addresses the tribunal's powers and, potentially, its duty to undertake ex officio investigations (Chapter 2, C).

0.23 In line with the above definition of fact-finding, the Chapter 3 goes on to evaluate the current practice of determining facts, i.e., the taking of evidence. In Chapter 3, A, the study first addresses the modalities of submitting evidence, the most relevant means of evidence (Chapter 3, B), as well as questions relating to the admission thereof (Chapter 3, C). Next, it proceeds to examine the standard of proof (Chapter 3, D) and the assessment of evidence, including facilitations of evidence, such as circumstantial evidence, adverse inferences and *prima facie evidence* (Chapter 3, E).

39. *See* below, Chapter 1.

0.24 The conclusion will then sum up the main findings and summarize the transnational rules of fact-finding in International Arbitration (i.e., the *Lex Evidentiae*) as suggested by the present study.

CHAPTER 1

Conceptual Foundations of Transnational Fact-Finding Rules

1.1 Modern international arbitration law is more than a compromise between different legal cultures. Rather than simply representing the presumed middle ground between the approaches of common law and civil law,[40] international arbitration has established its own institutions, structures and rules, which are continuously transforming international arbitration into a (largely) self-sufficient dispute resolution system, which creates, develops and consolidates its legal framework.[41]

1.2 Accordingly, the current developments in international arbitration are putting the traditional understanding of law to the test. Arbitration law, in the traditional positivist[42] sense (i.e., municipal and international laws on arbitration procedure), primarily has the function of defining minimum requirements and setting boundaries, rather than properly guiding parties and tribunals through the proceedings. The international consensus is that states must interfere with arbitration procedures as little as possible.[43] Moreover, the essence of the laws lies in the fact that they are formulated broadly and abstractly, in order to cover a wide range of similar proceedings and situations. The level of abstractness leaves tremendous room for variety in the practical application.[44]

1.3 Most relevant procedural steps in international arbitration and, in particular, in fact-finding procedures are thus usually not specified by municipal or international arbitration laws. Regularly, these do not contain detailed instructions on the submission of the initial pleadings and the requirements, the exchange of documents and information or the taking of evidence. Nonetheless, despite the lack of detailed

40. *See* below, Chapter 1, B.I.
41. *See* below, Chapter 1, B.II.
42. *See* below, Chapter 1, A.I.
43. *See* below, Chapter 1, A.III.2.
44. Klaus Peter Berger, *The Creeping Codification of the New Lex Mercatoria* (2nd edn, Kluwer Law International 2010) 46.

state-made laws, modern international arbitration can rely upon a robust framework with comprehensive and elaborated rules, many of which result from the very practice of arbitration rather than any formal legislative process.

1.4 This, in turn, does not suggest that there exists one big, unified body of rules indiscriminately applicable to all procedures. Rather, the sources[45] of rules and principles are manifold. Being largely procedural in nature, fact-finding rules are understood to mainly derive from the *lex arbitri*, the arbitration rules (be they institutional or ad hoc), the parties' specific agreements, and the tribunal's discretion.[46] Other fact-finding rules, in particular the burden of proof, are considered to be substantive issues, thus deriving from the applicable *lex causae*.[47] Moreover, some issues are found to be in the 'grey-zone',[48] thus somewhere between procedural and substantive rules, rendering the determination of the applicable law or set of rules even more challenging. Beyond that, as part of the international public policy, due process rules,[49] specifically the right to be heard and the right[50] to equal treatment[51] must also always be upheld.[52]

1.5 Accordingly, while different rules are potentially applicable, many issues that arise throughout the arbitration proceeding are not expressly regulated by state-made laws. Even where specifics are spelt out, these rules are seldomly mandatory and leave many details to the parties' freedom of choice as well as the tribunal's discretion. In this regard, it is vital to recognize party autonomy as a key feature of international arbitration and one of its unique selling points – 'Arbitration is a creature of consent'.[53]

1.6 Regardless of the procedural liberties, parties are neither interested in nor have the resources for designing an individual procedure for each dispute. The same is true for the tribunal, which must ensure that the proceeding is conducted efficiently, fairly and, above all, predictably. This combination of comprehensive freedom, the need for efficiency and the requirement of legal certainty provides a fertile ground for the development of arbitration rules (and specifically fact-finding rules) outside the sphere

---

45. Note that the term 'source of law' is commonly used in positivist concepts of law, and requires certain amendment in the ambit of transnational law, *see* Hans Kelsen, *Introduction to the Problems of Legal Theory: A Translation of the First Edition of the Reine Rechtslehre or Pure Theory of Law* (Bonnie Litschewski Paulson and Stanley L Paulson trs, Clarendon Press; Oxford University Press 1992) 67; Rodrigo Octávio Broglia Mendes, *Arbitragem, Lex Mercatoria E Direito Estatal: Uma Análise Dos Conflitos Ortogonais No Direito Transnacional* (Quartier Latin do Brasil 2010) n 131; James Bernard Murphy, *Philosophy of Positive Law – Foundations of Juris: Foundations of Jurisprudence* (Yale University Press 2012) 3, 4; Berger, *The Creeping Codification of the New Lex Mercatoria* (n. 44) 141; Francesco Galgano, 'The New Lex Mercatoria' (1995) 2 Annual Survey of International & Comparative Law 99, 102, 103.
46. Pauker (n. 19) 1–4, *see also* Art. 19 Model Law.
47. *Ibid., see also* Art. 28 Model Law.
48. Mavromati (n. 19) 195; Pauker (n. 19) 19.
49. Franco Ferrari, Friedrich Rosenfeld and Dietmar Czernich (eds), *Due Process as a Limit to Discretion in International Commercial Arbitration* (Kluwer Law International 2020) 3, 4.
50. *Ibid.*, 19–30.
51. *Ibid.*, 30–32.
52. For one of the key provisions in international arbitration, *see* Art. 18 Model Law.
53. Karton (n. 16) 296.

of influence of national states and their mandatory laws. In other words, it is the driving factor for developing transnational rules in international arbitration. Stakeholders strive to shape their expectations by referring to practices that have been tried and tested in the past. Best practices are thus established, applied and reapplied, consolidated, codified, reformed or – if proven impractical – simply abolished and forgotten.

1.7 Without being passed as law by any municipal or international legislator, these practices shape the parties' and tribunal's understanding of how a proceeding shall and must be conducted, thus stabilizing the stakeholders' expectations. The rules that emerge in this way are characterized, as will be demonstrated, by a comprehensive adaptability and flexibility.[54] The much-cited and controversially discussed IBA Rules on the Taking of Evidence are a vital example of this development. Their flexibility, as well as their (presumably)[55] non-binding nature, however, seems to create difficulties in describing and classifying them in terms of traditional legal theory. Although they are frequently discarded as mere 'soft law', the current study will demonstrate that these rules must, as a matter of fact, be understood as actual and true transnational law.

1.8 The below provides an outline of two basic concepts of transnational law (*A*), before linking the theoretical underpinning to the international arbitration practice and, in particular, fact-finding procedures (*B*).

A TRANSNATIONALIZATION OF ARBITRATION LAW: A BRIEF OUTLINE

1.9 When analysing the body of fact-finding rules in international arbitration, one can, in fact, identify a large number of laws and rules which might be classified as transnational. The existence, dogmatic foundations and questions pertaining to the concept of transnational law remain highly disputed, which, as a first step, warrants a closer look into the origins of the term.

1.10 The prefix 'trans' derives from Latin ('across', 'beyond'), which serves to distinguish the term from 'inter'-national law,[56] i.e., the law between national (or national-rooted) entities.[57] Transnational law thus describes the law which 'extends or

54. Gunther Teubner, 'Globale Bukowina' (1996) 15 Rechtshistorisches Journal 255, 281, 282; English translation: Gunther Teubner, 'Global Bukowina' in Gunther Teubner (ed.), *Global Law Without a State* (Dartmouth 1997) ch 1.
55. *See* below, Chapter 1, A.II. and Chapter 2, B.III.1.a.
56. Samantha Besson and John Tasioulas, *The Philosophy of International Law* (Samantha Besson and John Tasioulas eds, Oxford University Press 2010) 9, 10.
57. *Ibid.*, 17: ' it makes good sense to speak of international law governing the relations between sovereign states through norms and institutions enabling co-operation in matters such as financial regulation, trade agreements, scientific and technological advances, environmental protection, telecommunications, economic development, disaster relief, and the international propagation and protection of human rights, even in the absence of a global sovereign'.

goes beyond national boundaries'.[58] The term was first proposed by *Jessup*, who later became a judge of the International Court of Justice,[59] and famously described transnational law as:

> all law which regulates actions or events that transcend national frontiers. Both public and private international law are included, as are other rules which do not wholly fit into such standard categories.[60]

1.11 Not only is the existence of transnational law highly disputed in the ambit of international arbitration, but among its proponents, there also seems to be little agreement as to its theoretical underpinning. The below briefly outlines two (of many) principal theories, namely first, the concept of positive transnational law (I), and second pluralistic theories of transnational law (II), before addressing the implications of transnational law in the arbitration practice (III).

I Positivist Theories of Transnational Law

1.12 The first approach is the so-called Transnational Positivist Trend.[61] As suggested by its denomination, it is largely based on concepts of positive law. Traditionally contrasted with natural law and customary law,[62] positive law (from Latin *ponere*;[63] to put) commonly describes the law which is "laid down" or imposed by the supreme authority within a political community'.[64] The legal positivism of the twentieth century, despite its many facets and varieties,[65] is often associated with *Kelsen* and *H.L.A. Hart*.

1.13 In *Kelsen's* hierarchical understanding of law, all 'valid' law must be traceable to and validated by a 'basic norm' (*Grundnorm*):

> The Pure Theory of Law works with this basic norm as a hypothetical foundation. Given the presupposition that the basic norm is valid, the legal system resting on it is also valid. *The Basic norm confers on the act of the first legislator – and thus on all other acts of the legal system resting on this first act – the sense of 'ought' [den Sinn des Sollens]*, that specific sense in which legal condition is linked with legal consequence in the reconstructed legal norm, the paradigmatic form in which it must be possible to represent all the data of positive law.[66]

---

58. Graff-Peter Calliess, 'Reflexive Transnational Law' (2002) 23 Zeitschrift für Rechtssoziologie 185, 186.
59. *Ibid.*
60. Philip Jessup, *Transnational Law* (Yale University Press 1956) 1.
61. Gaillard, *Legal Theory of International Arbitration* (n. 34) 45–52.
62. Murphy (n. 45) ix.
63. *Ibid.*, 26.
64. *Ibid.*, 18.
65. *Ibid.*, 2.
66. Hans Kelsen, *Reine Rechtslehre: Einleitung in Die Rechtswissenschaftliche Problematik (Studienausgabe Der 1. Auflage 1934)* (Matthias Jestaedt ed, Mohr Siebeck GmbH & Co KG 2008) 66 (77); English translation: Kelsen (n. 45) 58, emphasis added.

1.14 According to *Kelsen*, legal norms thus do not apply by virtue of their content, but because they have been produced in a particular way, i.e., in accordance with the *Grundnorm*.[67] That is, the *Grundnorm* is the hypothetical basis for the validity of the legal system,[68] as it validates the actions of the first legislator and hence all other acts of the legal order based on it.[69]

1.15 Another main proponent of modern legal positivism, *Hart*, in his famous 1958 essay, suggests that:

> laws are commands of human beings (...),
>
> there is no necessary connection between law and morals or law as it is and ought to be, [and] (...)
>
> a legal system is a 'closed logical system' in which correct legal decisions can be deduced by logical means from predetermined legal rules without reference to social aims, policies, moral standards (...)[70]

1.16 Based on a division between primary and secondary rules, similar to *Kelsen*, *Hart* advocates a hierarchical concept of norms:

> [W]hile primary rules are concerned with the actions that individuals must or must not do, these secondary rules are all concerned with the primary rules themselves. They specify the ways in which the primary rules may be conclusively ascertained, introduced, eliminated, varied, and the fact of their violation conclusively determined.[71]

1.17 As the 'ultimate rule of a system',[72] a (secondary) 'rule of recognition'[73] shall determine 'whether some suggested rule is legally valid'.[74] That is, both in *Hart*'s and *Kelsen*'s traditional understanding of positivism, all 'valid' norms can ultimately be traced back to a confirming decision of the legislator, thus to the competent national state, which itself is validated by a '*Grundnorm*' or 'rule of recognition'.[75]

1.18 Against this backdrop, it seems that positivism, which emphasizes the dominant (or rather, omnipotent) role of national states in creating legal norms, leaves no room for the emergence of transnational – i.e., a-national – legal rules and orders. Nevertheless, even among legal positivists, there are influential proponents who seek to combine these concepts. According to 'Transnational Positivist Trend', transnational law in arbitration is derived from the interaction between international treaties (i.e.,

67. Kelsen (n. 66) 74 (85); English translation: Kelsen (n. 45) 64.
68. As the 'source of law' ('Rechtsquelle'), *see* Kelsen (n. 66) 76, 77 (85); English translation: Kelsen (n. 45) 67.
69. Kelsen (n. 66) 66 (77); English translation: Kelsen (n. 45) 58.
70. Herbert Lionel Adolphus Hart, 'Positivism and the Separation of Law and Morals' (1958) 71 Harvard Law Review 593, n 25.
71. Herbert Lionel Adolphus Hart, *The Concept of Law* (3rd edn, Oxford University Press 2012) 94.
72. *Ibid.*, 107.
73. *Ibid.*, 100 et seq.
74. *Ibid.*, 107.
75. Murphy (n. 45) 215.

the 'collective normative activity of the states') and a-national sets of procedural rules:[76]

> Th[e] representation [of arbitration as a transnational system] recognizes the source of legitimacy of arbitration as rooted in the views developed collectively by the community of nations through instruments such as the 1958 New York Convention, the UNCITRAL Model Law and numerous guidelines which express a common view as to how an arbitration should be conducted so as to be recognized as a legitimate means of adjudication. In other words, in this vision, the source of validity and legitimacy of the arbitral process is found in the collective normative activity of states.[77]

1.19 The 'three-dimensional' concept of international arbitration,[78] in turn, which seems to oscillate between rather traditional positivism and a form of legal pluralism,[79] advocates that arbitration is neither completely national nor truly transnational. In this view, arbitration derives its legitimacy from the 'horizontal' cooperation of 'sovereign legal systems'. However, the theory recognizes that 'the premise of law as within the exclusive dominion of States has for some time been shaken', as its 'vertical dimension reveals itself when more than one legal order occupies the same space'.[80] Even though it stresses the importance of state legislation in the creation of law, the theory also recognizes that non-state entities like ICANN[81] and CAS[82] 'unmistakably – even assertively – view themselves as legal orderings'.[83] This is based on the observation that they 'legislate, they establish adjudicatory bodies involving formal adversarial procedures (...) and they expect that their array of internal sanctions is such that they need no assistance of State officials to make their outcomes effective'.[84]

1.20 Nevertheless, the approach takes issue with the notion of arbitration as an 'autonomous legal order'. The approach considers it a 'great paradox' that international arbitration seeks 'the cooperation of the very public authorities from which it wants to free itself':[85]

76. *See* Gaillard, *Legal Theory of International Arbitration* (n. 34) 45 et seqq.
77. Emmanuel Gaillard, 'International Arbitration as a Transnational System of Justice' in AJ van den Berg (ed.), *Arbitration: The Next Fifty Years* (Kluwer Law International 2012) 68.
78. Jan Paulsson, *The Idea of Arbitration* (Oxford University Press 2013) 48 et seq.
79. *Ibid.*, 48: 'It would be childish to adopt a broad posture of either favouring or opposing the primacy of states. Historical processes are at work and cannot be ignored. Insight is more likely to emerge from the starting point of agnostic and non-committed views as to desirable social structures. The power of organizations that cut across the horizontal lines of purported state authority is to be seen not only in industrial and social or religious organizations, but also of course in regional political unions to which considerable portions of sovereignty are overtly ceded. What is important is to understand the capacity of a variety of social institutions for authoritative decision-making.'
80. *Ibid.*
81. Internet Corporation for Assigned Names and Numbers.
82. Court of Arbitration for Sport.
83. Paulsson (n. 78) 48.
84. *Ibid.*
85. *Ibid.*, 30.

> States have never accepted that the norms of the international community are derived from 'progressive tendencies' embraced by other states; they insist on their own individual adhesion. They are even less likely to embrace such amorphous norms as limitations on their national laws, in their national space, when dealing with a private-law feature like arbitration.[86]

1.21 The main proponents of positivist theories of transnational arbitration law, therefore, agree that transnational law was a given in practice and could be traced back to the cooperation of domestic states on an international level. Nevertheless, there is still disagreement about the concrete relationship between states and transnational arbitration law, as well as the theoretical and factual implications. As one can observe, both theories emphasize the sovereignty of municipal states but recognize at least the practical application of laws and rules which emerge outside the formal legislative process.

II Pluralistic Theories of Transnational Law

1.22 The positivist approach is opposed by various pluralistic legal theories. Their main premise is that legal norms and laws can emerge and develop outside the scope of municipal or international state legislation. While the common idea is that law-making without the state is possible, they neither deny the de facto powers of national states nor the coercive force of domestic or international state law. Rather, pluralist theories accept and advocate a variety of 'co-existing and overlapping regulatory regimes'.[87]

1.23 From a pluralist point of view, different regimes may thus apply to the same issue, each claiming the authority to provide an adequate solution. In particular, different regimes may arise out of self-governance in areas with (i) little regulation, (ii) limited state intervention and/or in areas (iii) for which the municipal laws do not provide satisfactory solutions.[88]

1.24 The IBA Rules on the Taking of Evidence may serve as an illustrative example. They are practice-made rules which seek to regulate a highly relevant issue in international arbitration, namely the organization of evidential procedures.[89] This issue is not governed by any national or international law, at least not in detail. For this reason, stakeholders in international arbitration strive to establish and have recourse to

---

86. *Ibid.*, 41.
87. Peer Zumbansen, 'Transnational Legal Pluralism' (2010) 1 Transnational Legal Theory 141, 144; Similarly, Berger, *The Creeping Codification of the New Lex Mercatoria* (n. 44) 51 describes the New Lex Mercatoria as a '"third" legal system between domestic and international law'; Paul Schiff Berman, *Global Legal Pluralism: A Jurisprudence of Law Beyond Borders* (Cambridge University Press 2012) 3 et seq.; Calliess (n. 58) 187.
88. Berger, *The Creeping Codification of the New Lex Mercatoria* (n. 44) 46: 'Due to their high degree of abstraction, domestic legal rules are inapt to provide workable regulatory frameworks for the increasingly complex business world. Privatized rule-making is effected by specialists in the field.'
89. *See* below, Chapter 1, B.II.

specific protocols which are capable of meeting their needs and providing legal certainty. As will be analysed in more detail below, the rules on document production, for example, have become an almost integral part of international arbitration proceedings, and even more so in investment arbitration.[90] The IBA Rules are frequently applied even if there is no express legal basis for their application. This suggests that, especially in international arbitration, the rules created through conduct and established practices can be binding upon the stakeholders without ever having been sanctioned by any legislator, thus amounting to 'law' in a transnational sense.

Pluralistic theories of transnational law accordingly seek to shift the focus away from national legislation, emphasizing the role of spontaneous rulemaking (*1*). These thus established rules are found to oscillate between law and social norms (*2*). Accordingly, pluralistic theories of transnational law are apt to regard international arbitration as an emerging transnational legal order (*3*).

1 *Decentralized and Spontaneous Rulemaking*

1.25 Both of the positivist approaches towards transnational law outlined above agree that, to a certain degree, the creation of norms in transnational arbitration transcends national jurisdictions. Both concepts recognize the limitations of traditional, essentially positivist theories of law to describe the phenomenon of transnational law. Nonetheless, the underlying positive theories uphold the authority of national states to create and enforce laws. Non-state and particularized creation of norms, however, is the very essence of transnational law:

> [T]o invoke an idea of transnational law is to suggest that law has new sources, locations and bases of authority.[91]

1.26 In other words: transnational law is, by its very definition, non-state law. Law that is rooted in collective normative activity of domestic legislators, in turn, is to be classified as international law.[92]

1.27 Rather than being created as 'top-down' law – i.e., passed by a sovereign onto the citizens as regulatory subjects – transnational law emerges 'bottom-up' out of a specific situation.[93] It is solution-driven and usually surfaces when stakeholders are confronted with a particular issue which is not appropriately governed by positive laws. If an adequate solution is found, and if subsequently the same conflict emerges, the

90. *See* below, Chapter 2, B.III.1.a.
91. Roger Cotterrell, 'What Is Transnational Law?' (2012) 37 Law & Social Inquiry 500, 502.
92. *Ibid.*: 'From this viewpoint, transnational law, when properly called law, is an extension of national sovereign jurisdictions, or the creation (through recognised mechanisms of international law) of law by international agencies or through international instruments ultimately validated by the express or tacit authority of sovereign states. Viewed in such a perspective, a category of transnational law apart from municipal or international law might seem redundant.'
93. Gralf-Peter Calliess and Peer Zumbansen, *Rough Consensus and Running Code: A Theory of Transnational Private Law* (Hart Publishing 2010) 125; Berger, *The Creeping Codification of the New Lex Mercatoria* (n. 44) 43; Berman (n. 87) 242, 243.

stakeholders may repeat their conduct. In doing so, the stakeholders may test and, where necessary, adapt the solution. Through ongoing repetition, the individual case thus becomes a practice, and the practice becomes a binding usage.

1.28 In the past decades, pluralistic theories on commercial matters have mainly concerned the *New Lex Mercatoria* (NLM), mapping out a transnational legal order in international trade. The findings are highly relevant for the purposes of this study on transnational rules in international arbitration because they rely upon the same mechanism. In fact, the law of international arbitration is at times referred to as procedural *lex mercatoria*[94] or *lex mercatoria arbitralis*.[95]

1.29 Goldman, one of the founding fathers of the NLM,[96] defines it as 'the law proper to international economic relations'.[97] Its rules were:

> mainly, if not exclusively, transnational and the origin is customary and thus spontaneous, notwithstanding the possible intervention of interstate or state authorities in their elaboration and/or implementation.[98]

1.30 A comparable observation – albeit not specifically referencing commercial transactions – was already made by *Ehrlich* in the early twentieth century. Based on his analysis of legal interaction in his remote and rural home region (*Bukowina*), *Ehrlich* found that, in many instances, 'living law' (*gelebtes Recht*) held more significance for the stakeholders than the official state law (*Juristenrecht*):

> The effect of state norms for decision is usually very much over-estimated. The whole matter hinges upon action by the parties, who very often fail to act altogether. Often the statute remains unknown to a considerable part of the population; again the parties for whose benefit it was enacted often lack the material means to enforce their claim, or, because of the actual distribution of power, they lack self-confidence or confidence in the authorities.[99]

1.31 With express reference to *Ehrlich*, *Teubner* finds the same to be true on a global level in modern society ('Global Bukowina'). Here, the living law was frequently more forceful and binding upon the stakeholders than any municipal or international law:

> On the global level, Eugen Ehrlich seems to be vindicated in his opinion that a centrally produced political law is marginal compared with the lawyers' law in

94. Luke R Nottage, 'The Procedural Lex Mercatoria: The Past, Present and Future of International Commercial Arbitration' [2006] Sydney Law School Research Paper No. 06/51.
95. Hans-Patrick Schroeder, *Die Lex Mercatoria Arbitralis: Strukturelle Transnationalität Und Transnationale Rechtsstrukturen Im Recht Der Internationalen Schiedsgerichtsbarkeit* (Sellier European Law Publishers 2007).
96. Berger, *The Creeping Codification of the New Lex Mercatoria* (n. 44) 1.
97. Berthold Goldman, 'The Applicable Law: General Principles of Law – The Lex Mercatoria' in Julian Lew (ed.), *Contemporary Problems in International Arbitration* (Springer Netherlands 1987) 113.
98. *Ibid.*, 114.
99. Eugen Ehrlich, *Grundlegung Der Sociologie Des Rechts* (1913) 297; English translation: Eugen Ehrlich, *Fundamental Principles of the Sociology of Law* (Walter L Moll tr, Routledge 2017) ch XVI.

> practical decision-making and especially with the living law of the Bukowina (Ehrlich, 1913). Therefore, political theories of law will be of little use in understanding legal globalization. This is true for positivist theories which stress the unity of state and law as well as for those critical theories which tend to dissolve law into power politics.[100]

1.32 While different approaches may view the issue from different angles, they have in common that they perceive and understand transnational law as emerging spontaneously, separate from the state's governmental powers. Accordingly, they recognize decentralized, private rulemaking and private governance as the core of social and commercial interactions.

1.33 Importantly, the conduct thus established is marked by a high degree of flexibility and adaptability to the changing practical needs, which itself contributes to providing a reliable framework ('Lex mercatoria is soft law, not weak law').[101] This is of particular importance in light of the ongoing debate on the overregulation of the international arbitration proceeding,[102] which is otherwise marked by extensive liberties.

1.34 Pluralistic theories of transnational law, therefore, prove helpful in describing and analysing the current events in the ambit of international arbitration. Here, one can observe a constant process of uniformization of the procedural conduct, driven by the stakeholders themselves. Said uniformization evolves largely without any interference from domestic jurisdictions and their legislators. The more stakeholders repeat their practices, the more binding they seem to become upon on them. By the same token, the practices thus established lose their authority if no longer referred to and relied upon. This illustrates both the strength and flexibility of private governance as a form of spontaneous law-making.

2 *Between Law and Social Norms*

1.35 Establishing the legitimacy of spontaneous law and decentralized legal orders remains a great challenge, especially because of the degree to which this concept breaks from traditional concepts of law. Due to the very nature of transnational law as non-state law, it seems inadequate to seek its ultimate validation in domestic or international legislation.[103] Against this backdrop, pluralistic theories of transnational law analyse the social and factual mechanisms which turn informal practices into binding usages. Yet, the dogmatic foundations remain in dispute.

---

100. Teubner, 'Globale Bukowina' (n. 54) 260; English translation: Teubner, 'Global Bukowina' (n. 54) ch 1.
101. Teubner, 'Globale Bukowina' (n. 54) 281, 282; English translation: Teubner, 'Global Bukowina' (n. 54) ch 1.
102. Daniel Greineder, 'The Limitations of Soft Law Instruments and Good Practice Protocols in International Commercial Arbitration' (2018) 36 ASA Bulletin 907, 907 et seq.; Ugo Draetta, 'The Transnational Procedural Rules for Arbitration and the Risks of Overregulation and Bureaucratization' (2015) 33 ASA Bulletin 327, 340.
103. *See* above, Chapter 1, A.II.

1.36 In the ambit of the pluralist theories of transnational law, some commentators have recourse to theories of customary law,[104] according to which law is found to exist where a certain practice can be observed (objective element) which the relevant stakeholders consider to be law (subjective element).[105] In international arbitration, however, it remains challenging to identify a consensus as to the legal quality of different recurring practices (such as the application of the IBA Rules[106]). Therefore, lacking the required subjective element, the theories of customary law do not seem to be promising to describe transnational law in international arbitration.

1.37 The theory of 'reflexive transnational law', however, suggests shifting the focus from 'sanctions' and 'social control' to 'communication',[107] in order to explain these acts of spontaneous rulemaking. Mainly based on *Luhmann's* Systems Theory,[108] *Teubner*[109] advocates that the legal system, like all social systems (such as economy, science, religion), was created and developed through the basic operation of communication.[110] This notion, i.e., the legal system based on communication, allows for the conceptualization of law-making outside the state legislative process. Within the theory of reflexive law, accordingly, (transnational) legal norms[111] emerge and are confirmed through repetitive communication:

> Norms will just come naturally with the decisions, ie, as the ratio decidendi of adjudication. *Norms as the structure of a legal system are thus produced by communication, as a by-product of processing legal acts.* However, a single judgment might not be sufficient to produce a norm, for norms are abstract. They

104. Goldman (n. 97) 114: 'The criterion for determining the ambit of lex mercatoria that I would follow thus does not solely reside in the object of its constituent elements, but also in its origin and its customary, and thus spontaneous nature.'
105. *See, e.g., North Sea Continental Shelf* [1969] ICJ Reports 3 [77]: 'Not only must the acts concerned amount to a settled practice, but they must also be such, or be carried out in such a way, as to be evidence of a belief that this practice is rendered obligatory by the existence of a rule of law requiring it. The need for such a belief, i.e., the existence of a subjective element, is implicit in the very notion of the opinio juris sive necessitatis.'
106. Cf. below, Chapter 2, B.III.1.
107. Teubner, 'Globale Bukowina' (n. 54) 270 et seq; Gunther Teubner, 'Introduction to Autopoietic Law', *Autopoietic Law: A New Approach to Law and Society* (de Gruyter 1988) 3.
108. Luhmann's Systems Theory can be described as a grand theory which strives to describe all aspects of social life (i.e., the society) in one comprehensive theoretical framework. Luhmann has developed his theory in over more than 600 publications including 40 books as well as in his famous 'note box' (Zettelkasten), consisting of more than 90,000 documents. The Niklas Luhman-Archive can be accessed online via https://niklas-luhmann-archiv.de, *see*, for instance, Niklas Luhmann, *Introduction to Systems Theory* (Dirk Baecker ed, Peter Gilgen tr, Polity 2013); Niklas Luhmann, *Das Recht der Gesellschaft* (1st (reprint), Suhrkamp 2002).
109. *See, inter alia,* Teubner, 'Introduction to Autopoietic Law' (n. 107); Gunther Teubner, 'Global Private Regimes: Neo-Spontaneous Law and Dual Constitution of Autonomous Sectors in World Society?' Paper prepared for the Workshop on 'Globalisation and Public Governance' 17/18 March 2000 European University Institute, Florence; Teubner, 'Globale Bukowina' (n. 54).
110. Calliess (n. 58) 195, 196.
111. Luhmann describes norms as structures which are resistant to disappointment, i.e., expectations that are maintained even if they are initially frustrated, *see* Luhmann, *Das Recht der Gesellschaft* (n. 108) 61, 62, 80, 81.

> are generalizations of several judgments, and they are more stable than a single case decision.[112]

1.38 Validation in a positivist sense was not required as long as the relevant parties adapted their conduct to the expectations created by the thus constituted norms.[113] As observed by *Callies* and *Renner*, these norms oscillate 'between law and social rules', being imperative on the stakeholders without being sanctioned by any national state.[114]

1.39 While the theory of reflexive law is indeed helpful in describing the spontaneous recreation of rules independent of a centralized legislator, the test to be applied may be too subtle to provide the necessary foreseeability and legal certainty. In practice, it will be difficult to establish if certain 'communications' have been sufficiently consolidated to create 'norms' in the sense of the theory.

1.40 Other approaches, therefore, draw less on communication than on the very agreement of the stakeholders. Particularly in modern transactions, it is 'the contract which assumes the genuine function of a source of law'.[115] Due to the trend towards self-governance and in contrast with the view of traditional legal positivism, the contract must be considered a proper 'source of law'.[116] In that regard, it is not necessary to conclude multi-lateral agreements as a means of validation, since the lack of 'consensual density'[117] is compensated for by the repetitive use of specific practices, which have thus been stabilized and consolidated. Especially in the ambit of international arbitration, this approach is promising since arbitration is a creature of consent[118] and deeply rooted in party autonomy. As a matter of course, autonomy has become a 'veritable leitmotif of international arbitration'.[119] Likewise, the constant exchange of ideas within the arbitration community and the efforts towards more transparency[120] help to consolidate the spontaneously created rules in international arbitration.

1.41 Nonetheless, the question arises of how one can ensure compliance with the so constituted, presumably transnational rules. In particular, the mere 'normative force of usages',[121] even if confirmed by agreement, is found to be insufficient:

---

112. Calliess (n. 58) 195, 196, emphasis added.
113. Teubner, 'Introduction to Autopoietic Law' (n. 107) 4: 'Circularity replaces extra-legal foundations of law as does Kelsen's fictitious Grundnorm.'
114. Gralf-Peter Calliess and Moritz Renner, 'Between Law and Social Norms: The Evolution of Global Governance' (2009) 22 Ratio Juris 260, 263 et seq., 277.
115. Berger, *The Creeping Codification of the New Lex Mercatoria* (n. 44) 141.
116. Galgano (n. 45) 102, 103.
117. Berger, *The Creeping Codification of the New Lex Mercatoria* (n. 44) 143.
118. Karton (n. 16) 296, 297; Margaret L Moses, *The Principles and Practice of International Commercial Arbitration* (2nd edn, Cambridge University Press 2012) 18.
119. George A Bermann, 'The Self-Styled "Autonomy" of International Arbitration' (2020) 36 Arbitration International 221, 232.
120. *See, e.g.*, the UNCITRAL Rules on Transparency in Treaty-Based Investor-State Arbitration.
121. Royston Miles Goode, Ewan McKendrick and Herbert Kronke, *Transnational Commercial Law: Text, Cases, and Materials* (2nd edn, Oxford University Press 2015) 1.64 et seq.

> There is, however, the world of difference between a course of conduct that is frequently, or even habitually, followed in a particular commercial community as a matter of grace and a course which is habitually followed, because it is considered that the parties concerned have a legally binding right to demand it. As Ungoed-Thomas J. pointed out in Cunliffe-Owen v. H Teather & Greenwood [1967] 1 W.L.R. 1421, 1438: 'What is necessary is that for a practice to be a recognised usage it should be established as a practice having binding effect.'[122]

1.42 Rather, 'external validation of some kind – whether by legislation, jurisprudence, or doctrine' is 'an essential prerequisite' for transnational law.[123] From a practical point of view, this is reasonable, particularly considering the need of all stakeholders for legal certainty and reliability in international arbitration. Independent of the theoretical underpinning, it is in the interest of all stakeholders to have robust and predictable structures that can be relied upon.

1.43 And in fact, as will be detailed below, the arbitration community has developed various means of ensuring compliance with its rules. Apart from informal sanctions within the business community – such as "black lists," withdrawal of membership rights, forfeiture of bonds'[124] – arbitral tribunals are equipped with far-reaching powers to control the conduct of the proceedings. Tribunals may, for example, apply inner-procedural mechanism to enforce their decisions, such as drawing adverse inferences from the party's conduct[125] or punishing a non-compliant party on the costs.[126] These mechanisms have proven to be highly efficient, as, in the vast majority of cases, the parties fulfil the tribunal's decisions without being subject to any coercive force.

1.44 It follows that the international arbitration community is capable of creating its own rules (in particular through decentralized agreements and ongoing efforts of consolidation) specifically designed to meet its particular needs and is well-equipped to ensure their observation. The legal certainty thus provided allows these rules to be classified not only as informal practices but, in fact, as transnational law.

III Transnational Arbitration Law in Practice

1.45 In practice, the concept of transnational law is still sharply opposed by its critics. The main objection is that transnational law lacked legitimacy, since any real law had to be validated by a national or international legal order. Specifically, only the national state was able to exercise coercive powers within a defined territory, which is the

122. *General Reinsurance Corp v Forsakringsaktiebolaget Fennia Patria [1983] QB 856* 874.
123. Goode, McKendrick and Kronke (n. 121) para. 1.66.
124. Berger, *The Creeping Codification of the New Lex Mercatoria* (n. 44) 139.
125. *See* below, Chapter 3, E.II.3.
126. Brendan Casey and others, 'Abuse of Document Production in International Arbitration: Remedies When the Adverse Inference Falls Short' (2020) 86 Arbitration: The International Journal of Arbitration, Mediation and Dispute Management 394, 405, 406.

necessary basis for the creation of laws.[127] Accordingly, to this day, objections are raised against the very concept of transnational arbitration law.[128] Even advocates of transnational tendencies in international arbitration struggle with the idea of non-state law-making.[129]

1.46 As explained in the above section, the positivist objections can readily be addressed with a shift of paradigm: focusing on the repetitive conduct and internal 'checks and balances'[130] rather than on state legislation and coercive force helps to conceptualize the emergence of transnational arbitration law beyond the municipal state's control.[131] Nevertheless, independent of the theoretical classification, it is vital to examine the 'substance of the legal phenomena' of transnational law, despite any potential disagreement as to its '*nomen juris*'.[132] In other words, independent of their theoretical underpinning, international arbitration practitioners must accept that certain (transnational) rules exist and are imperative within the arbitration community without being 'validated' by national states and their rules of recognition.

1.47 This has been recognized in practice by various awards and decisions (*1*). Where conflicts between domestic law and transnational arbitration law arise, the arbitration community can respond with different tactics, through adaptation, reconciliation or evasion (*2*). Despite the (mostly) private character of the evolving legal framework, in practice, the rules are largely binding upon the parties, secured by different means of enforcement, including the enforcement of awards (*3*).

1 Transnational Arbitration Law in Awards and Decisions

1.48 The positivist dismissive attitude to transnational law does not do justice to the practice. Even from a traditional, positivist point of view, it is difficult to ignore the recent phenomenon that globally imperative rules emerge on a private, rather than on a public level. This is particularly true in the ambit of international arbitration where many of these a-national norms, rules and principles are frequently more binding upon the stakeholders than most domestic arbitration laws. In fact, the latter are, to a large degree, dispositive and usually a mere fall back option in case of lacunas. As will be

127. Cf. the concise summary of common objections in Teubner, 'Global Bukowina' (n. 54) 7; *see* for a detailed discussion of the usual criticism Berger, *The Creeping Codification of the New Lex Mercatoria* (n. 44) 64–148.
128. *See, e.g.*, Dr Husain M Al-Baharna, 'International Commercial Arbitration in a Changing World' (1994) 9 Arab Law Quarterly 144, 145: 'So long as the lex mercatoria lacks the sanctions of national or international law, it is presumptuous to say that the ICA is governed by it. Such a point of view would be unsustainable in legal theory, besides being unacceptable to most governments. The cause of the ICA would not be served any better by a theory which runs in the face of governmental opposition.'
129. *See* above, Chapter 1, A.I.
130. Berger, *The Creeping Codification of the New Lex Mercatoria* (n. 44) 47.
131. *See* above, Chapter 1, A.II.
132. Draetta (n. 102) 329.

analysed extensively in the below sections on fact-gathering[133] and fact-determination,[134] nearly the entire arbitral process was designed through private governance, while domestic arbitration laws mainly serve to ensure that basic procedural guarantees are respected.

1.49 This is confirmed in practice by a number of awards and court decisions. These can be divided into two groups, namely (i) those which address and apply transnational rules in international arbitration and (ii) those which address international arbitration as a transnational legal order.

1.50 Already in 1982, the tribunal in *Kuwait v AMINOIL* dealt with the transnational character of international arbitration and the procedural liberty following therefrom:

> Having regard to the way in which the Tribunal has been constituted, its international or rather, transnational character is apparent. It must also be stressed that French law has always been very liberal concerning the procedural law of arbitral tribunals, and has left this to the free choice of the Parties who, often, have not had recourse to any one given national system. French law has thus befriended arbitrations the transnational character of which has been well in evidence. This tendency has been enhanced for the future by recent French legislation (Decree n° 81-500 of 12 May, 1981) which, even more specifically than before, affords recognition to transnational arbitration.[135]

1.51 In a similar vein, the tribunal in *Dallah Real Estate v Pakistan*, an ICC proceeding, found it adequate to apply 'transnational general principles' to determine the validity of the arbitration agreement:

> Judicial as well as Arbitral case law now clearly recognize that, as a result of the principle of autonomy, the rules of law, applicable to an arbitration agreement, may differ from those governing the main contract, and that, in the absence of specific indication by the parties, such rules need not be linked to a particular national law (French Cour de Cassation, 1er-civ., Dec. 20, 1993, Dalico), but may consist of those transnational general principles which the Arbitrators would consider to meet the fundamental requirements of justice in international trade.[136]

1.52 Subsequently, however, the courts of England and Wales denied the enforcement of the award. In particular, it was found that while transnational law may be part of the French law,[137] the tribunal had misapplied the law when assuming that the defendant

133. *See* below, Chapter 2.
134. *See* below, Chapter 3.
135. *Government of the State of Kuwait v The American Independent Oil Company (AMINOIL), Ad-Hoc Award of 24 May 1982* [1984] IX Ybk Comm Arb 71, 73.
136. *ICC Case No 9987, Partial Award of 2001* [2010] 2(4) International Journal of Arab Arbitration 339, 358. Note, however, that two arbitrators declared their reservations regarding 'the concept of a transnational procedural law independent of all national laws'.
137. *Dallah Real Estate and Tourism Holding Company v The Ministry of Religious Affairs, Government of Pakistan* [2010] 3 WLR 1472 [15].

had consented to the arbitration agreement.[138] This illustratively shows the conflicts which may arise between transnational law and domestic law, and which will be analysed in the section below.[139]

1.53 More recently, different awards have addressed and confirmed the existence of a transnational public policy. As a famous example, the Tribunal in *World Duty Free v Kenya* reviewed different international treaties, initiatives, court decisions and awards to conclude that the prohibition of corruption was a fundamental element of transnational public policy:

> In light of domestic laws and international conventions relating to corruption, and in light of the decisions taken in this matter by courts and arbitral tribunals, this Tribunal is convinced that bribery is contrary to the international public policy of most, if not all, States or, to use another formula, to transnational public policy. Thus, claims based on contracts of corruption or on contracts obtained by corruption cannot be upheld by this Arbitral Tribunal.[140]

1.54 Corresponding decisions can also be found in domestic case law. In 1994, the Swiss Federal Tribunal, for example, asserted the existence of:

> transnational or universal public policy including 'fundamental principles of law which are to be complied with irrespective of the connections between the dispute and a given country'.[141]

1.55 The French courts in particular have gone even further and have issued a series of arbitration-friendly decisions, emphasizing the autonomy of international arbitration and its transnational character.[142] In a number of proceedings, the courts have had to decide whether an award vacated in one jurisdiction could still be readily enforced in other jurisdictions.[143] Different French courts have found that this was the case, since international arbitration was delocalized and the awards did not depend on any specific jurisdiction. In *Hilmarton Ltd v Omnium de Traitement et de Valorisation* it was held that:

> the award rendered in Switzerland is an international award which was not integrated in the legal system of that State, so that it remains in existence even if

138. *Ibid.*, 88 et seq.
139. *See* below, Chapter 1, A.III.2.
140. *World Duty Free Co Ltd v The Republic of Kenya, ICSID ARB/00/7* Award of 4 October 2006 [157]; *see* for further examples Jean-Michel Marcoux, 'Transnational Public Policy as an International Practice in Investment Arbitration' (2019) 10 Journal of International Dispute Settlement 496, 507, 508.
141. *SFT, Judgment of 19 April 1994* BGE 120 II 155 167; translation by Gaillard, *Legal Theory of International Arbitration* (n. 34) 60.
142. *See* for an overview on French case law, Gaillard, *Legal Theory of International Arbitration* (n. 34) 60 et seqq.
143. Meik Thöne, 'Delocalisation in International Commercial Arbitration' [2016] SchiedsVZ 257, 258.

> set aside and its recognition in France is not contrary to international public policy.[144]

1.56 The decision in *Putrabali Adyamulia v Rena Holding* stimulated a subsequent debate on an international level,[145] which will be addressed in more detail in the following section. Here, the Cour de Cassation also confirmed the position that an award which had been set aside in another country (England) could be readily enforced in France:

> An international arbitral award, which is not anchored in any national legal order, is a decision of international justice whose validity must be ascertained with regard to the rules applicable in the country where its recognition and enforcement are sought.[146]

1.57 The court thus emphasized that the arbitral award is rooted in neither domestic jurisdiction but is a product of transnational law and thus of a transnational arbitration order.

1.58 This brief survey of different awards and decisions reflects a certain tendency in parts of the international practice to recognize the existence of transnational law in the ambit of international arbitration. While the specific recognition by states is not a constituent element, the overview shows that transnational arbitration is not a mere theoretical construct but a given in practice. The survey confirms that in practice, transnational laws, rules and principles have been applied on different levels and in different stages of the arbitral proceeding, namely to (i) define the relationship between the tribunal and the parties, (ii) interpret legal duties and assess the parties' legal relationship, (iii) establish issues of transnational public policy as limitations for both the parties and the tribunal and (iv) define the relationship between international arbitration and municipal laws.

2 Conflicts Between Domestic Law and Transnational Arbitration Law

1.59 As a matter of course, the co-existence of different regulatory regimes commonly leads to conflicts of power. These conflicts lie at the very core of legal pluralism.[147]

1.60 One objection to the transnational viewpoint is that it failed to acknowledge that parties have selected the seat and the applicable substantive law deliberately.[148]

---

144. *Omnium de Traitement et de Valorisation v Hilmarton, Cour d'Appel, Versailles, Decision of 29 June 1995* [1996] XXI YBK Comm Arb 524, 526.
145. Philippe Pinsolle, 'The Status of Vacated Awards in France: The Cour de Cassation Decision in Putrabali' (2008) 24 Arbitration International 277; Richard W Hulbert, 'When the Theory Doesn't Fit the Facts' (2009) 25 Arbitration International 157; Thöne (n. 143).
146. *Société PT Putrabali Adyamulia v S A Rena Holdings, Cour de cassation, 29 June 2007, (2007) Revue de l'Arbitrage* 507, 514; translation by Gaillard, *Legal Theory of International Arbitration* (n. 34) 63.
147. Berman (n. 87) 23 et seq.
148. Thöne (n. 143) 260, 261.

Moreover, it is found to be paradoxical that international arbitration proclaimed autonomy while still seeking the assistance of domestic courts to enforce awards.[149] Therefore, different jurisdictions continue to struggle with the concept of a transnational law, emphasizing the states' sovereignty and final word.[150] This is particularly true for the courts of England and Wales. In *Bank Mellat v Helleniki Techniki*, for example, the court found:

> Despite suggestions to the contrary by some learned writers under other systems, our jurisprudence does not recognise the concept of arbitral procedures floating in the transnational firmament, unconnected with any municipal system of law.[151]

1.61 Yet, independent of the seat of arbitration, arbitral tribunals are in fact known to be concerned with implementing the party agreements, since party autonomy becomes all the more important as the influence of the state diminishes.[152] Further, it is often precisely the desire of parties in international arbitration to limit state courts' intervention rather than to extend it.[153] The fact that in individual cases, domestic states may deny the enforcement of international awards does also not allow any conclusions to be drawn regarding the legal quality of international arbitration. Rather, owing to the New York Convention,[154] international awards have substantially higher chances of being enforced in foreign jurisdictions than judgment issues in domestic litigation proceedings.[155] Finally, the objection that only some jurisdictions have accepted the notion of transnational law whereas others have rejected it[156] does not change the findings which are presented in this study. Since transnational law evolves and emerges out of usages, agreements and ongoing established practices, the validation or recognition by national states is not a constituent element of transnational law.[157]

1.62 When a domestic court determines that an arbitral tribunal has gravely exceeded its authority, it will deny enforcement and set aside the award. International arbitration may respond to this with strategies of (i) adaptation (i.e., complying with a respective ruling in future), (ii) reconciliation (i.e., identifying a common denominator between

149. Paulsson (n. 78) 30.
150. *Ibid.*, 42 et seq.; *see* for the current practice in Luxembourg Michael Wietzorek, 'Luxembourg's Rejection of the French Approach to the Recognition and Enforcement of Annulled Arbitral Awards' (2019) 37 ASA Bulletin 316, 331–334.
151. *Bank Mellat v Helliniki Techniki SA* [1984] QB 291, 301.
152. Karton (n. 16) 296.
153. *See, e.g.*, Arjit Oswal, 'Limiting Judicial Intervention (Another Pro International Arbitration Step)' (*Young ICCA Blog*, 19 November 2014).
154. *See* below, Chapter 1, A.III.3.
155. On a side note, presumed difficulties of enforcing an individual domestic judgment do not allow any assumptions to be made about the legal quality and autonomy of the jurisdiction where it was rendered.
156. Paulsson (n. 78) 42–44.
157. *See* above, Chapter 1, A.II.1.

municipal and transnational rules)[158] or (iii) evasion (i.e., avoiding certain jurisdictions at the enforcement stage[159] or already when drafting arbitration agreements[160]).

1.63 In sum, conflicts between transnational law and municipal (or international) law in arbitration are inevitable as a result of overlapping regulatory regimes. However, the international arbitration community has proven itself robust and resilient, able to rely on different strategies to solve or avoid these conflicts.

3 Enforcement and Recognition of Awards

1.64 As pointed out, a main issue that positivist theories take with the concept of transnational law is the question of the enforceability of awards which are rendered based on transnational law.[161] While under the above theories on transnational law, enforcement of awards through the use of states' coercive powers is not a constituent element,[162] from a practical point of view it is vital to emphasize that enforcement of the awards is the rule, rather than the exception.

1.65 In fact, in most cases, the losing party respects the decision of the tribunal without the need for recourse to the coercive powers of a national state. A 2008 study showed that in only 11% of cases, the participants needed to enforce the award.[163] It is suggested that the main reason for compliance with awards is not the threat of legal enforcement, but rather the need 'to preserve a business relationship'.[164] That is, the parties' practical considerations often make it necessary to implement the award, which in turn creates an informal form of coercion.

158. In *Texaco Overseas Petroleum Company v The Government of the Libyan Arab Republic, Ad-Hoc Award of 19 January 1977* https://www.trans-lex.org/261700 [III.1.C] the sole arbitrator, Prof. René-Jean Dupuy presided over a contractual dispute, which in his view was subject to both Libyan law and 'principles of international law'. In his decision he held: 'The application of the principles of Libyan law does not have the effect of ruling out the application of the principles of international law, but quite the contrary: it simply requires us to combine the two in verifying the conformity of the first with the second.' Accordingly, rather than choosing between either domestic or international (or more properly, transnational) law, Dupuy found a common denominator and reconciled the approaches. This is of course less challenging if one can align the domestic substantive law with transnational principles.
159. *See* above, Chapter 1, A.III.1.
160. It is for good reason that practical guides on arbitration law in different jurisdictions regularly mention whether or not a particular jurisdiction is arbitration-friendly. *see, e.g.*, Nils Schmidt-Ahrendts and Aaron de Jong, 'The "Right" Place of Arbitration: How Germany Might Profit from Brexit' [2018] SchiedsVZ 281, 282.
161. *See* above, Chapter 1, A.III.2.
162. *See* above, Chapter 1, A.II. and III.
163. Queen Mary University of London, 'International Arbitration Survey 2008: Corporate Attitudes: Recognition and Enforcement of Foreign Awards' 10; *see also ibid.* 8: '84% of respondents indicated that the opposing party had honoured the award in full in more than 76% of cases. Only 3% reported that an award debtor had failed to comply with the award. During the interviews, corporate counsel reported that more than 90% of the awards were honoured by the non-prevailing party.'
164. Queen Mary University of London (n. 163) 8 This also seems to be sector-specific: 'The highest level of compliance appears in the re-insurance, pharmaceuticals, shipping, aeronautics and oil and gas sectors.'

1.66 Apart from the mostly voluntary compliance, the nexus between international arbitration and (inter)national law comes into play. Due to the pro-arbitration approach of the New York Convention adopted in 169 jurisdictions,[165] where necessary, the enforcement of awards is the rule rather than the exception. This is generally the case, independent of whether a tribunal applies domestic law, international law or transnational principles,[166] as long as considerations of (transnational) due process and public policy (Article V (1)(b);(2)(b) New York Convention)[167] are safeguarded, and the tribunal gave rise to parties' agreements on the composition of the arbitral authority and the arbitral procedure (Article V(1)(d) New York Convention). The global pro-enforcement approach is the very basis of the coexistence of national laws and transnational arbitration, confirming that they are complementary rather than mutually exclusive.

1.67 It follows that the enforcement of arbitration awards, independent of whether they are based on national or transnational law, is duly secured, providing the legal certainty and reliability necessary for the further development of the transnational legal framework.

IV Conclusion

1.68 Both the general question of whether transnational law exists, and the theoretical justification of transnational law remain two highly controversial issues.

1.69 While positivist theories of transnational law refer to soft law as well as the collective normative activity of the states, different pluralistic theories of transnational law suggest that law can come into being spontaneously, without the need for a centralized national legislator. Rather, law in a transnational sense emerges where stakeholders are faced with specific issues in practice, find an adequate solution and subsequently reapply said solution if the issue reoccurs. Thus, the individual case becomes a practice, and the practice becomes a binding usage. At the same time, transnational law is highly flexible and adaptive. Best practices are subject to ongoing revision and adaptation in order to suit the requirements of an ever-changing legal and commercial environment. Furthermore, the practices established in this way are backed by internal means of enforcement. Thus, constant repetition and consolidation of certain practices stabilizes the expectations of the stakeholders and ultimately leads to the emergence of law without the involvement of domestic legislatures.

1.70 In practice, while a certain reluctance is still evident, different tribunals and domestic courts (especially in Switzerland and France) have confirmed the existence of transnational arbitration law. The courts of England and Wales, however, remain more

165. *See* for a list of contracting states, https://www.newyorkconvention.org/list+of+contracting+states.
166. *See* for the further requirements, Art. V New York Convention.
167. Ferrari, Rosenfeld and Czernich (n. 49) 4; Charles T Kotuby and Luke A Sobota, *General Principles of Law and International Due Process: Principles and Norms Applicable in Transnational Disputes*, vol 6 (Oxford University Press 2017) 72, 73.

reluctant and emphasize their own final say and ultimate power. As has been pointed out, the acceptance of transnational law by domestic states is not a constituent element. Further, in every pluralistic legal environment where different legal regimes potentially govern the same subject, conflicts of power will be found. To negotiate the interaction between domestic states and transnational arbitration, the arbitration community has developed three strategies to resolve or avoid these clashes. It may accordingly either (i) adapt to the conflicting rules or decisions of a domestic jurisdiction, (ii) reconcile different approaches, or (iii) evade a specific jurisdiction, the rules of which are in conflict with (transnational) arbitration law.

B THE EMERGENCE OF A TRANSNATIONAL *LEX EVIDENTIAE*

1.71 In 1994, as a result of an extensive survey of evidentiary rules before international arbitration tribunals, *Brower* expressed his wish for the emergence of a (transnational) '*lex evidentia*':

> [I]t is perhaps justified to entertain some hope that just as a lex mercatoria has developed to a certain extent to provide common principles of international commercial dealing, a *lex evidentia* is emerging that will embrace common principles for the submission of evidence by parties and for the evaluation of evidence by international tribunals.[168]

What has happened since then?

1.72 Dealing with a multitude of legal traditions and cultures, understandings and approaches, each arbitration proceeding may potentially still be governed by an individual composition of fact-finding rules. While it might be true that no fact-finding procedure is like the other, this is not to say that arbitration proceedings are inherently unreliable or unpredictable. Rather, tribunals and parties are both able to make use of their procedural liberties by having recourse to a comprehensive body of soft laws and best practices, both codified and uncodified. As will be shown below, in many aspects of the procedure, this leads to an extensive synchronization of the fact-finding rules in international arbitration.

1.73 Based on the network of rules, experiences and practices, the arbitral process becomes streamlined and uniformized through repetitive application of and recurrence of established practices. Through this process, especially (but not only), the rules applicable to fact-finding procedures in modern arbitration are forming a fluid, non-uniform body of rules. In countless international arbitrations every year, the rules are tested, evaluated, reapplied, or eventually, abolished and forgotten. Again, the driving force behind this development is not the legislative acts of national courts but the very arbitral practice. As will be analysed in more detail below, these rules – to

168. Charles N Brower, 'Evidence Before International Tribunals: The Need for Some Standard Rules' (1994) 28 The International Lawyer 47, 58.

borrow the term from Brower[169] – form the new *Lex Evidentiae*[170] in international arbitration.

1.74 As will be detailed in this section, as an important step toward creating a genuine arbitral law, the international arbitration community is slowly overcoming the 'Common Law versus Civil Law' dichotomy (*I*). The thus developing best practices are frequently codified by non-state formulating agencies, which further consolidate the fact-finding rules (*II*).

I Overcoming the 'Common Law Versus Civil Law' Dichotomy

1.75 For decades now, many studies on international arbitration have been based on a comparison between common law and civil law approaches towards different legal issues. Recently, however, the question was raised whether this 'global paradigm' has finally come to an end.[171] As this study shall elaborate, the necessary answer to this question is yes, for two main reasons.

1.76 First, the 'Common Law versus Civil Law' paradigm is frequently imprecise and thus prone to errors. Within both the 'legal families'[172] of common law and civil law a multitude of different jurisdictions can be identified, which are in themselves hardly comparable. Some civil law jurisdictions, for example, are largely based on the Romanistic tradition, whereas other civil law jurisdictions derive from the German or

169. *See* for further references to 'lex evidentia' (in particular in the context of adverse inferences) Jeremy K Sharpe, 'Drawing Adverse Inferences from the Non-Production of Evidence' (2006) 22 Arbitration International 549, 552; Menalco J Solis, 'Adverse Inferences in Investor–State Arbitration' (2018) 34 Arbitration International 79, n 145; Karyl Nairn, Timothy G Nelson and Paula Henin, 'Evidentiary Inferences: Do Choice of Law and Seat Make a Difference?' in Neil Kaplan and Michael J Moser (eds), *Jurisdiction, Admissibility and Choice of Law in International Arbitration: Liber Amicorum Michael Pryles* (Wolters Kluwer 2018) 163–173; *see also* Pauker (n. 19): 'Though the applicability of doctrines like lex evidentia (92) or voie directe exceed the scope of this article, it is submitted that if those doctrines are to be accepted, the borderline nature of a legal issue or question as located with the grayzone between substance and procedure may well be taken into account within that discretion.'

170. Wilhelm Halbfass and Klaus Held, 'Historisches Wörterbuch Der Philosophie, Evidenz' (Schwabe Verlag 2017): The terminology is based on Latin lex, legis (law) and evidentia, evidentiae. Evidentia was first introduced into Latin by Cicero, based on Greek ἐνάργεια. Historically, it describes the 'evidence' in the sense of an apparent truth, which does not require any proof. However, the terminology has undergone a certain transformation. Over the course of time, it has been used both in a subjective (assigned to the perceiving subject) and an objective sense (with an emphasis on the objective binding nature of the perceived). That is, 'evidentia' can describe both an objective reason for subjective certainty, and as subjective basis of what is objectively certain. Because of this wide scope, the term 'evidentia' seems suitable to describe the law of evidence in international arbitration in a broad sense, i.e., all norms relating to fact-gathering and fact-determination.

171. Klaus Peter Berger, 'Common Law vs. Civil Law in International Arbitration: The Beginning or the End?' (2020) 36 Journal of International Arbitration, 295.

172. *See* for the terminology, H Patrick Glenn, 'Comparative Legal Families and Comparative Legal Traditions' in Mathias Reimann and Reinhard Zimmermann (eds), *The Oxford Handbook of Comparative Law* (2nd edn, Oxford University Press 2019) 436 et seq.

Nordic legal tradition.[173] Nonetheless, despite their, at times, tremendous differences, they are classified as 'civil law'. By contrast, common law jurisdictions – despite their joint tradition – have evolved autonomously from each other and developed distinct features. Typical US civil litigation, for example, differs markedly from civil litigation in England and Wales, especially since the Woolf Reforms.[174] Nonetheless, for practical reasons, authors often focus their studies on a few (presumably) representative jurisdictions. The analysis and conclusions thus drawn may, however, be different, if two (or more) other representative jurisdictions of the respective legal family are selected. Beyond that, the 'common law versus civil dichotomy' is based on a Eurocentric[175] perspective, as it largely ignores other legal traditions, such as different religious laws or the diverse Far Eastern legal systems. This, accordingly, contributes to the impreciseness of the approach.

1.77 As a second reason to set aside the classic paradigm, the analysis of modern and independent transnational arbitration law requires the examination of arbitral practice in particular reflected awards, legal commentary, arbitration rules and best practices, rather than ascertaining the trends within different national jurisdictions.[176] While modern arbitration rules have, without a doubt, been inspired and influenced by the laws and practices applicable before domestic courts,[177] the arbitration community has since emancipated itself. The current legal framework is more than a mere compromise between presumed common law and civil law practices;[178] it has outgrown domestic procedural rules and reflects many features which can be found in neither common law nor civil law litigation, but which are proprietary features of arbitration. In fact, this is necessary, since organizing international, private proceedings pose challenges which are at times very different from the requirements of standardized civil proceedings in domestic courts.

1.78 This does not mean that comparisons of different domestic rules of civil procedure were utterly superfluous. Rather, they may help to understand and outline specific issues in question, before going into the analysis from an arbitration point of view. However, and importantly, one must accept that the answers or solutions are not necessarily to be found in common law, civil law or a presumed compromise between these legal traditions. Accordingly, the analysis of the transnationalization of international arbitration requires a paradigm shift with regard to the very transnationality of rules in international arbitration. Analysing document production in international

173. *See* for an extensive overview on the evolution of legal system taxonomies, Mariana Pargendler, 'The Rise and Decline of Legal Families' (2012) 60 American Journal of Comparative Law 1043, 1056-1060.
174. *See* below, Chapter 2, C.I.
175. Glenn (n. 172) 433-436.
176. As suggested by Gaillard, *Legal Theory of International Arbitration* (n. 34) 50 et seq. in particular on substantive issues.
177. *See*, for an extensive study on the US-American influence, Pedro J Martínez-Fraga, *The American Influence on International Commercial Arbitration: Doctrinal Developments and Discovery Methods* (Cambridge University Press 2009) 51 et seq.
178. As, for example, rather humbly suggested by Peter Ashford, *The IBA Rules on the Taking of Evidence in International Arbitration: A Guide* (Cambridge University Press 2012) 9.

arbitration, for example, does not require an examination of document production before civil courts, as the arbitration community has found its own way and established its own rules, which nowadays are applicable independent of whether US law requires broad discovery and/or German law allows the parties to withhold adverse information.[179]

1.79 This holds true for other issues that may arise during the arbitral procedure.[180] In many instances, the arbitral law itself provides elaborated solutions that fit the requirements of stakeholders in international arbitration, which often differ from domestic solutions. It follows that these issues must be addressed from an inner-arbitral perspective and be guided by the prevailing principles, guidelines and requirements of international arbitration – rather than seeking answers in domestic litigation procedures.

II Codification by Formulating Agencies

1.80 International arbitration relies heavily on best practices. While these best practices are initially established through the reproduction of the stakeholder's experience or the recourse to legal commentary and awards, it is in particular the private formulating agencies who stabilize their application by closely following and observing the practice and proposing rules based thereon. The conduct thus established oscillates 'between laws and social norms',[181] which explains the general difficulty of analysing and classifying them by means of traditional positivist theories. Commonly, they are referred to as '"Notes", "Rules", "Guidelines", "Checklists", "Principles", or "Protocols", and "best practices standards'",[182] and collectively as 'soft law'.[183]

1.81 As a first prominent and successful example of codified best practices in international arbitration proceedings, tribunals frequently have recourse to the IBA Rules on the Taking of Evidence in International Arbitration ('*IBA Rules*').[184] The aim of these Rules is to bridge the gap between the diverging practices in the taking of evidence (*see* Foreword to the IBA Rules).[185] According to Article 1(1) IBA Rules, they can be applied either based on the parties' agreement or the tribunal's decision. In practice, however, the rules are seldom incorporated into the arbitral agreement but are usually adopted by the tribunal of its own accord. According to the 2015 Queen Mary Survey on International Arbitration, 77% of the respondents have seen the IBA

179. *See* below, Chapter 2, B.III.
180. *See, e.g.*, the pleading requirements in international arbitration, below Chapter 2, A, or rules pertaining to different means of evidence, below Chapter 3, B.
181. Calliess and Renner (n. 114) 263 et seq.
182. Berger, 'Common Law vs. Civil Law in International Arbitration: The Beginning or the End?' (n. 171) 304.
183. *See* above, Chapter 1, A.II.2.
184. *See* in particular below, Chapter 1, A.III.3.
185. Cf. Amy Cohen Kläsener and Alexander Dolgorukow, 'Die Überarbeitung Der IBA-Regeln Zur Beweisaufnahme in Der Internationalen Schiedsgerichtsbarkeit' [2010] SchiedsVZ 302, 302.

Rules being used in arbitrations,[186] while 69% have found them to be effective.[187] Importantly, they contain provisions on the consultation of evidentiary issues (Article 2), document evidence and document production (Article 3), witness evidence (Article 4), expert evidence (Articles 5 and 6), the conduct of the evidentiary hearing (Article 8) and the admissibility and assessment of evidence (Article 9). Since the IBA Rules were first issued in 1999, they have been subject to two revisions in 2010 and 2020.[188] The 2020 revision included, *inter alia,* a specific provision on remote hearings (Article 8.2), which exemplifies the rules' ability to adapt to an ever-changing legal and factual environment.

1.82 While the IBA Rules are generally perceived to be a success, especially non-common lawyers have voiced their concerns regarding their application. It is argued that the IBA Rules reflect a certain bias towards common law practices and thus do not sufficiently consider other legal traditions.[189] In particular, the document production procedure[190] as well as the examination of witnesses[191] under the IBA Rules are perceived to closely resemble common law disclosure (or, respectively, discovery) procedures,[192] which are foreign to many other jurisdictions.[193]

1.83 As a reaction to the criticism, the drafters of the Prague Rules proposed a new set of soft law with a palpable focus on presumed civil law practices. Like the IBA Rules, the Prague Rules contain specific provisions regarding documentary evidence (Article 4), witness evidence (Article 5), expert evidence (Article 6) and the conduct of the hearing (Article 8). Notably, the Prague Rules seek to strengthen the tribunal's proactive role (*see* Article 2)[194] by confirming the Tribunal's mandate to direct the course of the proceeding – to notify the parties of relevant issues (Article 2.4), to express preliminary views (Article 2.4.e), to promote settlements (Article 9), and to know and apply the law *(iura novit curia,* Article 7).

1.84 As another important force in promoting the uniformization of international arbitration proceedings (and with this, of course, fact-finding rules), the United Nations Commission on International Trade Law (UNCITRAL) has published and updated non-binding legislative texts which may serve as a template, or at least an

186. Queen Mary University of London, 'International Arbitration Survey 2015: Improvements and Innovations in International Arbitration' 35.
187. *Ibid.*, 36.
188. *See* for an overview, 1999 IBA Working Party, 2010 Rules of Evidence Review Subcommittee and 2020 IBA Rules of Evidence Review Task Force, *Commentary on the Revised Text of the 2020 IBA Rules on the Taking of Evidence in International Arbitration* (2021).
189. Kabir Duggal and Rekha Rangachari, 'A Challenger Approaches: An Assessment of the Prague Rules on the Efficient Conduct of Proceedings in International Arbitration' (2020) 37 Journal of International Arbitration 27, 27, 28.
190. *See* below, Chapter 2, B.III.1.a.
191. *See* below, Chapter 3, B.
192. Duggal and Rangachari (n. 189) 29, 30.
193. To put this criticism into perspective, while document production proceedings under the IBA Rules – if not handled properly – may result in extensive exchange of documents, their scope is, compared to proper discovery proceedings, fairly limited, *see* below, Chapter 1, C.1.a.
194. Berger, 'Common Law vs. Civil Law in International Arbitration: The Beginning or the End?' (n. 171) 298; Duggal and Rangachari (n. 189) 34, 42–44.

orientation, for national arbitration acts and rules of international arbitration institutions. Importantly, the Model Law on International Commercial Arbitration was first published in 1985 and updated in 2006. Moreover, in 2012, UNCITRAL released a digest of case law on the Model Law to further promote its uniform application. Thus far, the Model Law has been voluntarily adopted in eighty-three different jurisdictions.[195] Other jurisdictions (such as Brazil),[196] while not fully harmonizing their arbitration laws with the Model Law, have integrated individual key provisions into their national arbitration acts. Despite the differences between jurisdictions and legal cultures, this astonishing number indicates a far-reaching synchronization of arbitration proceedings on a global level, which supersedes the frequently cited 'common law versus civil law' dichotomy.[197]

1.85 Equally importantly, the UNCITRAL Arbitration Rules were first published in 1976 as 'the product of representatives of the international community of States, irrespective of national ideologies and economic power'.[198] Subsequently, in 2010 and 2013, they underwent a comprehensive revision. While the UNCITRAL Arbitration Rules only apply where parties have made a respective agreement (*see* Article 1 (1)), in practice, they exceed the mere character of rules for ad hoc arbitrations. In an extensive survey, the UNCITRAL identified twenty-six arbitration institutions which have adopted institutional rules based on or inspired by the UNCITRAL Arbitration Rules.[199]

1.86 The interaction between the UNCITRAL Model Law, UNCITRAL Rules, arbitration acts and institutional rules is not linear (i.e., from UNCITRAL to the practice) but, in fact, circular. Just as legislators, institutions and other codifying agencies seek inspiration from the UNCRITRAL, the UNCITRAL follows the events and recent developments in international arbitration and revises their rules accordingly.[200] This contributes to the above-described formation of transnational structures in international arbitration.

1.87 As a further example, in 2004, UNIDROIT, in cooperation with the American Law Institute (ALI), published the ALI/UNIDROIT Principles of Transnational Civil Procedure ('*ALI/UNIDROIT Principles*'). In 1999, *Stürner* drafted the first feasibility study,[201] laying out the objective of harmonizing international procedural law based on an

195. 'Status: UNCITRAL Model Law on International Commercial Arbitration (1985), with Amendments as Adopted in 2006' https://uncitral.un.org/en/texts/arbitration/modellaw/commercial_arbitration/status.
196. André Abbud, Daniel Levy and Rafael Francisco Alves, *Brazilian Arbitration Act: A Case Law Guide* (Kluwer Law International 2019) ix.
197. Berger, 'Common Law vs. Civil Law in International Arbitration: The Beginning or the End?' (n. 171).
198. Paulsson and Petrochilos (n. 14) v.
199. 'Arbitration Centres | United Nations Commission on International Trade Law' https://uncitral.un.org/en/texts/arbitration/contractualtexts/arbitration/centres.
200. Jan Paulsson and Georgios Petrochilos, *Revision of the UNCITRAL Arbitration Rules* (2006) para. 5.
201. For an outline of the developments leading to the formation of a working group, *see* Rolf Stürner, 'The Principles of Transnational Civil Procedure, An Introduction to Their Basic Conceptions' (2005) 69 Rabels Zeitschrift für ausländisches und internationales Privatrecht 201, 204 et seqq.

extensive study of the approaches in domestic codes and other sets of rules.[202] The result is a comprehensive body of principles, addressing all relevant issues that arise in civil proceedings and arbitrations alike and, accordingly, different matters of fact-finding (especially pleadings and evidence). While the focus of the project was to promote harmony in transnational litigation, the principles are also applicable to 'international arbitration, except to the extent of being incompatible with arbitration proceedings'.[203] The Principles are supplemented by a model set of rules ('Rules of Transnational Civil Procedure', the '*ALI/UNIDROIT Rules*') which neither UNIDROIT nor the ALI have formally adopted but reflect the Reporters' model implementation of the Principles (*see* Appendix; Reporters Study). The ALI/UNIDROIT Principles, while thus far seldom referred to in international arbitration, play an important role in harmonizing fact-finding procedures.

1.88 Besides these rather comprehensive projects, there is also a multitude of other notes, guidelines and sets of rules which cover specific areas of the arbitral proceeding, such as the IBA Rules on Transparency, Notes on Organizing Procedures, and ICC Rules on Virtual Hearings. These are just a few of many examples, which, to a varying degree, influence the arbitration practice and the conduct of the proceedings.

1.89 Lastly, and as an equally powerful instrument that must not be overlooked when analysing the origins and the codification of transnational law in international arbitration, tribunals frequently lay out the basic terms of the arbitration via the first procedural order.[204] Said procedural order is seldom hand-drafted in view of that very proceeding but is usually based on either publicly available models or procedural orders from prior proceedings. Accordingly, by relying on prior models, tribunals confirm and consolidate certain procedural rules which have proved to be efficient. This contributes to the codification of best practices, albeit in a less coordinated and thus more spontaneous way.

III Conclusion

1.90 The above findings suggest that international arbitration is currently subject to an ongoing process of transnationalization.

1.91 Applying the above theoretical findings to the current development of arbitration law, especially with regard to fact-finding, one finds that best practices emerge which are continuously applied, adapted or rejected, thus contributing to the emergence and ongoing development of a transnational *Lex Evidentiae*. It is noteworthy that the practice relies less and less on rules from domestic civil litigation but establishes an independent conduct suitable for the needs of international arbitration. So-called

202. Rolf Stürner, 'Transnational Rules of Civil Procedure – Study LXXVI – Doc 1 – Feasibility Study' 4, 5.
203. American Law Institute (ALI) and UNIDROIT, *ALI/UNIDROIT Principles of Transnational Civil Procedure* (Cambridge University Press 2006) para. P-D.
204. Berger, 'Common Law vs. Civil Law in International Arbitration: The Beginning or the End?' (n. 171) 312.

formulating agencies closely follow recent events in international arbitration and codify, and thus consolidate, successful best practices. The IBA Rules on the Taking of Evidence, the Prague Rules and the ALI/UNIDROIT Principles are important examples of this.

1.92 Although the resulting rules do not originate from domestic legislators, they are for the most part more binding and imperative on the parties than the largely dispositive provisions of domestic arbitration acts. On an inner-procedural level, the tribunal may ensure their application by either drawing adverse inferences in case of non-compliance or by punishing the respective party on the costs. However, experience shows that, in most cases, parties voluntarily comply with these rules and usually respect the tribunal's decisions and awards without coercive powers needing to be employed. In any case, the arbitral-friendly approach of most jurisdictions guarantees enforcement in more than 150 countries across the globe.

CHAPTER 2

Introduction of Facts into the Proceedings

2.1 While the term 'fact-finding' is often used as a synonym for the taking of evidence, this is only half the story. Before a tribunal takes evidence, it must hear both parties' versions of the story, potentially allow for certain disclosure procedures and then link the facts so introduced into the dispute with a legal rule. Only those facts which may have an influence on the application of the law require further examination. This means that, in an essential first step of each proceeding, all potentially relevant factual materials and issues are fed into the proceedings. Only then may the tribunal proceed to determine the 'truth' (in a procedural sense)[205] through the taking of evidence, i.e., the second relevant phase of fact-finding.

2.2 The rules on fact-finding are largely developed by practice. Against the backdrop of the above theoretical underpinning, in international arbitration, there is a strong trend towards a body of transnational rules on the gathering of facts, as the first pillar of the *Lex Evidentiae*. Specifically, in modern arbitration, facts are introduced through the parties' pleadings (*A*), through the mandatory exchange of information, such as document production (*B*), and potentially through investigations of the tribunal (*C*).

A PLEADING OF FACTS

2.3 Every dispute is initiated by a statement of claim[206] in which the claimant pleads the facts that they seek to rely upon. This is followed by the statement of defence,[207] by means of which the defendant shall comment on the assertions and present their version of the facts. These pleadings of facts are essential for each arbitration as they both define the scope of the dispute and provide information based on which the tribunal can apply the law and ultimately render a decision. No tribunal will initiate

205. *See* below, Chapter 2, B.II.2.
206. *See, e.g.*, Art. 23 Model Law, or respectively, a Request for Arbitration, *see* Art.4 ICC Rules.
207. *See, e.g.*, Art. 23 Model Law, or respectively, an Answer to the Request, *see* Art. 5 ICC Rules.

proceedings on its own motion, nor will it take evidence on matters it was not informed about.[208]

2.4 Nonetheless, the issue of pleadings of facts and the specific requirements in international arbitration proceedings has been given little attention thus far, and there is little commentary and case law available. Likewise, most arbitration rules only reflect the very basic requirements of pleadings by stating that the parties must 'plead the facts they rely upon'; or plead 'all relevant facts and circumstances'.[209] More technical issues, such as the required level of detail, the burden to address all assertions as well as fiction of admission are not expressly governed. Yet, while the burden of proof and other evidence-related topics are frequently debated in the international arena, the importance of the parties' pleadings must not be underestimated. In fact, the burden of proof is 'one in a series of legal burdens':

> Far and away the most important burden is that of initiating the proceedings in which proof will count. This is the burden of suing, filing, applying, petitioning, charging or claiming and, in general, all other burdens follow it.[210]

2.5 Before the tribunal can even think about taking evidence, it is crucially in the parties' own interest to properly plead their specific cases as a basis for the entire proceeding. In legal terms, this is referred to as the 'burden of pleading'.[211] The applicable pleading standard will necessarily influence the likelihood of each party's success: a claimant that has only minimal knowledge on the relevant facts and seeks to obtain information during an arbitration proceeding will be at a disadvantage if it is required to provide full details from the outset. A respondent, who may simply contest a claimant's allegation, will have a higher chance of success than a defendant who must present his own version of the story and is required to offer evidence for each of its assertions. Thus, defining and knowing the applicable pleading standards is paramount for parties seeking to properly make their case. The same is true for the tribunal. It must be aware of the requirements and apply them uniformly to both parties to ensure a fair proceeding.

2.6 Despite the importance of the issue, arbitration laws and rules, as well as soft law, only demand very basic requirements (*I*). Yet, certain other rules and guidelines can be distilled under the prevalent regime of fact pleading in international arbitration (*II*). Moreover, the distribution of the burden of pleading generally follows the burden of proof but is ultimately subject to the tribunal's discretion (*III*). Lastly, tribunals are encouraged to set cut-off dates to enhance the efficiency of rounds of submissions and thus the arbitral proceedings as a whole (*IV*).

---

208. *See* below, Chapter 2, C.
209. *See* below, Chapter 2, A.I.
210. Stephen Wexler and Jack Effron, 'Burden of Proof and Cause of Action' (1983) 29 McGill Law Journal 468, 469 on litigation in common law.
211. *See, e.g.*, American Law Institute (ALI) and UNIDROIT (n. 203) para. P-21A.

I Minimum Pleading Requirements under Arbitration Laws and Rules

2.7 Despite current trends to strengthen the role of the tribunal during the fact-finding procedure,[212] a survey of different arbitration laws and rules confirms that it remains largely the parties' burden to introduce the facts they seek to rely upon into the dispute. That being said, most arbitration laws and rules contain few specific provisions. As the below survey shows, they only stipulate minimum requirements for factual pleadings in the parties' statements of case, namely by stating in slightly varying language that parties shall set out the basic facts in support of their respective position.

2.8 For instance, Article 23 (1) Model Law stipulates that 'the claimant shall state the facts supporting his claim' and 'the points at issue', while 'the respondent shall state his defence in respect of these particulars, unless the parties have otherwise agreed as to the required elements of such statements'. Nearly the same wording can be found in the German Arbitration Law under section 1046 (1) ZPO. The English Arbitration Act generally leaves it to the tribunal to decide 'whether any and if so what form of written statements of claim and defence are to be used' and 'when these should be supplied' (*see* Articles 34.1, 34.2(c)).

2.9 Not only the arbitration laws but also many arbitration rules stipulate only very basic requirements as regards the content of the pleadings. Article 20.2 (a), (b), 21.2 of the UNCITRAL Rules (and, in the same language, Article 20.2 (b), (c), 20.2 of the SCAI Rules) demand that the statements of claim and defence contain a 'statement of the facts supporting the claim' as well as the 'points at issue'. Article 4.3 (c) of the ICC Rules orders the claimant to submit 'a description of the nature and circumstances of the dispute giving rise to the claims', while the respondent shall submit 'its comments as to the nature and circumstances of the dispute giving rise to the claims and the basis upon which the claims are made' (Article 5.1 (c) ICC Rules). Moreover, under Article 23.1 (c) of the ICC Rules, the parties are required to include 'a summary of the parties' respective claims' into the terms of reference. According to Article 16.2, 17.2 of the HKIAC Rules as well as Articles 20.1 and 21.1 of the PCA Rules, the claimant's statement of case shall include 'a statement of facts supporting the claim', to which the respondent 'shall reply'.

2.10 Similarly, Article 1.1 (iii) of the LCIA Rules requires 'a statement briefly summarising the nature and circumstances of the dispute' and 'the transaction(s) at issue' in order to commence the arbitration. This is to be supplemented at a later stage by a Statement of Case 'setting out in sufficient detail the relevant facts and legal submissions on which it relies' (Article 15.2 LCIA Rules). The respondent shall accordingly submit its 'confirmation or denial of all or part of the claim advanced by the Claimant in the Request' (Article 2.1.(ii) LCIA Rules). Absent a full confirmation, the respondent shall submit 'a statement briefly summarising the nature and circumstances of the dispute, (...), the transaction(s) at issue and the defence advanced by the Respondent' (Article 2.1.(iii) LCIA Rules). Subsequently, the respondent may either elect to 'have its

212. *See* below, Chapter 2, C.

response treated as its Statement of Case', or submit 'its written Statement of Defence and (if applicable) Statement of Counterclaim setting out in sufficient detail the relevant facts and legal submissions on which it relies' (Article 15.3 LCIA Rules).

2.11 Under Article 29.1 and 29.2 of the SCC Rules, the parties shall submit the 'factual and legal basis'. Article 5.2. (v) and Article 7.4 of the DIS Rules stipulate that a request for arbitration as well as the answer to the request shall contain a 'description of the facts and circumstances' on which the claim and, respectively, the answer 'is based'. Under the plain language of Article 7.2.2 of the Vienna Rules, the claimant shall make 'a statement of the facts' while under Article 8.2.2 of the Vienna Rules, the respondent shall comment 'on the request for relief and the facts upon which the Statement of Claim is based'. Moreover, Article 9.2 of the Vienna Rules states that the parties 'shall make all factual arguments in their written submissions (...)'.

2.12 The ICDR Rules in their Article 24 provide a more flexible approach with an emphasis on the tribunal's power to direct the proceeding. They allow the tribunal to 'manage the exchange of information between the parties with a view to maintaining efficiency and economy' (Article 24.1 ICDR Rules). Further, they state that '[t]he parties may provide the tribunal with their views on the appropriate level of information exchange for each case, but the tribunal retains final authority. To the extent that the parties wish to depart from this Article, they may do so only by written agreement and in consultation with the tribunal' (Article 24.2 ICDR Rules).

2.13 The above survey shows that generally only the formal and organizational aspects of pleadings based on the procedural role of the parties (claimant and respondent) are governed by the analysed sets of rules. In particular, the rules and acts do not address dogmatic issues such as the distribution of the burden of pleading, or other specifics like a defending party's reaction or fiction of admission where it fails to address an allegation. It is further notable that none of the rules address the scope of the parties' obligations of truth or potential consequences if a party were to make false representations. The legal framework is thus designed to allow for a flexible handling of the parties' pleadings, without limiting the tribunal's authority to direct the proceeding as it deems adequate.

2.14 More guidance is given by the ALI/UNIDROIT Principles and Rules. During the process of drafting the Principles, the research group carefully analysed different pleading models prevalent in various jurisdictions.[213] Unlike the above arbitration laws and rules, the ALI/UNIDROIT Principles, therefore, stipulate quite an elaborate framework for pleadings.[214] While they grant the trier of fact certain powers of

213. *See, e.g.*, Antonio Gidi, 'Transnational Rules of Civil Procedure – Study LXXVI – Doc 3 – Report on the First Session, Rome, 22 to 26 May 2000' 46.

214. *See* for further details, Geoffrey Hazard and Michele Taruffo, *Transnational Rules of Civil Procedure – Study LXXVI – Doc 2 – Preliminary Draft Rules and Comments* (Joint American Law Institute / UNIDROIT Working Group 2000) 6, 7; American Law Institute (ALI) and UNIDROIT (n. 203) no Preface; Edward H Cooper, 'Transnational Civil Procedure: Fact Pleading or Notice Pleading – A Viewpoint from the USA Harmonising Transnational Civil Procedure: The ALI/UNIDROIT Principles and Rules: II – Stages and Problem Areas in Transnational Litigation'

investigation, under the ALI/UNIDROIT Principles, the responsibility to introduce facts into the dispute lies with the parties.[215] Importantly, the ALI/UNIDROIT Principles demand a certain level of detail to be provided and specifically spell out the requirements. They also deal with the consequences if a party fails to sufficiently plead its case or reply to the opposing party. Pursuant to Principle 11.3, the parties must 'present in reasonable detail the relevant facts'. Rules 12.1 and 13.2 provide that the claimant[216] and the defendant 'must state the facts on which the claim is based (...) so far as reasonably practicable, [and] set forth detail as to time, place, participants, and events'. Accordingly, unlike other sets of rules, they expressly spell which details are considered relevant, thereby giving clear instructions to both the parties and the tribunal on the expected content of the submissions.

2.15 This is supplemented by Rule 12.4 Second Sentence, according to which, '[i]n connection with an objection that a pleading lacks sufficient detail, the [tribunal][217] should give due regard to the possibility that necessary facts and evidence will develop in the course of the proceeding'.

2.16 Moreover, blanket denials are not permissible. According to Rule 13.1 First Sentence, the respondent must either 'admit, admit with explanations, or allege an alternative statement of facts, and deny allegations defendant wishes to controvert'. Furthermore, any '[f]ailure explicitly to deny an allegation' shall be 'considered an admission for purposes of the proceeding and obviates proof thereof' (Rule 13.1 Second Sentence).

2.17 The provisions on pleadings are further complemented by Rule 25.2, which expressly links the pleading stage with the taking of evidence. It states that 'the facts and legal claims and defenses in the pleadings determine relevance'[218] for the admission of evidence under Rule 25. Lastly, according to Rule 12.4 First Sentence, 'a party who is justifiably uncertain of a fact or legal grounds may make statements about them in the alternative'.

2.18 In summary, while the ALI/UNIDROIT Principles and Rules provide an elaborate pleading regime, the arbitration laws and rules are largely silent as to the specifics. As will be detailed below, tribunals may be guided by the provisions of the Principles and Rules when assessing the parties' pleadings.[219] It is in any case strongly recommended

---

[2001] Uniform Law Review 857; LJ Priestley, 'Transnational Civil Procedure – Fact Pleading v. Notice Pleading: Its Significance in the Development of Evidence Harmonising Transnational Civil Procedure: The ALI/UNIDROIT Principles and Rules: II – Stages and Problem Areas in Transnational Litigation' [2001] Uniform Law Review 841.

215. *See, e.g.*, American Law Institute (ALI) and UNIDROIT (n. 203) para. P-21A.
216. Referred to as Plaintiff under the ALI/UNIDROIT Principles and Rules.
217. The original wording refers to the court. As noted under American Law Institute (ALI) and UNIDROIT (n. 203) P-E, the ALI/UNIDROIT Principles and Rules shall be equally applicable to international arbitration, except to the extent of being incompatible with arbitration proceedings.
218. For further elaboration of the term 'relevance' *see* below, Chapter 2, B.III.1.a.iii.
219. *See* below, Chapter 2, A.II.2.

that the tribunal clarifies the applicable pleading standard beforehand, so that all parties are able to meet the expectations.

II Fact Pleading Versus Notice Pleading

2.19 In domestic litigation procedures throughout the jurisdictions, pleading standards are highly diverse. In particular, the structure of proceedings and the different procedural phases (including the general exchange of information)[220] have a major impact on the question of how detailed facts must be. Broadly speaking, in jurisdictions where the parties are required to exchange and disclose substantial information during discovery,[221] the (initial) pleadings are usually more concise. The aim of the pleadings is not to fully inform the trier of facts but to roughly outline the dispute.[222] In contrast to this, in jurisdictions where parties are not subject to discovery duties (in which they may therefore withhold information, documents and evidence), the pleading requirements are more specific and detailed.[223]

2.20 US litigation, for example, operates in three phases. The first pleading phase is followed by an extensive discovery phase, which is then followed by the trial phase.[224] The same roughly applies in England and Wales; the parties first exchange pleadings,[225] subsequent to which the court orders disclosure of documents and information (where appropriate),[226] after which the action goes to trial.[227] In the Romance legal family, even though the parties do not engage in discovery, the proceedings also consist of three phases, namely first, the 'written introductory phase', followed by the taking of evidence, which is mainly controlled by an instructing judge, and finally, the oral hearing without taking evidence.[228] Conversely, proceedings in Germany are only

220. Stürner (n. 202) 3: 'Nearly all national civil procedural laws know the division of proceedings into two stages. In the Anglo-American law family, the pre-trial with its discovery is used to gather all the facts and to find new evidence, to determine the crucial issues for trial, and in most cases to settle the dispute by a lawyers' agreement. The German pretrial stage prepares the final hearing and the taking of evidence at trial without any chance of fishing expeditions. The French and Italian civil procedure is divided into a stage of judicial fact finding and the final hearing as a stage of legal decision. The variety of the structures makes the mutual understanding of the foreign procedural law more difficult and produces misunderstandings when evidence is to be taken abroad.'
221. *See* below, Chapter 2, B.II.1.
222. Priestley (n. 214) 842 et seq.
223. Gidi (n. 213) 23.
224. Stürner (n. 201) 224; Christoph G Paulus, 'Die Beweisvereitelung in der Struktur des deutschen Zivilprozesses – rechtsgeschichtliche und rechtsvergleichende Betrachtungen' (1997) 197 Archiv für die civilistische Praxis 136, 154.
225. *See* CPR 7.2; 7.4. and CPR 9.
226. *See* in particular CPR 31.
227. *See* CPR 39, *see* however Stürner (n. 201) 224, 225, who suggests that the modern English system rather resembles the German two-part regime.
228. *Ibid.*, 223.

bipartite, i.e., only consist of the pleading phase and the hearing phase, during which evidence is taken,[229] lacking any form of (broad) discovery or disclosure.[230]

2.21 Importantly, these general differences in structure translate to different requirements and modes of pleading. Due to extensive discovery, traditional[231] common law litigation makes use of 'notice pleadings'. This regime requires the parties to only introduce 'very general allegations',[232] as the parties are expected to exchange further details during the discovery phase.[233] In *Tchenguiz v Grant Thornton UK LLP*, an English case, Leggatt J struck out an unsolicited pleading based on its seemingly excessive length by stating:

> Statements of case must be concise. They must plead only material facts, meaning those necessary for the purpose of formulating a cause of action or defence, and not background facts or evidence. Still less should they contain arguments, reasons or rhetoric. These basic rules were developed long ago and have stood the test of time because they serve the vital purpose of identifying the matters which each party will need to prove by evidence at trial.[234]

2.22 Nonetheless, the requirements are slowly changing both in England and Wales[235] and the US. In the US, Rule 8(a)(2) FRCP generally requires 'a short and plain statement of the claim showing that the pleader is entitled to relief'. In *Bell Atlantic Corp. et al. v Twombly*, the Supreme Court of the United States interpreted the above provision as requiring the statement of claim to also be 'plausible', albeit without specifying the requirements.[236] The plausibility test was subsequently further specified in *Iqbal*, with the statement that a 'claim has facial plausibility when the pleaded factual content

229. Note that, in Germany, the phases are handled quite flexibly. That is, the oral hearing does not necessarily mark the end of a proceeding but may require the parties to submit further pleadings and evidence to be tested in a further hearing. If, during the hearing, the court notifies the parties of issues that the parties have not properly dealt with, it may require additional post-hearing submissions in which the parties may supplement their pleadings, *see* sec. 139 (5), 283 ZPO.
230. Stürner (n. 201) 225 refers to this approach as the 'main hearing model'.
231. For further details on 'code pleading' which preceeded the regime of notice pleading in the US *see* Cooper (n. 214) 868.
232. Priestley (n. 214) 841.
233. *Ibid.*
234. *Tchenguiz & Ors v Grant Thornton UK LLP & Ors* [2015] EWHC 405 (Comm) [1].
235. Lacking an abstract rule, the CPR provides specific requirements for specific causes of action, namely where a party claims interest (*see* CPR 16.4.(1)(b) and 16.4.(2)), aggravated damages or exemplary damages (16.4.(1)(c)). CPR PD 16 stipulates further specifics to be pleaded in case of personal injury claims (para. 4), fatal accident claims (para. 5) and hire purchase claims (para. 6). Yet, these concrete provisions do not allow for a generalization to develop abstract requirements. Nonetheless, the CPR does not encourage the parties to excessively plead facts. Rather, the parties are expected to restrict themselves to the necessary basics.
236. The court emphasized that the test was not meant to introduce a probability requirement to at the pleading stage, i.e., to anticipate the taking of evidence: 'Asking for plausible grounds does not impose a probability requirement at the pleading stage; it simply calls for enough fact to raise a reasonable expectation that discovery will reveal evidence of illegal agreement. (…) Here, the Court is not requiring heightened fact pleading of specifics, but only enough facts to state a claim to relief that is plausible on its face. Because the plaintiffs here have not nudged their claims across the line from conceivable to plausible, their complaint must be dismissed', *see Bell Atlantic Corp v Twombly* (550 US 544) [1(b)].

allows the court to draw the reasonable inference that the defendant is liable for the misconduct alleged'.[237]

2.23 The regime of notice pleading can be contrasted with the regime of fact pleading, which calls for 'the assertion of detailed facts' and 'exactly specified means of evidence during the pleading phase of the proceedings'.[238] In Germany, for example, the parties exchange information through the interplay of the pleading burdens (burden of presentation, *Darlegungslast*; burden of substantiation, *Substantiierungslast*; secondary burden of presentation, *sekundäre Darlegungslast*)[239] rather than through formalized methods of disclosure (i.e., document production, interrogatories or depositions). Based on the respective initial submissions, parties are required to repeatedly address and specify their allegations. Frequently, this makes several rounds of submissions necessary, thus protracting the pleading phase and rendering the course and duration of the proceeding unpredictable.[240] Accordingly, in Germany, where the parties have no means of discovery available,[241] and where parties may withhold adverse information,[242] pleadings are of paramount importance. In fact, in only 8.9% of the cases resolved before Higher Regional Courts in Germany, evidence was taken.[243] The remaining 91.1% of proceedings, the vast majority, were resolved solely on the basis of the pleadings.[244] As a consequence, German case law has established a highly elaborate, complex and distinct pleading regime, stipulating different rules and exceptions to guide the parties.[245]

2.24 Despite the importance of the conduct of the proceeding, none of the above-examined arbitration laws and rules expressly address the required level of detail to be provided. As shown, only the ALI/UNIDROIT Principles give more guidance. As set out

237. *Ashcroft v Iqbal* (556 US 662) 2(c): '[D]etermining whether a complaint states a plausible claim is context-specific, requiring the reviewing court to draw on its experience and common sense. (…) A court considering a motion to dismiss may begin by identifying allegations that, because they are mere conclusions, are not entitled to the assumption of truth. While legal conclusions can provide the complaint's framework, they must be supported by factual allegations. When there are well-pleaded factual allegations, a court should assume their veracity and then determine whether they plausibly give rise to an entitlement to relief.'
238. *See* Stürner (n. 201) 233 with reference to French, Italian and Spanish law; Priestley (n. 214) 841.
239. Hanns Prütting, 'ZPO § 286' in Thomas Rauscher and Wolfgang Krüger (eds), *Münchener Kommentar zur ZPO* (6th edn, C.H. Beck 2020) paras 137–139.
240. In practice, courts make use of their extensive liberties to set further periods for submissions (*see, e.g.*, sec. 283 ZPO. Unlike in modern arbitration proceedings, civil litigation in Germany does not operate with a procedural calendar to set the sequence of the proceedings up front. Rather, the courts assess after each round of pleadings if it seems adequate and necessary to grant further periods of submissions which results in a pendulum-like structure of the proceedings, that continuously requires the party to provide further factual details.
241. *See* below, Chapter 2, B.II.1.
242. *See* below, Chapter 2, B.II.2.
243. Statistisches Bundesamt (Federal Statistical Office), 'Publikation: Justiz & Rechtspflege; Zivilgerichte (2019)' 60.
244. For the sake of clarity, this includes all forms of resolution of the proceedings, e.g., judgments (including default judgments), orders, admissions of the claims, withdrawals of claims, and settlements, *see ibid.*, 48.
245. *See* above, Chapter 2, A.II.

in Principle 9, the proceedings envisaged by the principles are based on a tripartite model, consisting of a pleading phase (*see* Rules 11–16), an interim phase for case management and potential discovery proceedings (*see* Rules 17–32), and a final hearing phase (*see* Rules 29–32). While the content and scope of the Principles rather resemble the proceedings of modern common law litigation, they do state that the organization of the proceedings ought to be handled with the necessary flexibility 'according to the nature of the particular case'.[246] That being said, the Principles are based on a 'fact pleading' model rather than following the traditional American 'notice pleading' approach.[247]

2.25 Since domestic pleading requirements are, contrary to popular belief, not applicable in international arbitration (*1*), the below describes the current regime of fact pleading, seeking to distil different rules and guidelines to render the pleading phase more predictable (*2*).

1 No Recourse to Domestic Pleading Requirements

2.26 Despite trends towards the uniformization of procedural rules in international arbitrations, some practitioners continue to rely on domestic standards of pleading. For instance, in *Pac Rim Cayman LLC v Republic of El Salvador*, an ICSID proceeding under the CAFTA, the respondent argued that the claimant was required to fulfil a heightened pleading standard, i.e., the one of 'plausibility' based on US doctrine developed in *Iqbal*. The tribunal rejected the argument and held that the requirement was not applicable, especially because FRCP and ICSID procedures were not comparable. This meant that individual elements could and should not be transferred from American civil procedure to international arbitration:

> The Tribunal was not materially assisted by comparisons between these provisions and national court procedures in one Contracting Party, the USA, as evidenced by its President's Message of 2005 and several decisions of US courts, including the decisions of the US Supreme Court in Neitzke v. Williams and Ashcroft v. Iqbal. Not only is that message from one Contracting Party not replicated by other Contracting Parties to CAFTA, there is also no reason to equate such common law court procedures to provisions in CAFTA agreed by Contracting Parties with different legal traditions and national court procedures.[248]

2.27 Similarly, a Scottish court found in a challenge to an award that the tribunal had not been required to adhere to domestic pleading standards:

246. American Law Institute (ALI) and UNIDROIT (n. 203) 28.
247. *Ibid.*, R12A; Gidi (n. 213) 23: 'It was manifested some concerns that the project has a very strong common law basis to which Hazard explained that the three most fundamental characteristics of American procedure (jury trial, notice pleading, and comprehensive discovery) are repudiated in the draft.'
248. *Pac Rim Cayman LLC v Republic of El Salvador, ICSID ARB/09/12* Decision on the Respondent's Preliminary Objections under CAFTA Articles 10204 and 10205 of 2 August 2010 [117].

> Pleadings in arbitration need not, indeed normally should not, follow the form of pleadings in common use in the Court of Session. It is for the arbitrator to decide questions as to the admissibility, relevance, materiality and weight of any evidence: R28(1)(b).[249]

2.28 Despite the incompatibility, it remains quite common for German qualified practitioners to seek to apply the domestic burden of substantiation in arbitration proceedings. As pointed out, the substantiation standard is a moving target and requires the parties to adapt the details of their submissions to the level of detail of the counterparty.[250] In this context, it has been noted that the domestic pleading requirements have become 'second nature' to many German attorneys and judges, which they seek to introduce into pleadings in international arbitration as well.[251] This is especially true for practitioners who frequently act in domestic litigation proceedings.

2.29 Some commentators argue that tribunals are necessarily required to reject 'unsubstantiated' submissions,[252] thus relying on the standard applicable in German domestic litigation. Others seem to go so far as to advocate the strict application of domestic rules on pleading and evidence.[253] German courts ultimately leave the decision to the tribunal's discretion. In different decisions, it has been confirmed that the arbitral tribunals have the power to reject a party's submission if it is considered to be 'unsubstantiated', measured against German standards.[254] In another decision, the OLG Frankfurt rejected challenges of arbitral awards where a tribunal had based its

249. *Arbitration Application No3 of 2011* [2011] CSOH 164 29, emphasis added; Hew Dundas, 'Challenge to Arbitral Award and Survey of Scottish Arbitral Jurisprudence' (2017) 83 The International Journal of Arbitration, Mediation and Dispute Management 368, 373.
250. *See* above, Chapter 2, A.II.
251. Markus S Rieder, 'Sekundäre Darlegungs- Und Beweislast Im Schiedsverfahren?' in Rolf A Schütze and Reinhold Geimer (eds), *Fairness, Justice, Equity: Festschrift Für Reinhold Geimer Zum 80. Geburtstag* (C.H. Beck 2017) 557, 563 et seq. With reference to the 'secondary burden of pleading', Rieder notes that it has become the second nature of German practitioners, but speaks out against the application of domestic standards in international arbitrations.
252. Rolf A Schütze, Eckart Brödermann and Ulrich Theune (eds), *Institutionelle Schiedsgerichtsbarkeit: Kommentar* (3rd edn, Carl Heymanns Verlag 2018) 306; Wolfgang Kühn and Katharina Walter, 'The Burden of Substantiation and Proof in Continental European Civil Procedure and the Taking of Evidence in International Arbitration' (*Best Lawyers Legal Insights*, 31 August 2017).
253. *See, e.g.*, Münch, 'ZPO § 1049' in Thomas Rauscher and Wolfgang Krüger (eds), *Münchener Kommentar zur ZPO* (5th edn, C.H. Beck 2017) para. 65, who, for instance, argues that tribunals operating under the German Arbitration Act were required to not accept copies of documents as real evidence but rather as party pleading (as in German litigation). Note, however, that the author argues the contrary in para. 44, namely that the tribunal was not bound to apply domestic rules to the means of evidence.
254. For domestic awards, *see OLG Köln, Order of 21 November 2008* [2009] BeckRS 4423 [Para II.2.c]; *OLG Köln, Order of 4 August 2017* [2018] NJOZ 949 [36]; for international awards, *see OLG Frankfurt aM, Order of 17 February 2011* [2013] SchiedsVZ 49 [I.3]; Stefan Kröll, 'Kröll: Die Schiedsrechtliche Rechtsprechung 2016 Und 2017' [2018] SchiedsVZ 201, 208, 209; *OLG München, Order of 18 November 2004* [2004] OLG München 34 Sch 19/04, [2006] SchiedsVZ 111.

decision on submissions that may not have met the German standard of substantiation.[255] Thus, according to the case law of German courts, the tribunal is free to determine whether it finds the standard to be adequate and applicable. It is not bound to adhere to domestic rules. Yet, the application thereof lies within the tribunal's discretion.

2.30 Commentators in Switzerland have likewise observed that tribunals frequently apply similar domestic standards of pleading and substantiation in arbitration proceedings. For instance, it was noted that under Swiss Law, there were 'no conceptual differences between arbitration and litigation as regards the burden of substantiation'. Nonetheless, arbitral tribunals usually were 'more generous' in the application of such pleading standards.[256]

2.31 A preferable course of action would be for international tribunals to refrain from having recourse to domestic pleading standards, as they cater to the needs of their procedural system[257] and are usually incompatible with the information model which is prevalent in international arbitration. Due to the differing configurations of civil proceedings and arbitration, the application of domestic pleading requirements in arbitration is liable to cause difficulties and errors throughout the process.[258] The standard of substantiation, for example, which requires the parties to continuously supplement their pleadings may clash with cut-off dates, subsequent to which submissions are no longer admissible.[259] The same is true for the US standard of plausibility, which may have its merits within the structure of the US proceedings for which it was developed, but should not be strictly applied in proceedings that function without US-style discovery.

2.32 Only in domestic arbitration proceedings, where all parties are from the same jurisdiction, and where the tribunal conducts the proceeding in a litigation-style manner, may it be justified to order the application of domestic pleading standards. In any event, where a tribunal intends to organize the exchange of pleadings in a litigation-inspired manner, it shall duly inform the parties beforehand, e.g., by including a rule to that effect into the first procedural order.

---

255. *OLG München, Order of 18 November 2004* (n. 254) 159; *OLG Frankfurt a M, Order of 2 February 2017* [2018] NJOZ 584, 586; both decisions where made in enforcement proceedings of international awards.
256. Manuel Arroyo, *Arbitration in Switzerland: The Practitioner's Guide* (2nd edn, Kluwer Law International 2018) para. 93; equally, Michael Bösch and Patrick Rohn, 'Switzerland' in Amy Cohen Kläsener (ed.), *The Guide to M&A Arbitration* (Global Arbitration Review 2018) 170 note that 'if the substantive law applicable to the dispute is Swiss law, the tribunal will generally also apply the Swiss concept of burden of proof and concurrently the closely connected concept of burden of substantiation'.; *see also* Simon Gabriel, 'Dealing with "Challenged Documents"' [2011] ASA Bulletin 823, 824.
257. This is in line with the above observations on the secondary burden of pleading, *see* Rieder (n. 251) 563–565.
258. *Ibid.*
259. *See* above, Chapter 1, A.IV.

2 *Fact Pleading in International Arbitration: Specific Pleading Requirements*

2.33 The fact that domestic standards do not apply prompts the question of how facts must then be pleaded in international arbitration. In particular, the need for legal certainty renders a more uniform standard desirable, as in the case of the burden of proof.

2.34 Despite its practical relevance, this issue has thus far not been given a great deal of attention by the international arbitration community. Nevertheless, it is not seldom that some of the main issues, if not entire cases, are decided on the basis that one party's pleading is insufficient to order the taking of evidence. Any attempt to define a more uniform standard must necessarily consider the overall structure of the proceedings as well as the requirements set out in the prevalent arbitration rules.[260] At the same time, as with any procedural issue that is generally left to the tribunal's discretion, any such solution must provide the necessary flexibility, rather than imposing an overly regulated, litigation-like regime.[261]

2.35 Against this backdrop, modern arbitration proceedings demand a reasonably specific account of the facts, i.e., fact pleadings rather than mere notice pleadings. This is especially true since the parties are not subject to extensive discovery duties.[262] Rather, as will be detailed below, they are restricted to arguably moderate forms of document production.[263] It follows that in international arbitration, more weight is given to the parties' submissions as to the facts, which, accordingly, must be more specific than in traditional common law notice pleading. However, the availability of document production, albeit limited, means that pleadings are not the only source of information. Thus, they do not have to be as detailed as in, for example, German or Swiss litigation, where discovery is not available, and facts are gathered by reciprocal factual submissions only. This leaves international arbitration pleadings somewhere in between common law and civil law pleadings, i.e., reasonably specific but not overly detailed.

2.36 This was recently confirmed by the Supreme Court of Austria, which found that a notice of arbitration lacking the necessary details had not properly initiated an arbitration proceeding:

> The informational purpose [of the notice of arbitration] can only be achieved if the respondent is informed of the dispute to which it is to become a party. The required information about the claim is not yet the same as the requirements for the description of the subject matter of the dispute in the context of the subsequent arbitration action. Therefore, it is correctly argued in the literature not to apply 'too strict standards' (…). According to the purpose of a notice of arbitration, however, it is in any case necessary that the demand is circumscribed for the defendant to

260. *See* above, Chapter 2, A.II.1.
261. *See* above, Chapter 1, A.II.2.
262. *See* below, Chapter 2, B.III.
263. *See* below, Chapter 2, B.III.

such an extent that he can recognize what is demanded of him in order to be able to set a reaction adequate to the proceedings.[264]

2.37 In short, a satisfactory level of detail was deemed necessary to allow the respondent to assess the litigation and cost risk and to choose both specialized counsel and arbitrator.[265]

2.38 Beyond this, based on their rather broad language, the arbitration laws and rules analysed here, as well as the soft laws, leave it largely to the tribunal to define the specific pleading requirements.[266] Nonetheless, there is common ground between these rules. All of these, in varying wording, require the parties to 'state the facts', or 'the points at issue' supporting the claim or defence, or to set out in 'sufficient detail the relevant facts and legal submissions' on which the parties rely. It follows that parties are required to positively spell out the facts they seek to rely upon and that each party shall address the opposing parties' submissions. The language used, combined with the above observations on the structure of the proceedings, which demands reasonably but not overly specific factual submissions, allows the following guiding rules and principles to be distilled:

- Independent of distribution of the pleading burden, both the claimant and the respondent, in their own interest, are expected to plead all facts that they seek to rely on.[267]
- The parties shall provide a level of detail which allows for an understanding of the issues in dispute. Where the data is available, this usually requires addressing the time, location, involved persons and specific events.[268]
- If a party acknowledges a fact submitted by the opposing party, the tribunal shall generally[269] consider said fact to be undisputed.[270]

264. *OGH, Judgment of 6 February 2018* 18 ONc 4/17h [II.4].
265. *Ibid.*
266. *See* above, Chapter 2, A.I.
267. *See, e.g.*, Art. 20.2 (a), (b), 21.2 UNCITRAL Rules (and, in the same language, Art. 18.2 (b), (c), 19.2 SCAI Rules) which demand that the statements of claim and defence shall contain a 'statement of the facts supporting the claim' as well as the 'points at issue'.
268. *See, e.g.*, ALI/UNIDROIT Rules 12.1 and 13.2 which provide that the claimant and the defendant 'must state the facts on which the claim is based (...) so far as reasonably practicable, set forth detail as to time, place, participants, and events'. *See also* Art. 15.2 of the LCIA Rules, according to which the statement of claim shall 'out in sufficient detail the relevant facts (...)'.
269. An exception may apply if the parties agree on an apparently wrong fact, Chapter 2, C.III.2.
270. *See, e.g.*, ALI/UNIDROIT Rule 13.1 First Sentence which states that the respondent must either 'admit, admit with explanations, or allege an alternative statement of facts, and deny allegations wishes to controvert'. *See also* Art. 2.1.(ii) of the LCIA Rules, stating that the respondent shall accordingly submit its 'confirmation or denial of all or part of the claim advanced by the Claimant in the Request' (Art. 2.1.(ii) LCIA Rules). Absent a full confirmation, the respondent shall submit 'a statement briefly summarising the nature and circumstances of the dispute, (...), the transaction(s) at issue and the defence advanced by the Respondent' (Art. 2.1.(iii) LCIA Rules).

- Unless due to a justifiable lack of knowledge, a party shall seriously contest an opposing party's allegation.[271] A failure to address an allegation of the opposing party may be considered an admission.[272]
- In case of disagreement, a party must accordingly put forward its version of the story. Consequently, general blanket denials, by means of which a party denies all of the opposing party's allegations if not expressly confirmed are not admissible.

2.39 If a party fails to comply with these basic requirements, the tribunal is free to either notify the parties that the case is not sufficiently pleaded,[273] draw inferences it deems appropriate,[274] or, in extreme cases, strike out the pleadings as insufficient.[275]

III Distribution of the Burden of Pleading

2.40 Closely intertwined with the question of the necessary details to be pleaded, the distribution of the burden of pleading defines which party may be required to address a specific issue. Like the burden of proof,[276] the burden of pleading is a rule of risk distribution. If, by the end of the proceeding, relevant facts have not been pleaded (or otherwise introduced), this goes to the detriment of the burdened party. In other words, the burden of pleading defines the duty of the parties to plead all facts relevant to their position.[277] Accordingly, if a party fails to plead facts that give rise to its claim or defence, the tribunal will make an adverse decision.

2.41 In an ICC proceeding, for example, the tribunal rejected the claimant's additional claims relating to 'costs in connection with the Customs Duty Case', finding that:

> the allegations made in this respect are so general in nature, that Claimant's burden of allegation cannot be deemed discharged thereby.[278]

2.42 Despite its vital role, the burden of pleading has thus far been given little attention in the context of international arbitration. As has been pointed out, none of the arbitration acts or rules specifically address dogmatic issues regarding the burden

271. Allan Redfern and others, 'Special Section: The Standards and Burden of Proof in International Arbitration' (1994) 10 Arbitration International 317, 338, *see* further ALI/UNIDROIT Rule 13.1 First Sentence; Art. 2.1 LCIA Rules.
272. *Ibid.*, *see* further ALI/UNIDROIT Rule 13.1 First Sentence; Art. 2.1 LCIA Rules.
273. *See* below, Chapter 2, C.II.3 and 4.
274. *See* below, Chapter 3, E.II.3.
275. *OGH, Judgment of 6 February 2018* (n. 264) para. II.4.
276. *See* below, Chapter 3, A.II.
277. Note that little material is available on the doctrine of the burden of pleading in international arbitration. *See*, however, for references Redfern and others (n. 271) 328, 338; Mateus Aimoré Carreteiro, 'Burden and Standard of Proof in International Arbitration: Proposed Guidelines for Promoting Predictability' (2016) XIII Revista Brasileira de Arbitragem 82, 84, 85; Anne Véronique Schlaepfer, 'The Burden of Proof in International Arbitration' (2015) 18 Legitimacy: Myths, Realities, Challenges, ICCA Congress Series 127, 128; *ICC Case No 17730/CYK/RD, Final Award of 2014* Arbitrator Intelligence Materials [250].
278. *ICC Case No 20065, Final Award* [2019] XLIV Ybk Comm Arb [102, 103].

of pleading and its distribution.[279] The rules stating that parties shall plead the facts they seek to rely on are not concerned with the burden of pleading in a technical sense. Rather, these provisions reflect that it is in the interest of the parties to introduce facts that support their positions. They do not expressly set out which party must plead which issue.

2.43 In international arbitration, the distribution of the burden of pleading is found to follow the distribution of the burden of proof, and thus largely follows the transnational principle of *actori incumbit*.[280] Accordingly, a party must plead all facts that are favourable to its position, i.e., those that give rise to claims or affirmative defences.[281] This is in line with the prevalent litigation practice in, *inter alia*, Germany,[282] France,[283] as well as in the United States.[284] The same applies in England and Wales, where, for instance, it was found in *BPE Solicitors & Anor v Hughes-Holland* that:

> [t]he legal burden of proving any averment of fact lies upon the person who is required to assert it as part of his case. In the ordinary course, this means that the claimant has the burden of pleading and proving his loss, whereas the defendant has the burden of proving facts (such as failure to mitigate) going to avoid or abate the consequent liability in damages.[285]

2.44 While there seems to be very little case law in international arbitration, the rule that the burden of proof follows the burden of pleading was confirmed, *inter alia*, by the final award in *Crain Walnut Shelling, Inc. v SPC Group*. In the ICC proceeding seated in California, the tribunal applied the 'burden of pleading and proving' according to the applicable substantive law, in that case Californian law.[286]

> [U]nder California law, the defendant (and in this arbitration the Respondents) bears the burden of pleading and proving a defence based on the avoidable consequences doctrine.

2.45 The link between the burden of pleading and the burden of proof is also acknowledged by legal commentary[287] and is consistent with the approach taken by the ALI/UNIDROIT Principles. While the language of the ALI/UNIDROIT Principles or Rules does not make any explicit statement regarding the distribution of the pleading burden, they are based on the general rule that the 'burden of pleading goes with the

---

279. *See* above, Chapter 2, A.I.
280. *See* below, Chapter 3, A.II.
281. *See* below, Chapter 3, A.II.
282. Leo Rosenberg, *Die Beweislast: auf der Grundlage des Bürgerlichen Gesetzbuchs und der Zivilprozessordnung* (5th edn, Beck 1965) 44; Prütting, 'ZPO § 286' (n. 239) paras 137–139.
283. Article 6 NCPC: 'A l'appui de leurs prétentions, les parties ont la charge d'alléguer les faits propres à les fonder.'
284. Wexler and Effron (n. 210) 469.
285. *BPE Solicitors & Anor v Hughes-Holland (in substitution for Gabriel) (Rev 1)* [2017] UKSC 21 [53].
286. *ICC Case No 17730/CYK/RD, Final Award of 2014* (n. 277) para. 250.
287. Schlaepfer (n. 277) 128; Aimoré Carreteiro (n. 277) 85, 86; for the German Arbitration Act, *see also* Karl-Heinz Böckstiegel, Stefan Kröll and Patricia Nacimiento (eds), *Arbitration in Germany: The Model Law in Practice* (2nd edn, Kluwer Law International 2015) 173.

burden of proof'.[288] Accordingly, in the application of Principle 21.1, *mutatis mutandis*, the burden of pleading lies upon a party which substantially asserts the affirmative of an issue, and each party must plead all the material facts that are the basis of that party's case.[289]

2.46 As will be further elaborated below, the application of *actori incumbit* requires a determination of whether a specific rule relied upon is an affirmative claim, an affirmative defence, or a mere negation of such an affirmative.[290] This is, in turn, defined by the applicable substantive law. It follows that the tribunal shall have due regard for the *lex causae* when analysing the distribution of the burden of pleading. Nonetheless, care must be taken not to treat the pleading requirements as a substantive issue, despite their interplay with substantive law.[291] Rather, forming a central element of the organization of the procedures, the specific pleading requirements are an inherently procedural issue.[292] In other words: while the distribution of the burden of pleading follows the substantive law, the incidence of the burden of pleading (i.e., the question of whether and how the burden applies at all) is a procedural matter. In particular, the tribunal is not required to adhere to any domestic particularities, such as modifications of the distribution of pleading burden in specific procedural situations.[293]

2.47 The task of defining adequate pleading requirements, including the distribution of the burden of proof, is, in the absence of any specific rules or party agreements, largely left to the due discretion of the tribunal. In light of the tribunal's broad powers to conduct the proceedings, the trend towards semi-inquisitorial features[294] and the parties' information duties,[295] the tribunal may therefore rely on the general distribution of burden of pleading but also make amendments in specific cases based on its due discretion. Further, it may also always order a party to provide further details on specific issues, especially if these stem from said party's sphere of information, independent of the distribution of the burden of proof.[296] Any such order is, of course, always subject to the right to be heard and procedural fairness.

IV Cut-Off Dates

2.48 At the beginning of a properly organized arbitral proceeding, and upon consultation with the parties, the tribunal will usually issue a procedural calendar. The

288. American Law Institute (ALI) and UNIDROIT (n. 203) para. P-21A.
289. *See* below, Chapter 2, A.II.2.a.
290. *See* for English law, Adrian Keane and Paul McKeown, *The Modern Law of Evidence* (13th edn, Oxford University Press 2020) 78 et seq.; *See* for German law, Prütting, 'ZPO § 286' (n. 239) paras 113–116.
291. *See*, however, Redfern and others (n. 271) 328, who on the contrary state that: '[t]he burden of allegation is necessarily governed by the law applicable to the substance of the dispute'.
292. *See, e.g.*, on the German pleading standards, Rieder (n. 251) 565.
293. This is, as pointed out, in particular true for, e.g., the burden of substantiation or the secondary burden of pleading under German law, *see* above, Chapter 2, A.II.1.
294. *See* below, Chapter 2, C.II.
295. *See* below, Chapter 2, B.II.
296. *See* below, Chapter 2, C.II.3.

purpose of the procedural calendar is to determine the number of submissions and hearings, details on the production of documents and expert evidence (if applicable) as well as specific deadlines and dates, including cut-off dates. The procedural calendar thus provides structure for the proceedings, limits them to a specific time frame and provides predictability and legal certainty. Nevertheless, despite all careful planning, parties and tribunals in international arbitration frequently encounter issues surrounding subsequent amendments of the pleadings as well as of delayed submissions of facts.

2.49 One of the underlying issues is that fact-finding procedures are dynamic and depend on both parties' reciprocal contributions and the actions taken by the tribunal. Accordingly, many issues do not come up immediately, but are introduced, or properly addressed, only after two or three rounds of submissions have been exchanged. Usually, for example, the respondent will raise defences which require rebuttal by the claimant. The claimant's new submissions, in turn, may raise further issues that the respondent feels required to reply to. Thus, relevant issues are frequently only distilled over the course of the proceedings. At the same time, reasons of efficiency and cost-control demand that the tribunal must limit the pleading of facts to a specific period, after which the tribunal must disregard further submissions.

2.50 Different arbitration acts stipulate (in different wording) that parties may amend or extend their statements of case during the course of the arbitral proceedings, unless the arbitral tribunal considers it inappropriate to allow such amendment due to the delay in making it.[297] The same is true for many arbitration rules[298] and also provided for by ALI/UNIDROIT Principle 10.4.[299] As has been noted by the drafters, while issues of subsequent amendments are treated differently across different legal systems, the parties should be accorded 'some flexibility, particularly when new or unexpected evidence is confronted'.[300]

2.51 When assessing potentially delayed factual submissions, it is vital to consider whether the tribunal has defined (or the parties have agreed on) a specific number of pleading rounds, during which the party has failed to make the respective allegations.

297. *See, e.g.*, Art. 23 (2) Model Law, sec. 1046 (2) ZPO; the English Arbitration Act generally leaves it to the tribunal to decide to what extent statements can later be amended (*see* Art. 34.1, 34.2(c)).
298. *See* Art. 22 UNCITRAL Rules; Art. 22.1(i) LCIA Rules (emphasizing the tribunal's discretion to admit such amendment); Art. 30 SCC Rules; Art. 10 ICDR Rules; Art. 18 HKIAC Rules; Art. 20 SCAI Rules; Art. 22 PCA Rules; the DIS Rules and ICC Rules do not provide any specific rules on amendments.
299. Under Principle 10.4 of the ALI/UNIDROIT Principles, a party 'upon showing good cause, has a right to amend its claims or defences upon notice to other parties, and when doing so does not unreasonably delay the proceeding or otherwise result in injustice'.
300. American Law Institute (ALI) and UNIDROIT (n. 203) para. P-10C.

The DIS Rules[301] as well as the Prague Rules, *inter alia*, suggest discussing any limitation on the rounds at the beginning of the proceeding.[302] This goes hand-in-hand with the above-mentioned practice of scheduling the course of the proceedings in advance through procedural calendars.[303]

2.52 As a measure for organizing and focusing the proceedings, tribunals frequently stipulate cut-off dates. Where a cut-off date has been set, all new pleadings and evidence must, in the ordinary course, be rejected as delayed after the cut-off date has lapsed. The laws and rules surveyed here generally do not contain any specifics regarding cut-off dates. There are, however, exceptions. For instance, Article 28.2 of the Vienna Rules suggests the use thereof.[304] Likewise, Article 2.5 of the Prague Rules states that the tribunal shall, upon consultation with the parties, consider setting a 'cut-off date for submission of evidence and not accepting any new evidence after that date, save for under exceptional circumstances'.[305]

2.53 While the use of cut-off dates becomes increasingly popular and may help to expedite the proceedings,[306] the tribunal must always carefully examine whether a party's delay to plead facts or provide evidence is reasonably justifiable. In doing so, the tribunal must consider that enforcing a cut-off date may restrict the right to present the case and thus may violate the right to be heard. The latter is usually not a concern if a party has had the opportunity to make the respective submissions (of allegations or evidence) at an earlier stage. On rare occasions, a party may learn new facts or find new evidence at a later stage. Relevantly, a party that seeks to rely on such an exception will be required to plead and prove the underlying circumstances.[307]

2.54 In an ICC proceeding between a Taiwanese buyer and a German seller, the tribunal discussed whether to admit evidence to the file after the lapse of the cut-off date. In this case, the claimant had presented delayed evidence in response to a late (but still timely) submission of the respondent. The tribunal allowed for an exception. It found that:

> the (...) statement [i.e. the evidence in question] was not available before the cut-off date. Again, it appears to be rather Respondent's than Claimant's responsibility that the issue of the YYY Contract only arose after the Rejoinder. Had Respondent from the very beginning of the present arbitration proceedings

---

301. *See* Annex 3 E DIS Rules.
302. Article 2.5 Prague Rules.
303. Article 27.4 DIS Rules, Art. 24.2 ICC Rules, cf. also Art. 28.2 SCC Rules according to which the tribunal shall 'schedule' the proceedings.
304. Article 28.2 Vienna Rules: 'Subject to advance notice, the arbitral tribunal may inter alia consider pleadings, the submission of evidence, and requests for the taking of evidence to be admissible only up to a certain point in time of the proceedings.'
305. Further, *see* Art. 15.6 LCIA Rules, according to which no party may submit any further written statement following the last of the written statements allowed by the LCIA Rules, unless otherwise ordered by the Arbitral Tribunal.
306. *See also* the suggestion in ICC Commission on Arbitration and ADR Task Force, *Report on Reducing Time and Costs in Arbitration* (2nd edn, ICC 2012) para. 73.
307. This follows from the *actori incumbit* principle. *See* on the general distribution of the burden of proof below, Chapter 3, A.2.

> pleaded a consistent factual argument, Claimant would have been obliged to submit any evidence in this respect in due course. In the present exceptional constellation, however, the late submission (...) is comprehensible and can be excused.[308]

2.55 In order to safeguard the respondent's right to make its case, the tribunal accordingly granted the opportunity of an extended deadline for submissions.[309]

2.56 Under similar circumstances, in *FinnHEMS Oy v Skärgårdshavets Helikoptertjänst AB*,[310] a related issue arose. The question was whether a tribunal that set a cut-off date, to which the parties consented, was itself bound by it. In this case, the respondent had raised issues after the lapse of the cut-off date, which the tribunal, nonetheless, then considered in the award. Upon the claimant's request, the District Court of Helsinki set aside the award, arguing that the tribunal 'had set a binding cut-off date after which new claims or evidence could not be presented'. Moreover, the 'parties had expressly accepted at a pre-hearing conference that the parties must raise all claims and facts the sole arbitrator may base their decision on'. Considering that these new issues had therefore exceeded the tribunal's authority, the Court of Appeal of Helsinki confirmed the decision, finding that by considering delayed submissions, the tribunal had failed to allow the claimant to sufficiently present its case.

2.57 The above rulings are indicative of the problems that may arise. Where a party is not able to justify its delayed submissions, adhering to a cut-off date is a matter of procedural fairness, as both parties must be equally granted the right to present their case. If a tribunal considers one party's belated evidence whereas the opposing has respected the cut-off date, the tribunal fails to uphold the principle of equal treatment.

2.58 Moreover, *FinnHEMS* raises a further, highly relevant question, namely whether a procedural calendar including cut-off dates, which the tribunal has coordinated with the parties, amounts to a 'party agreement' in the sense of Article V (1) (d) of the New York Convention. If this were the case, the Tribunal would forfeit a considerable part of its procedural discretion by cooperating with the parties. However, it is submitted that care is required in determining the existence of a party agreement, especially if not expressly labelled as such. In recent years, it can be observed that different institutions have encouraged stronger cooperation between the parties and the tribunal to ensure more efficient proceedings.[311] If, however, tribunals run the risk of compromising their powers to direct the proceedings as they deem fit, they may seek to reduce the parties' involvement in preparing procedural decisions. In any case, for practical reasons, it is

---

308. *ICC Case No 18671, Final Award of 2013* [2017] XLII Ybk Comm Arb 204 [29].
309. *Ibid.*
310. *See* the summary in *FinnHEMS Oy v Skärgårdshavets Helikoptertjänst AB, Court of Appeal of Helsinki, Case No S 18/854, Decision No 626 of 23 May 2019* ITA Arbitration Report.
311. *See, e.g.*, Art. 27 and Annex 3 DIS Rules, Art. 24 and Appendix IV ICC Rules.

recommended that the tribunal clarifies that, despite consulting the parties, the ultimate decision regarding dates and deadlines lies with the tribunal.[312]

2.59 In light of the above, one can conclude that, as a general principle in international arbitration, the tribunal may set cut-off dates to expedite the proceedings. Once a cut-off date is set, no party may submit further facts or evidence. Likewise, the tribunal may not admit such delayed submission of facts or evidence. An exception only applies if, under due consideration of all circumstances, the delay is sufficiently reasonably justified, in particular (i) if the respective issue was first introduced, or (ii) if the submitting party has only learned of the particular fact or means of evidence at a late stage of the proceeding, thus rendering timely submission impossible.

V Conclusion

2.60 Pleadings are key to every proceeding. The written legal framework on the pleading of facts remains relatively vague, since most arbitration laws only demand in varying language that parties must plead the facts they seek to rely upon. The same holds true for the arbitration rules which have been analysed above. They do not specify which pleading regime applies (i.e., notice pleading, fact pleading or, for that matter, a hybrid solution), or which party bears the burden of introducing specific issues (burden of pleading). Despite the lack of an express legal basis, the respective rules – which in many cases can determine a party's victory or defeat – have become increasingly synchronized in recent years. In practice, there is a trend towards a specific arbitral pleading regime independent of the pleading requirements in domestic litigation, which demands a reasonable degree of detail and an explicit response to the opposing party's submission.

2.61 This is underpinned by the best practice of linking the burden of pleading with the burden of proof. Accordingly, a party that invokes an affirmative (either claim or defence) must plead the facts that support it.

2.62 Another notable best practice in this regard is the fixing of a reliable procedural calendar, including cut-off dates, in order to render the course of the proceedings predictable and clarify to the parties by which exact date they must have provided the material they seek to rely upon. Cut-off dates accordingly apply both to pleadings and the submission of evidence. Once a cut-off date is set and has lapsed, the parties may make new submissions only under exceptional circumstances. Likewise, the tribunal is barred from considering late submissions without good cause.

B DISCLOSURE DUTIES

2.63 The (compulsory) exchange and disclosure of information and documents remains one of the most contentious issues in international arbitration. At the same

312. The same is true for other procedural decisions and orders which the tribunal coordinates with the parties.

time, it is also a procedural phase which strikingly illustrates the transnationalization of arbitration law, as illustrated above.

2.64 This section will first analyse the legal framework based upon which parties may be obliged to disclosure of information (*I*). Subsequently, it will describe the general model of information exchange prevalent in international arbitration (*II*). The last part of the chapter examines the submission and disclosure of information (particularly documents and further material) in practice, with special emphasis on the modalities of document production under the IBA Rules (*III*).

I Legal Framework

2.65 While most arbitration laws provide only scant guidance on the mandatory exchange of information (*1*), arbitration rules and soft laws tend to be more specific (*2*).

1 Arbitration Laws

2.66 Most arbitration acts do not provide any, or only rather vague, provisions on the parties' disclosure duties, the tribunal's powers to order document production or the issue of the truth in a procedural context. The Model Law, for example, does not list any specific provisions that would allow or require the tribunal to order the production of documents or any other form of document exchange. Article 15 (2) Second Sentence of the Model Law merely states that each party must 'attach all papers and documents cited by it in the case'. The rule thus operates on the assumption that the parties are responsible for procuring the documents (and other means of evidence) that they require to support their case, rather than being entitled to access to the other party's sphere of information.

2.67 By contrast, Article 34 (2) (d) of the English Arbitration Act, seemingly inspired by the traditional common law model, specifically stipulates that the tribunals shall decide:

> whether any and if so which documents or classes of documents should be disclosed between and produced by the parties and at what stage.

2.68 The US Federal Arbitration Act states in its section 7 that:

> [t]he arbitrators selected either as prescribed in this title or otherwise, or a majority of them, may summon in writing any person to attend before them or any of them as a witness and in a proper case to bring with him or them any book, record, document, or paper which may be deemed material as evidence in the case.

2.69 Other arbitration laws indirectly address the tribunal's powers to order the production of documents. In Germany, Austria and Spain, for example, the tribunal may order the parties to provide relevant information and documents to an appointed expert.[313] While not containing any explicit provisions regarding the exchange of documents between the parties, these rules show that the tribunal is generally entitled to direct the parties to disclose information and documents.[314]

2.70 Other acts that do not provide rules on document disclosure, do, however, grant the tribunal powers to order the parties to produce means of evidence in their possession.[315] Under Article 1467 (3) of the French NCPC, for example, if a party is in possession of any (relevant) means of evidence, the arbitral tribunal may enjoin that party to produce it.[316] Likewise, under Article 22 of the Brazilian Arbitration Act, the tribunal may take the evidence of the parties, hear witnesses, and determine that expert opinions or other evidence is necessary, at the request of the parties or on their own initiative.[317] While these rules make no direct statements regarding the exchange of documents or information, they confirm the tribunal's wide authority to order the parties to produce relevant material.

2.71 The above shows that domestic national arbitration laws usually contain only sparse rules on the production of evidence, with the exception of English and American laws. Nonetheless, and importantly, the analysis confirms that under the prevalent laws the tribunal has the broad general authority to make such an order.

2 Arbitration Rules and Best Practices

2.72 Most arbitration rules have been adapted in the wake of international developments and expressly grant the tribunal the authority to order the production of documents and other potential means of evidence. Provisions to this effect can be found under the Rules of the LCIA,[318]

313. *See* sec. 1049 (1) Second Sentence ZPO, sec. 611 (1) (2) Austrian Code of Civil Procedure, Art. 22 (1) Lei de Arbitraje.
314. *See*, however, for the German Arbitration Act Münch, 'ZPO § 1049' in Thomas Rauscher and Wolfgang Krüger (eds), *Münchener Kommentar zur ZPO* (5th edn, 2017) para. 71, who, from a rather German domestic perspective seems to struggle with the notion of a general duty to disclose documents. In any case, considerations of confidentiality aside (*see* below Chapter 2, B.III.1.v.[a]) it is submitted that does not make any difference whether a party is required to provide information to an expert, who forwards this information to the tribunal, or of the party is required to provide said information directly to the tribunal and the opposing party. For the parties' general information duties *see* below, Chapter 2, B.II.
315. For a more extensive overview, *see* below, Chapter 2, B.II.
316. Article 1467 (3) NCPC: 'Si une partie détient un élément de preuve, le tribunal arbitral peut lui enjoindre de le produire selon les modalités qu'il détermine et au besoin à peine d'astreinte.'
317. Article 22 Brazilian Arbitration Act: 'The sole arbitrator or the arbitral tribunal, either ex officio or at the parties' request, may hear parties' and witnesses' testimony and may rule on the production of expert evidence, and other evidence deemed necessary.'
318. Article 22 (1) LCIA Rules: 'The Arbitral Tribunal shall have the power, (...) (iv) to order any party to make any documents, goods, samples, property, site or thing under its control available for inspection by the Arbitral Tribunal, any other party, any expert to such party and any expert to the Tribunal (...).'

SCC,[319] VIAC,[320] ICDR,[321] HKIAC[322] and SCAI.[323] Similar provisions can also be found under the Rules of the PCA[324] and ICSID.[325]

2.73 The ICC Rules, in Appendix IV (case management techniques), suggest the following measures to control time and costs under Item (d) Production of documentary evidence:

(i) requiring the parties to produce with their submissions the documents on which they rely;
(ii) avoiding requests for document production when appropriate in order to control time and cost;
(iii) in those cases where requests for document production are considered appropriate, limiting such requests to documents or categories of documents that are relevant and material to the outcome of the case;
(iv) establishing reasonable time limits for the production of documents;
(v) using a schedule of document production to facilitate the resolution of issues in relation to the production of documents.

2.74 While the DIS Rules do not provide any explicit rules on the tribunal's authority, they follow a rather German domestic approach, which is little compatible with international practice.[326] According to Annex 3 D of the DIS Rules, during the case management (the tribunal conference), the arbitral tribunal shall discuss with the parties whether the production of documents can be requested from a party that does

319. Article 31 (3) SCC Rules: 'At the request of a party, or exceptionally on its own motion, the Arbitral Tribunal may order a party to produce any documents or other evidence that may be relevant to the case and material to its outcome.'
320. Article 29 (1) Vienna Rules: 'If the arbitral tribunal considers it necessary, it may on its own initiative collect evidence, question parties or witnesses, request the parties to submit evidence, and call experts.'
321. Article 21 (4) ICDR Rules: 'The tribunal may, upon application, require a party to make available to another party documents in that party's possession not otherwise available to the party seeking the documents, that are reasonably believed to exist and to be relevant and material to the outcome of the case. Requests for documents shall contain a description of specific documents or classes of documents, along with an explanation of their relevance and materiality to the outcome of the case'; *see also* further provisions on Art. 21 ICDR Rules on the Exchange of Information.
322. Article 22.3 HKIAC Rules: 'At any time during the arbitration, the arbitral tribunal may allow or require a party to produce documents, exhibits or other evidence that the arbitral tribunal determines to be relevant to the case and material to its outcome. The arbitral tribunal shall have the power to admit or exclude any documents, exhibits or other evidence.'
323. Article 26.2 SCAI Rules: 'At any time during the arbitral proceedings, the arbitral tribunal may require the parties to produce documents, exhibits, or other evidence within a period of time determined by the arbitral tribunal.'
324. Article 27 PCA Rules: 'At any time during the arbitral proceedings the arbitral tribunal may require the parties to produce documents, exhibits or other evidence within such a period of time as the arbitral tribunal shall determine. The arbitral tribunal may also, after consultation with the parties, perform a site visit.'
325. Under Art. 43 (a) ICSID Convention, 'the Tribunal may, if it deems it necessary at any stage of the proceedings, call upon the parties to produce documents or other evidence'. The same is allowed under Rule 34.2 (a) ICSID Rules.
326. *See* below, Chapter 2, B.III.1.a.v.(c).

not bear the burden of proof. The tribunal shall further discuss the possibility of limiting document production requests in general.

2.75 In line with the common law tradition,[327] R-22 of the AAA Rules grants broad and detailed powers to order document production as well as an exchange of information.[328] Further, unlike the above international arbitration rules, the AAA Rules even allow for the possibility of taking depositions under Item (f) of Annex L-3:

> In exceptional cases, at the discretion of the arbitrator, upon good cause shown and consistent with the expedited nature of arbitration, the arbitrator may order depositions to obtain the testimony of a person who may possess information determined by the arbitrator to be relevant and material to the outcome of the case.

2.76 This is also in line with the approach identified by the ALI/UNIDRTOIT Principles of Transnational Civil Procedure. According to Principle 16.1 First Sentence, each party as well as the trier of fact:

> should have access to relevant and nonprivileged evidence, including testimony of parties and witnesses, expert testimony, documents, and evidence derived from inspection of things, entry upon land, or, under appropriate circumstances, from physical or mental examination of a person.

2.77 This is supplemented by Rules 21 and 22, on the 'Disclosure and Exchange of Evidence'. Similar to the IBA Rules,[329] the ALI/UNIDROIT Rules expect the parties to exchange documents and other evidence in a preliminary phase (ALI/UNIDROIT Rules

---

327. *See* below, Chapter 2, B.II.1.
328. R-22. Pre-Hearing Exchange and Production of Information:
   (a) Authority of arbitrator. The arbitrator shall manage any necessary exchange of information among the parties with a view to achieving an efficient and economical resolution of the dispute, while at the same time promoting equality of treatment and safeguarding each party's opportunity to fairly present its claims and defences.
   (b) Documents. The arbitrator may, on the application of a party or on the arbitrator's own initiative:
      i. require the parties to exchange documents in their possession or custody on which they intend to rely;
      ii. require the parties to update their exchanges of the documents on which they intend to rely as such documents become known to them;
      iii. require the parties, in response to reasonable document requests, to make available to the other party documents, in the responding party's possession or custody, not otherwise readily available to the party seeking the documents, reasonably believed by the party seeking the documents to exist and to be relevant and material to the outcome of disputed issues; and
      iv. require the parties, when documents to be exchanged or produced are maintained in electronic form, to make such documents available in the form most convenient and economical for the party in possession of such documents, unless the arbitrator determines that there is good cause for requiring the documents to be produced in a different form. The parties should attempt to agree in advance upon, and the arbitrator may determine, reasonable search parameters to balance the need for production of electronically stored documents relevant and material to the outcome of disputed issues against the cost of locating and producing them.
329. *See* below, Chapter 2, B.III.1.

21 and 22).[330] The document production is to be carried out through specific party requests, based upon which it is the tribunal's authority to 'order production of other evidence as necessary in the interest of justice' (ALI/UNIDROIT Rule 22.2 Second Sentence). While the working group found that Rules 21 and 22 reflected the 'philosophy (...) of the common-law countries other than the United States',[331] the provisions 'should be interpreted as striking a balance between the restrictive civil-law systems and the broader systems in common-law jurisdictions'.[332]

2.78 Apart from that, the scope of the parties' disclosure duties is further elaborated by Article 3 of the IBA Rules, the specific application of which will be discussed in detail below.[333] In contrast to the IBA Rules, Article 4 of the Prague Rules suggests limiting the exchange of documents to the bare minimum but has yet to prove itself as an adequate and practical solution in international arbitration.[334]

II Information Models

2.79 As shown by the above survey, arbitration laws and rules provide a solid legal framework for the prevalent information model in international arbitration, rendering the recourse to domestic approaches obsolete.

2.80 For the purposes of this study, the term 'information model' shall describe the approach within a contentious proceeding – such as arbitration – to the parties' duties and burdens to voluntarily or compulsory feed information and other relevant material into the dispute. There are two opposing approaches that are particularly known from domestic civil litigation, namely the Anglo-American 'full disclosure'-model, on the one hand, and the highly restrictive Germanic '*nemo tenetur*'-model on the other. Neither of these applies in international arbitration. Rather, as the chapter will further elaborate, international arbitrations are subject to an information model that contains different elements of both, without being a mere compromise between the two. International arbitration has developed a specific information model suitable to its needs, with due regard for the necessity of conducting the proceedings efficiently (*1*).

2.81 Closely related to this issue is the parties' (and witnesses') procedural duty to submit (or testify) the truth, whereby the establishment of the truth is necessarily compromised by subjective and objective factors in any proceeding (*2*).

1 *Full Disclosure Versus* Nemo Tenetur

2.82 It is no secret that the comparison of civil procedures in common law with other legal traditions reveals a cultural divide. While common law jurisdictions generally

330. American Law Institute (ALI) and UNIDROIT (n. 203) para. R-22A.
331. *Ibid.*, R-22C.
332. *Ibid.*, R-22E.
333. *See* below, Chapter 2, B.III.1.a.
334. *See* below, Chapter 2, B.III.1.b.

operate with an extensive pretrial exchange of information and documents (discovery or disclosure),[335] to other jurisdictions, this mandatory pretrial exchange of information (including adverse facts and documents) is foreign. In fact, some civil law jurisdictions, such as Germany,[336] go so far as to state that no party may be obliged to submit facts or means of evidence adverse to its position (so-called *nemo tenetur*).[337] This divide and its potential consequences have, naturally, been extensively discussed by the international arbitration community and shall, therefore, not be the focus of this study.[338]

2.83 The question of what effects these different approaches may bring to bear on international arbitrations remains contentious. While it is generally accepted that domestic rules on disclosure and discovery do not apply in international arbitration,[339] the application of the Germanic *nemo tenetur* principle continues to be advocated in international arbitration where German law applies to the merits of the dispute.[340] It is at times suggested that the *nemo tenetur* principle in Germany forms part of the substantive law, and is thus binding upon the tribunal in case German law governs the merits of the dispute.[341] In this context, it must, however, be noted that, from an international comparative perspective, the *nemo tenetur* is utterly outdated. Rather, it is a:

> universally accepted and fundamental rule that the court and the parties to litigation should generally have access to all relevant evidence. Insofar as Germany

335. *See* for the historical development, Alan K Goldstein, 'A Short History of Discovery' (1981) 10 Anglo-American Law Review 257, 257; David Mackie, 'Discovery in Commercial Litigation' in AAS Zuckerman and Ross Cranston (eds), *Reform of Civil Procedure: Essays on 'Access to Justice'* (Clarendon Press; Oxford University Press 1995) 139, 143–148; for a thorough analysis of discovery in English civil procedure leading to the Woolf Reforms, *see* Harry Woolf and Christopher Campbell-Holt, *The Pursuit of Justice* (Oxford University Press 2008) 315; of course, even within common law jurisdiction, the practice of discovery is a highly contentious issue, *see, e.g.*, Martin H Redish, 'The Allocation of Discovery Costs and the Foundations of Modern Procedure' in FH Buckley (ed.), *The American Illness: Essays on the Rule of Law* (Yale University Press 2013) 202: 'In many ways, discovery is reminiscent of the invention of fire. Like fire, if used properly the discovery system can dramatically improve our situation. If abused, however, discovery can cause immeasurable damage.'
336. *BGH, Judgment of 11 June 1990* [1990] NJW 3151 [III] with further references.
337. For an extensive examination of the Federal Court of Justice's approach, *see* Christian Gomille, *Informationsproblem Und Wahrheitspflicht: Ein Aufklärungsmodell Für Den Zivilprozess* (Mohr Siebeck 2016) 25, 35–38, 46–48 who comprehensively analyses that *nemo tenetur* is incompatible with sec. 138 (1) ZPO. Further, Gomille argues that the principle is not a necessary consequence of the burden of pleading, the subjective and objective burden of proof, or the generally adversarial nature of proceedings in Germany.
338. Blackaby and others (n. 14) 376 et seq., 380 et seq.; Gary Born, *International Commercial Arbitration* (3rd edn, Kluwer Law International 2021) 2493 et seqq.; Gabrielle Kaufmann-Kohler and Philippe Bärtsch, 'Discovery in International Arbitration: How Much Is Too Much?' [2004] SchiedsVZ 13; Stürner (n. 201) 235; Rolf Trittmann, 'The Interplay Between Procedural and Substantive Law in International Arbitration' [2016] SchiedsVZ 7.
339. *See* on the current practice below, Chapter 2, B.III.1.a.
340. *See, e.g.*, for the German Arbitration Act Münch (n. 253) para. 71, who, from a rather German domestic perspective seems to struggle with the notion of a general duty to disclose documents.
341. Trittmann (n. 338) 14, 15.

and some other continental or continental-influenced legal systems have not completely put this basic evidentiary conception into effect they have fallen behind the common standard.[342]

2.84 Moreover, as this present study shows, the fact-finding model in international arbitration is in the process of breaking away from domestic fact-finding rules. One can, in fact, observe the emergence and stabilization of an information model which offers distinct features in line with the specific needs of international arbitration which cannot be found in any domestic civil procedure. Rather than relying on (presumed) civil law or common law concepts, a unique transnational system is in the making.

2.85 Importantly, the information model prevalent in international arbitration rejects the overly liberal approach of *nemo tenetur*, as most arbitration laws and rules contain comprehensive information duties that oblige the parties to wide-ranging transparency rather than allowing them to withhold information.[343] This is confirmed by ALI/UNIDROIT Principle 16.1 First Sentence[344] as well as the authority of the tribunal – granted by most modern arbitration laws and rules – to order the parties to disclose information and other documents.[345] The ICSID Convention goes even further, expressly authorizing the tribunal to subsequently revise the award, if it emerges that one of the parties has concealed material facts.[346]

2.86 At the same time, the fact-finding model in international arbitration is distinct from domestic discovery and disclosure proceedings. It seeks to limit the exchange of information to what is considered reasonable to ensure efficient proceedings. For instance, the IBA Rules state, *inter alia*, that the tribunal must always bear in mind 'considerations of procedural economy, proportionality, fairness or equality of the parties that the arbitral tribunal determines to be compelling' (Article 9.2 (g)). Of course, the right balance between broad disclosure of information and efficiency remains the subject of ongoing discussions. Not only continental European[347] but also

342. Stürner (n. 201) 235.
343. *See* above, Chapter 2, I, *see* further Jeffrey Waincymer, *Procedure and Evidence in International Arbitration* (Kluwer Law International 2012) 831 et seq.
344. ALI/UNIDROIT Principle 16.1 First Sentence: 'Generally, the court and each party should have access to relevant and nonprivileged evidence, including testimony of parties and witnesses, expert testimony, documents, and evidence derived from inspection of things, entry upon land, or, under appropriate circumstances, from physical or mental examination of a person. The parties should have the right to submit statements that are accorded evidentiary effect.'
345. *See* above, Chapter 2, B.I.
346. Article 51 (1) ICSID Convention: 'Either party may request revision of the award by an application in writing addressed to the Secretary-General on the ground of discovery of some fact of such a nature as decisively to affect the award, provided that when the award was rendered that fact was unknown to the Tribunal and to the applicant and that the applicant's ignorance of that fact was not due to negligence.'
347. Trittmann (n. 338) 8.

US-based[348] lawyers tend to find that the current practice in international arbitration is more of a concession to the demands of common law practitioners. While the concept of document production procedures certainly originated from the common law sphere, as will be shown below, in international arbitration, the duties of the parties are comparatively restricted. In particular, there is neither an automatic exchange of document lists nor an automatic exchange of the listed documents.[349] Rather, it is the tribunal's task to carefully review the reasoned production request, as well as the objections, in order to make an individual decision on each category of documents.[350] Moreover, other important features of discovery (or disclosure) proceedings are virtually unknown in arbitration. This is especially true for the exchange of depositions and interrogatories, which are part of a comprehensive exchange of information but can significantly delay the procedures.[351]

2.87 From the above, it follows that the prevalent information model can be neither described as 'full disclosure' nor does it adhere to the principle of '*nemo tenetur*'. Rather, modern international arbitration proceedings usually rely on a finely balanced system of sufficiently detailed pleadings,[352] comprehensive but limited document disclosure,[353] and, as will be further addressed below, certain powers of the tribunal to proactively engage in fact-finding where this is deemed appropriate.[354] In modern arbitration, there is no room for overly liberal attitudes that allow relevant information to be withheld. The tribunal's powers trump overly adversarial approaches and confirm that the search for truth[355] is accorded higher priority than any rights to withhold adverse information.[356] At the beginning of the proceeding, the tribunal should thus establish and formulate what is expected from the parties, for example, by including an adequate provision in the first procedural order. (For example: 'The Parties are expected to make their submissions completely and truthfully, and may not withhold information, documents or evidence, even though it may be adverse to their position.')

348. Martínez-Fraga (n. 177) 67: 'Careful analysis establishes that discovery and the underlying tenets configuring the system commonly referred to as the Federal Rules of Civil Procedure, while conceptually and doctrinally distant from the civil code and the continental system, are close to arbitration and the underlying policies that sustain and define it as distinct from judicial proceedings because of its foundation rooted in party-autonomy. (...). Accordingly, discovery as framed, formed, and defined by the Federal Rules of Civil Procedure clearly comports with the nature of arbitration, and it is only because of the misperception arising from want of familiarity on the part of practitioners from other non-common law jurisdictions, and adherence to platitudes of discovery abuses by common law practitioners, judges, and commentators, that the affinity between discovery and arbitration has been obscured.'
349. *See* below, Chapter 2, B.III.1.a.i and ii.
350. *See* below, Chapter 2, B.III.1.a.ii.
351. *See* below, Chapter 2, B.III.2.
352. *See* above, Chapter 2, A.II.2.
353. *See* below, Chapter 2, B.III.1.
354. *See* below, Chapter 2, C.
355. *See* below, Chapter 2, B.II.2.
356. This is also corroborated by duty of good faith litigation frequently imposed on the parties in different arbitration laws and acts and also stipulated as a transnational principle under ALI/UNIDRTOIT Principle 11.1: 'The parties and their lawyers must conduct themselves in good faith in dealing with the court and other parties.'

2 Truth in a Procedural Context

2.88 Closely linked to the prevalent information model, due regard must be given to the meaning of the term 'truth' in the procedural context, which is more complex than it might appear at first sight.

2.89 In a fairly radical statement, a German judge declared that he was not 'interested in the truth' after denying a party's request to take evidence.[357] The requesting party felt they had been treated unfairly and challenged the judge. After the challenge was first rejected, the party found the support of the German Federal Constitutional Court. The Federal Constitutional Court agreed that a judge who expressly states his disinterest in the truth may, in fact, appear biased:

> The adversarial nature of the civil procedure leaves it to the responsibility of the parties to make the necessary factual allegations and to adduce evidence, which limits the task of the judge to investigate the facts (...). However, (...) it does not mean that the judge should not be interested in the truth in principle.[358]

2.90 The decision not only reflects the difficulties of dealing with truth in presumably adversarial[359] procedures but also raises the universal question of how the term 'truth' is to be defined in a legal and procedural context. As a matter of course, there is no independent concept of truth in arbitration. Commentators on international procedural law at times rely on correspondence theory,[360] which can be traced back to Aristotle's metaphysics.[361] In simple terms, it states that a fact is true if it corresponds to reality.[362] Similarly, as extensively analysed by *Twining*[363], the Anglo-Saxon common law tradition of evidence law is largely based on the rationalist approach to epistemology, which is likewise based on the correspondence theory of truth.[364] While this approach accepts that 'knowledge about past events is typically based upon incomplete evidence', it argues that 'the best way for discovering truth is reason'.[365]

357. *BVerfG, Order of 12 December 2012* [2013] BeckRS 45462 [16], translation by the author.
358. *Ibid.*
359. *See* for a definition of adversarial and inquisitorial procedures below, Chapter 2, C.I.
360. Moritz Brinkmann, *Das Beweismaß Im Zivilprozess aus rechtsvergleichender Sicht* (Heymanns 2005) 6; Peter-Andreas Brand, 'Grenzen Zivilprozessualer Wahrheit Und Gerechtigkeit' [2017] NJW 3558, 3561.
361. Marian David, 'The Correspondence Theory of Truth' in Edward N Zalta (ed.), *The Stanford Encyclopedia of Philosophy* (2020th edn, Metaphysics Research Lab, Stanford University) para. 1.
362. Brinkmann (n. 360) 5, translation by the author.
363. William Twining, *Rethinking Evidence: Exploratory Essays* (2nd ed, Cambridge University Press 2006) ch 3.
364. *See* further Terence Anderson, David A Schum and William Lawrence Twining, *Analysis of Evidence* (Cambridge University Press 2005) 78, 79; Donald Nicolson, 'Truth, Reason and Justice: Epistemology and Politics in Evidence Disclosure' (1994) 57 The Modern Law Review 726, 727; Donald Nicolson, 'Taking Epistemology Seriously: "Truth, Reason and Justice" Revisited' (2013) 17 The International Journal of Evidence & Proof 1.
365. Nicolson, 'Truth, Reason and Justice' (n. 364) 767.

2.91 Establishing the truth is considered the 'intrinsic goal of fact-finding'.[366] Notoriously, however, the quest for the objective truth in contradictory procedures is challenging, to say the least – for a number of reasons. To begin with, there is always the possibility that the parties' and witnesses' ethics and integrity are compromised. Where much is at stake, parties may be tempted to knowingly make or arrange for false statements.

2.92 Apart from this, issues of misidentification impose strict limitations on the fact-finding:[367] Even an honest party may be mistaken, and a truthful witness can misjudge, misremember or simply forget relevant parts of the story.[368] The longstanding history of scepticism traditions[369] suggests that the human mind mixes subjective impressions of a specific situation with subsequent impressions relating to that very situation,[370] be it photos, videos or oral descriptions of others. Basic psychological research and neuroscience studies indicate that memory is a reconstructive process that is highly susceptible to distortion:[371]

> Perceptions of reality are not simply given to us by our senses; we have to use subjective creativity to make sense of them.[372]

2.93 It follows that parties or witnesses can hardly be expected to submit or testify the 'objective truth'. Rather, as a general rule, the trier of fact must be satisfied with their (honest) versions of it, i.e., their 'subjective truth'.[373]

2.94 Further, in addition to these subjective limitations, arbitration proceedings are designed to serve justice while being both efficient and proportionate. The latter items necessarily compromise the quest for the material truth. Where a party has failed to address an allegation or is in default, the trier of fact may interpret this as an admission.[374] Where a party is in default, the trier of fact may decide based on the other party's version of the facts.[375] Moreover, under due consideration of proportionality, the scope of document production[376] and the use of expert witnesses can usually be

366. Moritz Brinkmann, 'The Synthesis of Common and Civil Law Standard of Proof Formulae in the Ali / Unidroit Principles of Transnational Civil Procedure' (2004) 9 Uniform Law Review 875, 881.
367. Ragnar Harbst, 'Die (Un-)Verlässlichkeit Der Zeugenerinnerung' 2021 SchiedsVZ 49, 50 et seq.
368. Twining (.n 365) 165–191.
369. William Twining, 'Some Scepticism about Some Scepticisms' (1984) 11 Journal of Law and Society 137, 138 et seq.: ' memory is unreliable, perception is unreliable, honest witnesses are suggestible, bias is unavoidable, non-rational techniques of persuasion are potent and so on'.
370. *Ibid.*
371. Joyce W Lacy and Craig EL Stark, 'The Neuroscience of Memory: Implications for the Courtroom' (2013) 14 Nature Reviews Neuroscience 649.
372. Nicolson, 'Taking Epistemology Seriously' (n. 364) 13.
373. Ragnar Harbst, *A Counsel's Guide to Examining and Preparing Witnesses in International Arbitration* (Kluwer Law International 2015) 184; Luc Demeyere and Bernard Hanotiau (eds), 'The Search for the Truth in Arbitration: Is It Possible to Start from a Definition of "Truth"?', *Do Arbitral Awards Reveal the Truth?: Reports from the Third Joint Cepani-Nai Colloquium Held on March 21, 2019* (2019) 6: 'formal legal truth'.
374. *See* above, Chapter 2, A.II.2.
375. *See, inter alia*, Art. 25 (b) Model Law.
376. *See* below, Chapter 2, B.III.1.a.v.(b).

limited.[377] The lower the meaning and value of a dispute, the leaner the procedure usually turns out to be. In other words, the objective truth is compromised if the investigation thereof might unduly delay the proceedings.

2.95 Beyond that, jurisdictions with broad disclosure duties in particular seek to achieve a balance by establishing complex systems of privilege, which are invoked in international arbitration as well. In other words, even where a piece of information or means of evidence is relevant and material and could be readily introduced, in many cases, the rules of privilege exempt the parties from the production.[378]

2.96 Lastly, party-dominated approaches to the exchange of information may further undermine the search for the truth. Adversarialism suggests that the trier of fact is bound by and restricted to the parties' factual submissions.[379] Where the parties agree on a fact, the trier of fact accepts it to be true, whether it is believable or not.[380] Likewise, adversarial techniques of preparing and examining evidence (such as cross-examination) may further obscure the truth.[381]

2.97 The truth in a procedural sense is thus a heterogeneous composition of facts that the court deems to be 'true' as the result of the taking of evidence, combined with facts that the parties have agreed upon, facts that are left undisputed, as well as facts considered to be true due to a party's shortcomings or negligence. The objective truth may be established only by chance during an arbitration, if at all.[382]

2.98 From the above, one can conclude that it is necessary for all stakeholders to acknowledge the challenges in the quest for truth. Even with the best efforts, no tribunal will overcome the inaccuracies which are owed to the subjectivity of perception and the requirements of efficiency. One must accept that, at the end of the proceeding, a trier of facts may, at best, have established the procedural truth, which is hopefully adequately close to the objective truth.

III The Exchange of Documents and Information in Practice

2.99 Most commonly, parties exchange relevant information via formalized document production procedures (*1*). The use of depositions and interrogatories, which features particularly in the Anglo-Saxon tradition, is rather less common, albeit generally subject to the tribunal's discretion (*2*). Lastly, the parties may have recourse to substantive information claims under the *lex causae* (where applicable). However, their application is usually difficult to reconcile with the prevalent information model in international arbitration (*3*).

377. *See* below, Chapter 3, A.B.II.
378. *See* below, Chapter 2, B.III.1.a.v.(a).
379. *See* for a definition of adversarial and inquisitorial procedures below, Chapter 2, C.I.
380. In the ambit of international arbitration, it is however submitted that the tribunal may disregard a party's agreement on the facts if it is obviously wrong, *see* below, Chapter 2, C.II.2.
381. Harbst (n. 367) 56, *see* further below, Chapter 3, B.2.a.
382. *See*, for German domestic law, Brand (n. 360) 3650 who relies on similar considerations.

1 *Document Production*

2.100 Over the last few decades, the practice of document production has changed considerably. When analysing the status quo, one must bear in mind that the current practice in arbitration, despite the changes it has undergone, is undeniably rooted in the common law tradition. To be more specific, it originated centuries ago in equity before the Court of Chancery, long before being adopted by common law courts.[383] At this time, litigious proceedings were certainly not as document driven as they have since become. If any document was involved at all, parties may have produced a single document from which the argument had arisen. Disputes revolving around millions of potentially relevant documents[384] were unthinkable – which likely holds equally true for disputes from only forty to fifty years ago. With the continuously growing amount of stored data, it is ever more challenging to strike a balance between the parties' right to information and transparency and the need for efficient proceedings.

2.101 While most arbitration rules allow the tribunal to order the production of documents, they usually do not reflect any specifics on the document production procedure.[385] In international arbitration, the stakeholders thus frequently have recourse to the IBA Rules on the Taking of Evidence, which reflect the currently prevalent, albeit not undisputed, best practice (*a*). As a countermodel, the Prague Rules seek to further limit document production (*b*).

i *Best Practice under the IBA Rules*

2.102 The IBA Rules are a stellar example of the transnationalization of international arbitration law.[386] They contain a fairly elaborate system of document production, which has never been sanctioned by any state legislator, but which is nonetheless widely applied in international arbitration proceedings across the globe.[387] As the IBA

383. Goldstein (n. 335) 263, who assumes that common law courts may have started to order disclosure in the period of the reign of Charles II (1660–1685).

384. To give an example of the challenges of e-disclosure and potential solutions other than limitations, in *Pyrrho Investments Limited, MWB Business Exchange Limited v MWB Property Limited, Rick Aspland-Robinson, Keval Pankhania, Richard Balfour-Lynn, Jagtar Singh* [2016] EWHC 256 (Ch) [33.(6)], the court had to decide whether the use of 'predictive coding' to search for documents was a suitable approach for E-Discovery under the CPR. In said case, the number of electronic documents amounted to over 3,000,000. The court considered that '[t]he cost of manually searching these documents would be enormous, amounting to several million pounds at least'.

385. *See* above, Chapter 1, B.

386. *See* above, Chapter 1, A.B.II, *see* further Klaus Sachs, 'Use of Documents and Document Discovery: "Fishing Expeditions" versus Transparency and Burden of Proof' [2003] SchiedsVZ 193, 199; István Varga, *Beweiserhebung in transatlantischen Schiedsverfahren: eine Suche nach Kompromissen zwischen deutscher und US-amerikanischer Beweisrechtstradition* (Nomos 2006) 138–153.

387. Queen Mary University of London (n. 186) 35.

Rules and their specific applications are the subjects of countless publications,[388] the present study shall limit itself to an outline of the basic concepts.

2.103 The IBA Rules confirm the general approach of allowing the parties to engage in the pretrial (or rather, pre-hearing) exchange of information and require all parties to show their hand. In comparison to common law proceedings, these disclosure obligations on the parties are nevertheless rather limited and are specifically designed to prohibit fishing expeditions.[389] In line with this, the working group noted that common law style discovery was 'generally inappropriate in international arbitration'.[390] Rather, 'requests for documents to be produced should be carefully tailored to issues that are relevant and material to the determination of the case'.[391]

2.104 Importantly, document production under IBA Rules is mainly a fact-gathering instrument, rather than being a matter of taking evidence. It serves the primary purpose of collecting all potentially relevant information and material, which, in case of doubt, must subsequently be verified through evidence in a later stage. Nonetheless, the documents thus exchanged may be used as means of evidence as well.

2.105 Unlike the FRCP,[392] the IBA Rules do not require any automatic disclosure or exchange of documents. Rather, they require each party to produce the documents they seek to rely on (Article 3.1) and allow the parties to make specific requests for documents to be produced by the opponent (Article 3.2–3.14). In these requests, the parties must (i) identify the document (or category of document) sought, (ii) give a sufficiently detailed description, (iii) indicate its materiality and relevance for the case, (Article 3.3.(a), (b) IBA Rules (*see* below)) and state why it assumes that the documents requested are in the possession, custody or control of another party. The IBA Rules then require the opposing party to comment on each request (Article 3.4 IBA Rules), after which the tribunal makes a decision on each individual request (Article 3.10 IBA Rules). In practice, the tribunal usually organizes the Article 3 procedures by means of so-called Redfern Schedules (attributed to Mr Alan Redfern), i.e., specific tables that reflect the parties' document requests, indicating the alleged relevance or materiality, the opponent's response or objection, the party's reply to the objection and

388. *See, inter alia,* Blackaby and others (n. 14) 376 et seq., 380 et seq.; Born (n. 338) 2493 et seqq.; Kaufmann-Kohler and Bärtsch (n. 338); Trittmann (n. 338).
389. 1999 IBA Working Party, 2010 Rules of Evidence Review Subcommittee and 2020 IBA Rules of Evidence Review Task Force (n. 188) 9.
390. 1999 IBA Working Party and 2010 Rules of Evidence Review Subcommittee, *Commentary on the Revised Text of the 2010 IBA Rules on the Taking of Evidence in International Arbitration* (2010) 7; 1999 IBA Working Party, 2010 Rules of Evidence Review Subcommittee and 2020 IBA Rules of Evidence Review Task Force (n. 188) 10, *see* further below, Chapter 2, A.B.III.iii and iv.
391. 1999 IBA Working Party and 2010 Rules of Evidence Review Subcommittee (n. 390) 7.
392. *See* Rule 34 (b) as well as Rule 26 (a) (1) (A) FRCP for initial disclosure: 'Except as exempted by Rule 26(a)(1)(B) or as otherwise stipulated or ordered by the court, a party must, without awaiting a discovery request, provide to the other parties (...) a copy - or a description by category and location - of all documents (...) that the disclosing party has in its possession.'

lastly, the decision of the tribunal.[393] More recently, the use of the 'Armesto Schedule' has been suggested, which reflects a number of modifications to the format, defines the criteria against which the requests should be measured and suggests the use of a standardized procedural order.[394] It remains to be seen whether the Armesto Schedule will prevail in practice.

2.106 The below will accordingly briefly outline the requirements of document production, starting with the question of whether it is an opt-in or an opt-out procedure (i). This is followed by an analysis of the formal requirements of the parties' requests, (ii), the standard of relevance (iii), and materiality (iv), potential objections to the opposing party's request, (iv) and the consequences of a party's non-compliance (v).

a Opt-In Versus Opt-Out

2.107 A question that frequently arises in international arbitration between parties with different legal backgrounds is whether document production proceedings are available to the parties by default. While in investment arbitration, document production is the rule rather than the exception,[395] and despite the wide acceptance of the IBA Rules,[396] the practice in international commercial arbitration is not quite as uniform. In particular, many non-common lawyers still view document production procedures to be excessive, overly burdensome, and inefficient.[397]

2.108 Most arbitration rules and laws grant tribunals the right to order the production of documents.[398] Consequently, no explicit party consent is required to allow document production and the tribunal may order a party to disclose documents against its will, even if the document contains adverse information.[399] Nonetheless, due to the lack of an explicit provision and in view of the undeniable cultural differences, there is also no inherent subjective right of the parties to demand document production; at least

393. Dominic Wong, 'Summary of Young-OGEMID Symposium No. 3: "Prove It! Evidence in International Arbitration (6–15 June 2016)"' (2017) 14 Transnational Dispute Management 20, 8.
394. *See* Mélanie Riofrio Piché and Sofia de Sampaio Jalles, 'The Armesto Schedule: A Step Further to a More Efficient Document Production' (*Kluwer Arbitration Blog*, 4 April 2020).
395. *See* ICDR, *Practice Notes for Respondents* (2015): 'The applicable rules regarding document disclosure are often agreed to by the parties or ordered by the Tribunal. Reference is frequently made to the IBA Rules on the Taking of Evidence in International Arbitration (2010) to guide the Tribunal's decision on whether documents should be disclosed and to what extent. In ICSID proceedings, document production applications are routinely addressed using a Redfern schedule (...).'; ICSID, 'Production of Documents – ICSID Convention Arbitration' https://icsid.worldbank.org/en/Pages/process/Production-of-Documents.aspx; 1999 IBA Working Party, 2010 Rules of Evidence Review Subcommittee and 2020 IBA Rules of Evidence Review Task Force (n. 188) 10.
396. Queen Mary University of London (n. 186) 36; Riofrio Piché and de Sampaio Jalles (n. 394).
397. *See* below, Chapter 2, B.2.
398. *See* above, Chapter 2, B.I.
399. Waincymer (n. 343) 831 et seq.

not in commercial arbitration proceedings. The steady practice in investment arbitration may suggest otherwise.[400] In commercial proceedings, the decision lies within the tribunal's discretion and is taken on a case-to-case basis, duly considering the common practice and the parties' legitimate expectations. Yet, in making the decision, the tribunal must take into consideration that there is a strong, albeit not undisputed, trend towards allowing document production in international arbitration. A party's objection to document production does not compromise the tribunal's discretion, as long as there is no exclusionary agreement between the parties.

b Requests and Identification of Documents

2.109 According to Article 3 (2) of the IBA Rules, any party may submit a request for production of documents to the Arbitral Tribunal and to the other parties within the timeframe ordered by the Arbitral Tribunal. The definition of 'document' is (in line with modern common law approaches)[401] rather broad and includes any 'writing, communication, picture, drawing, program or data of any kind, whether recorded or maintained on paper or by electronic, audio, visual or any other means'. Apart from all digitally stored information, it thus also comprises all types of digital communication, such as emails and chat protocols, including WhatsApp histories. Moreover, parties may also request the production of documents that have yet to be created,[402] such as accounts and other types of information which must first be compiled.

2.110 While only parts of the IBA working group found the right to demand production to be essential, there was a consensus to disallow fishing expeditions.[403] The IBA Rules, therefore, seek to limit the scope of document exchange by limiting requests to specific documents, or, where necessary, specific categories of documents. Article 3 (3) of the IBA Rules states that the request must contain either 'a description of each requested Document sufficient to identify it' or 'a description in sufficient detail (including subject matter) of a narrow and specific requested category of Documents that are reasonably believed to exist'. Note that in a similar vein, under Appendix IV (d) (iii) to the ICC Rules, the suggestion is made to limit 'requests to documents or categories of documents that are relevant and material to the outcome of the case'. Likewise, under Article 24.4 Second Sentence of the ICDR Rules, '[r]equests for documents shall contain a description of specific documents or classes of documents, along with an explanation of their relevance and materiality to the outcome of the case'. While 'classes' seems to be a broader term than 'categories', the language of the

400. *See* ICDR (n. 395): 'The applicable rules regarding document disclosure are often agreed to by the parties or ordered by the Tribunal. Reference is frequently made to the IBA Rules on the Taking of Evidence in International Arbitration (2010) to guide the Tribunal's decision on whether documents should be disclosed and to what extent. In ICSID proceedings, document production applications are routinely addressed using a Redfern schedule (...).'; ICSID (n. 395).
401. *See* below, Chapter 3, B.III.
402. Born (n. 338) 2527.
403. 1999 IBA Working Party, 2010 Rules of Evidence Review Subcommittee and 2020 IBA Rules of Evidence Review Task Force (n. 188) 10; 1999 IBA Working Party and 2010 Rules of Evidence Review Subcommittee (n. 390) 9.

ICDR Rules also requires the parties to include a sufficiently specific description thereof.

2.111 In the ambit of the IBA Rules, this is also referred to as the 'narrow and specific'-standard. As the Tribunal in *Landmark Ventures, Inc. v Insightec, Ltd.* emphasized in a procedural order, these are not 'mere formalities' but requirements which are vital in order to limit the document production to an adequate amount:

> In order to curtail expansive document production, the IBA Rules also require, in Articles 3(a)(ii) and 3(b), that requests to identify a 'narrow and specific' category of documents that are reasonably believed to exist, and that they include a statement as to how the documents requested are relevant to the case and material to its outcome. Again, these are not mere formalities. These requirements curtail so-called fishing expeditions. Furthermore, they are essential to containing the cost and burdens associated with document production(...).[404]

2.112 That being said, particularly the production of 'categories of documents' remains controversial,[405] owing to the challenges of striking the right balance between the parties' right to information and the need for efficiency. It is thus submitted that the specification of documents generally requires identification of the type of document, the author(s), (presumed) content, and/or location.[406] The well-known and frequently submitted formula of ''all documents' within a vague time frame, 'relating' to a broad topic' does not meet the standard.[407] There are, of course, situations in which such detailed information is not readily available to the requesting party. In that case, the requesting party may be expected to explain why it presumes the existence and content of the document. This ultimately leaves it to the tribunal to make an *ex-ante* assessment of whether such documents may exist and bear upon the outcome of the dispute.

2.113 The same standard of specificity must apply to e-documents, meaning that it is not sufficient to merely note a specific search term.[408]

c Relevance

2.114 The most important requirement for document production is the test of 'relevance and materiality'. According to Article 3.3.(b) of the IBA Rules, a requesting party must demonstrate why the documents are 'relevant to the case and material to its outcome'. It thus stipulates two complementary requirements, each of which must be met. The test is not exclusive to the IBA Rules, but can be found, in varying language,

404. *ICC Case No 18807/VRO/AGF, Procedural Order No 2 of 2013* Arbitrator Intelligence Materials [9].
405. The issue is also linked to the question of proportionality, *see* below Chapter 2, A.B.III.v.(b).
406. *See* Waincymer (n. 343) 11.7.2; 1999 IBA Working Party, 2010 Rules of Evidence Review Subcommittee and 2020 IBA Rules of Evidence Review Task Force (n. 188) 10.
407. Nathan D O'Malley, *Rules of Evidence in International Arbitration: An Annotated Guide* (2nd edn, Informa law from Routledge 2019) para. 3.35.
408. Waincymer (n. 343) para. 11.7.2.

in different sets of arbitration rules.[409] It reflects 'the pre-eminent test', which tribunals are encouraged to adhere to even outside the scope of the IBA Rules.[410]

2.115 While there is no uniform standard which determines whether a document is relevant to the case, generally, the test of relevance 'simply calls for the moving party to articulate convincingly why it believes that document Y will support contention X'.[411] A document is thus relevant if it renders a contention to be either more or less likely. A succinct definition is also contained in the commentary to the ALI/UNIDROIT Principles:

> In deciding upon admissibility of the evidence, the court makes a hypothetical evaluation connecting the proposed evidence with the issues in the case. If a probative inference may be drawn from the evidence to the facts, then the evidence is logically relevant.[412]

2.116 The requirement of relevance originates from common law proceedings.[413] While the tribunal should refrain from directly applying the common law test,[414] it may, in dubious cases, serve as an orientation. Under the classic common law definition, the test for 'relevance' is positive when:

> any two facts to which it is applied are so related to each other that according to the common course of events one either taken by itself or in connection with other facts proves or renders probable the past, present or future existence or non-existence of the other.[415]

2.117 Having recourse to the 'common course of events' means that the question of whether evidence is relevant usually requires an assessment based on common sense.[416]

409. *See, e.g.*, Art. 31 (3) SCC Rules; Art. 21 (4) ICDR Rules; Art. 22.3 HKIAC Rules, Art. 24.4 Second Sentence ICDR Rules.
410. O'Malley (n. 407) para. 3.8.2.
411. *Ibid.*, 3.7.2.
412. American Law Institute (ALI) and UNIDROIT (n. 203) para. R-25B.
413. The test of relevance was developed in common law jurisdictions. Traditionally, recourse was taken to the Peruvian Guano test, which was first established in 1882 in *Compagnie Financiere du Pacifique v Peruvian Guano Co* [1882] 11 QBD 55 [64] Lord Justice Brett famously held: 'It seems to me that every document which relates to the matters in question in the action, which not only would be evidence upon any issue, but also which, it is reasonable to suppose, contains information which may – not which must – either directly or indirectly enable the party requiring the affidavit either to advance his own case or to damage the case of his adversary. I have put in the words "either directly or indirectly" because, as it seems to me, a document can properly be said to contain information which may enable the party requiring the affidavit either to advance his own case or to damage the case of his adversary if it is a document which may fairly lead him to a train of enquiry which may have either of those two consequences.'
414. Waincymer (n. 343) 793.
415. James Fitzjames Stephen, *Digest of the Law of Evidence* (12th edn, Macmillan & Co 1936) Art. 1; cited after Keane and McKeown (n. 290) 23.
416. *Regina v Randall* [2003] UKHL 69 [20]: 'A judge ruling on a point of admissibility involving an issue of relevance has to decide whether the evidence is capable of increasing or diminishing

2.118 A typical (common law) example of (ir-)relevance can be found in *Holcombe v Hewson*, where the defendant argued that the plaintiff had delivered bad beer. In order to rebut the allegation, the plaintiff offered the witness evidence of other customers to demonstrate a general level of satisfaction. The court found the witness evidence to be irrelevant, stating:

> We cannot here enquire into the quality of different beer furnished to different persons. The plaintiff might deal well with one, and not with the others. Let him call some of those who frequented the defendant's house, and there drank the beer which he sent in.[417]

2.119 Importantly, it is the requesting party's task to lay out why it considers the requested document to be relevant. In *Landmark Ventures v Insightec*, the tribunal rejected a request for document production, as the party had failed to substantiate its request in this regard:

> Nearly all of the Claimant's requests fail to satisfy one or both of these standards [i.e. the relevance and materiality standards]. (...) Request No. 1, for instance, seeks 'all documents, including emails concerning, constituting, evidencing and pertaining to the negotiation of the Letter Agreement and any amendments thereto, as well as all correspondence between Claimant and Respondent relating thereto' on the basis that the 'documents are material and relevant to show the intention of the parties, and to explain the nature of the transaction within the context of investment banking norms and practices.' The problem with this request is that although extrinsic evidence *may* be necessary for proper interpretation of a contract, the Claimant has failed to tailor the request to the dispute at hand by isolating particular provisions or terms of the Letter Agreement as to which it (or, alternatively, the Respondent) contends negotiation history is relevant or material.[418]

2.120 A similar test of 'relevance and materiality' applies, as will be shown below, when deciding on the admission of evidence.[419] However, at the admission stage, the tribunal's perspective may be different and more advanced, as it occurs at a later phase of the proceedings when more information is available. Thus, as the tribunal stated in a procedural order in *Churchill Mining PLC and Planet Mining Pty Ltd v Republic of Indonesia*, the assessment of the tribunal during document production is necessarily of a prima facie character:

> At this stage of the proceedings [i.e. the document production phase], the Tribunal is only in a position to assess the *prima facie* relevance of the documents requested, having regard to the factual allegations the Parties made heretofore.

the probability of the existence of a fact in issue. The question of relevance is typically a matter of degree to be determined, for the most part, by common sense and experience.'

417. *Holcombe v Hewson* [1810] 2 Camp, KB 391.
418. *ICC Case No 18807/VRO/AGF, Procedural Order No. 2 of 2013* (n. 404) paras 10, 11.
419. *See* below, Chapter 3, C.II.

> This *prima facie* assessment does not preclude a different assessment at a later point of the arbitration, with the benefit of the entire evidentiary record.[420]

2.121 Accordingly, when assessing the relevance and materiality of requested documents, the tribunal must always keep in mind the preliminary nature of this early stage of the proceeding.

d Materiality

2.122 The requirement of relevance is supplemented by the requirement of materiality. Materiality determines whether the requested document is likely to bear upon the final award.[421] Like the requirement of relevance, the materiality test stems from common law litigation, where it is found to have been merged into the relevance test, thus retaining 'no independent viability'.[422] Similarly, in international arbitration, these two prerequisites are at times condensed into a single test.[423]

2.123 A closer examination, however, shows that the separate application of the materiality standard has its merits. In fact, there are various reasons why relevant information may not influence the outcome of the proceedings. For example, a piece of evidence can be immaterial if the record already contains sufficient evidence to determine a specific issue.[424]

2.124 Apart from that, some (mostly continental European) commentators suggest taking the burden of proof into consideration when determining materiality.[425] As will be detailed below, however, this approach must be rejected, especially since the burden of proof is a matter of taking evidence (i.e., of the later procedural phase) and is not to be taken into account during the fact-gathering process.[426]

2.125 In any case, the requirement of materiality should apply restrictively. While there truly is a need to contain the number of documents to be exchanged, especially at the beginning of the proceeding when documents are usually exchanged, it might be

---

420. *Churchill Mining PLC and Planet Mining Pty Ltd v Republic of Indonesia; ICSID ARB/12/14* Procedural Order No 5 of 19 March 2013 6.
421. O'Malley (n. 407) para. 3.78.
422. Konstantin Pilkov, 'Evidence in International Arbitration: Criteria for Admission and Evaluation' (2014) 80 Arbitration. The International Journal of Arbitration, Mediation and Dispute Management 147, 149; This is especially true for US litigation, where Rule 401 of the Federal Rules of Evidence states that '[r]elevant Evidence is relevant if: (a) it has any tendency to make a fact more or less probable than it would be without the evidence; and (b) the fact is of consequence in determining the action'.
423. *See, e.g., Churchill Mining PLC and Planet Mining Pty Ltd v Republic of Indonesia; ICSID ARB/12/14* (n. 420) para. 8: 'For purposes of this Order, the term "relevance" encompasses both the term "relevance" and "materiality".'
424. O'Malley (n. 407) para. 3.80; American Law Institute (ALI) and UNIDROIT (n. 203) para. R-25A.
425. *See* below, Chapter 2, B.III.1.a.v.(d).
426. *See* below, Chapter 2, B.III.1.a.v.(d) and Chapter 3, A.III.

difficult to assess whether the production of a specific document would bear on the outcome of the dispute.[427]

e Objections

2.126 Since the production of documents may be burdensome, time-consuming, and expensive, it is subject to certain limitations. These restrictions are particularly necessary due to the widespread misuse of document production as well as the ever-growing amounts of data available through e-discovery and e-disclosure.[428]

2.127 In particular, under the IBA Rules, parties may object to the production of documents where the information is privileged or confidential (a), where the production would be unreasonably burdensome, i.e., disproportionate (b), or where the documents stem from illegal sources (c). Moreover, some commentators suggest considering the burden of proof as a limitation to document production (d).

(i) Privilege and Confidentiality

2.128 Parties frequently rely on privilege to object to document production requests. The question of whether privilege is a matter of substantive law or procedural law remains disputed.[429] Its qualification has a decisive impact on the availability of evidence[430] and thus on the outcome of the proceeding. Based on a conflict of laws approach, no less than eight potentially applicable laws have been identified, namely:

- the law of the contract;
- the law of the seat of the arbitration (lex arbitri);
- the law of the jurisdiction where the party claiming the privilege resides;
- the law of the jurisdiction where the lawyer claiming the privilege resides;
- the law of the place where the communication/information was created;
- the law of the place where the lawyer with whom the communication took place is admitted;
- the law of the jurisdiction where enforcement of the award will be sought;
- general principles, without reference to any national law.[431]

2.129 Jurisdictions with far-reaching discovery or disclosure proceedings usually balance these with corresponding rules on privilege, ensuring that some information

427. Waincymer (n. 343) para. 11.7.1.2.

428. *See* above *Pyrrho Investments Limited, MWB Business Exchange Limited v MWB Property Limited, Rick Aspland-Robinson, Keval Pankhania, Richard Balfour-Lynn, Jagtar Singh* (n. 384) para. 33.(6).

429. *See* for an overview Klaus Peter Berger, 'Evidentiary Privileges: Best Practice Standards versus/and Arbitral Discretion' (2006) 22 Arbitration International 501, paras 506–513; Diana Kuitkowski, 'The Law Applicable to Privilege Claims in International Arbitration' (2015) 32 Journal of International Arbitration 65, 82 et seqq.

430. Kuitkowski (n. 429) 65.

431. *Ibid.*, 87; Michelle Sindler and Tina Wüstemann, 'Privilege Across Borders in Arbitration: Multi- Jurisdictional Nightmare or Storm in a Teacup' (2005) 23 ASA Bulletin 610, 618.

remains confidential. Other jurisdictions, in particular those that do not make allowances for any exchange of documents, usually provide no (or only very vague) legal bases for withholding documents (and other information).[432] In England and Wales, for example, while it is considered that 'the public interest' was 'served best by rigidly confining within narrow limits the cases where material relevant to litigation may be lawfully withheld',[433] there are a number of vital heads of evidence the parties may rely on. Specifically, these are the privilege against self-incrimination,[434] the legal professional privilege[435] and the so-called without prejudice privilege.[436] The latter covers communications made with the intention of seeking a settlement of the dispute with the opponent.[437] Moreover, under the English CPR, a party may apply for an order permitting it to withhold disclosure on the ground that disclosure would damage the public interest.[438]

2.130 Due to these differences, attempts have been made to stipulate uniform requirements of privilege in international arbitration.[439] This is to be welcomed as it may serve to enhance predictability. Due to the multitude of different jurisdictions that may apply, the closest connection test regularly causes problems in practice.[440] For reasons of equal treatment, it has been suggested to resort to the laws of the most favourable jurisdiction, i.e., the rule that 'provides the highest level of protection'.[441] Yet, this does not always seem to be the most adequate solution, particularly since the scope of privilege should correspond to the scope of document production. The international best practice of document production in arbitration is neither as broad as in common law nor as narrow as in civil law, so that the scope of privilege must, by necessity, also be different. Accordingly, neither the full application of English rules on privilege nor the application of any other jurisdiction's laws on privilege will satisfy the needs arising in arbitration.

2.131 That being said, privileges in international arbitration usually include the:

432. Kuitkowski (n. 429) 73, 74; for an extensive overview on the rules of privilege in different jurisdictions, *see* DLA Piper, *DLA Piper's Legal Professional Privilege Global Guide* (2019).
433. *Waugh v British Railways Board* [1979] 3 WLR 150, 165.
434. Keane and McKeown (n. 290) 713 et seq.
435. *Ibid.*, 725 et seq.
436. *Ibid.*, 749 et seq.
437. *Ibid.*
438. CPR 31.19 (1).
439. Olaf Meyer, 'Time to Take a Closer Look: Privilege in International Arbitration' (2007) 24 Journal of International Arbitration 365, 370 et seqq.
440. Kuitkowski (n. 429) 94 et seq.
441. *See, e.g.*, Art. 7 of the ICDR Guidelines for Arbitrators Concerning Exchanges of Information: 'The tribunal should respect applicable rules of privilege or professional ethics and other legal impediments. When the parties, their counsel or their documents would be subject under applicable law to different rules, the tribunal should to the extent possible apply the same rule to both sides, giving preference to the rule that provides the highest level of protection.' Likewise, Art. 25 ICDR Rules states: 'The arbitral tribunal shall take into account applicable principles of privilege, such as those involving the confidentiality of communications between a lawyer and client. When the parties, their counsel, or their documents would be subject under applicable law to different rules, the tribunal should, to the extent possible, apply the same rule to all parties, giving preference to the rule that provides the highest level of protection.'

- attorney-client privilege;[442]
- in-house privilege;[443]
- work-product privilege (referring to documents produced in anticipation of a dispute);[444]
- cabinet privilege (especially in proceedings involving states and public entities).[445]

2.132 However, as questions of detail keep arising, further standardization of the arbitration law on privilege is desirable. Thus far, beyond recognizing the existence of the above heads of privilege, it is difficult to clearly formulate more specific guidelines that may pertain to the body of transnational rules.[446]

2.133 Importantly, a party that relies on privilege bears the burden of proof for the underlying circumstances. As the tribunal found in *Glamis Gold, Ltd. v United States*:

> The Tribunal notes that the party asserting the privilege has the burden of proving that such privilege applies to each document (...) but, after that showing is made, the burden shifts to the other party to contest the privilege. The Tribunal recognizes that, when asserting this privilege, it is important to make clear that the attorney is indeed acting as such and providing legal advice, and is not acting as a policy-maker or corporate officer. Therefore, it is critical that, when invoking the privilege, the invoking party explain with sufficient specificity the role the attorney is taking.[447]

2.134 Aside from privilege, the Tribunal must also consider whether a request should be dismissed due to 'grounds of commercial or technical confidentiality' (Article 9.2.(e) IBA Rules). While any document submitted or produced by either parties or non-parties in the arbitration is to be kept confidential (Article 3.13 IBA Rules), a producing party may already suffer undue disadvantages if the receiving party alone gains insight into sensitive areas of its business. This especially affects documents that relate to the 'financial inner workings of a company' as well as 'formulas, know-how, trade secrets or other proprietary information'.[448] According to Article 9.5 of the IBA Rules, the tribunal may make, where appropriate, 'necessary arrangements to permit Documents to be produced, and evidence to be presented or considered subject to suitable confidentiality protection'. In doing so, the tribunal may order the parties to produce documents in a redacted form, between the counsel only ('attorneys-eyes

442. Frédéric Gilles Sourgens, Kabir AN Duggal and Ian A Laird, *Evidence in International Investment Arbitration* (Oxford University Press 2018) 242 et seqq.; Mélanie Riofrio Piché and Sofia de Sampaio Jalles, 'Model Procedural Order – Armesto Schedule' http://arbitrationblog.kluwerarbitration.com/wp-content/uploads/sites/48/2020/04/Procedural-Order-Model.pdf.
443. Sourgens, Duggal and Laird (n. 442) 248.
444. *Ibid.*; Riofrio Piché and de Sampaio Jalles (n. 442).
445. Sourgens, Duggal and Laird (n. 442) 245 et seq.
446. Berger, 'Evidentiary Privileges' (n. 429) 513 et seq.; Kuitkowski (n. 429) 99 et seq.; Born (n. 338) 2550 et seq., 2562.
447. *Glamis Gold Ltd v United States, UNCITRAL, Ad Hoc Final Award of 8 June 2009* ITA Board of Reporters [221].
448. O'Malley (n. 407) para. 9.8.3.

only' production), or to an independent third person.[449] The 2021 revision of the IBA Rules clarified that this applies both during the document production procedure and the production of documentary evidence at a later stage of the proceedings.[450]

(ii) Proportionality

2.135 To avoid overly extensive and time-consuming proceedings, the IBA Rules state that the arbitral tribunal may prevent the production of documents for 'considerations of procedural economy, proportionality, fairness or equality of the parties that the arbitral tribunal determines to be compelling' (Article 9.2 (g)). Whether a request is (dis)proportionate is always to be decided on a case-to-case basis. When determining proportionality, regard must be had for the efforts required to produce the document compared to its relevance and materiality (cost/benefit analysis).[451] If it is foreseeable that a document might be important to decide the case (material), the threshold is accordingly higher.

2.136 In *Railroad Development Corporation v Republic of Guatemala*, the tribunal rejected a document production request as disproportionate. Here, the claimant had requested at the beginning of the proceeding that the tribunal should order the opposing party to preserve a certain category of documents. Guatemala objected that such an order would amount to a pre-discovery-style fishing expedition, which was inadmissible in international arbitration. The tribunal rejected the request in its decision on provisional measures, stating that it would 'place an unfair burden on Guatemala because of its excessive breadth and that no need or urgency justified interim measures of protection'.[452] This was particularly true since it would require an 'undetermined number of government officials across the administration' to identify the documents.[453]

2.137 Moreover, the tribunal must always keep in mind the overall importance of the matter and the value of the dispute. Low-volume proceedings rarely ever justify extensive document proceedings that might cause legal fees higher than the amounts in dispute.

(iii) Illegality

2.138 There is no transnational or international consensus on the exclusion of illegally obtained evidence.[454] Considering the lack of a uniform rule, the 2020 Review Task Force of the IBA Rules left the decision to the tribunal: according to Article 9.3 of the

449. 1999 IBA Working Party, 2010 Rules of Evidence Review Subcommittee and 2020 IBA Rules of Evidence Review Task Force (n. 188) 30.
450. *Ibid.*
451. Waincymer (n. 343) para. 11.7.7.
452. *Railroad Development Corporation v Republic of Guatemala, ICSID ARB/07/23,* Decision on Provisional Measures of 15 October 2008 [36].
453. *Ibid.*, 33.
454. *See* below, Chapter 3, C.III.

IBA Rules, the tribunal 'may', at the request of a party or on its own motion, exclude evidence obtained illegally.[455] It is not obliged to do so, however.[456]

2.139 Ultimately, the tribunal will have to conduct a case-by-case analysis by weighing the importance of the evidence against the way it was obtained. As a typical example, a party may rely on documents which were leaked by a whistle-blower bearing evidence of illegal conduct such as corruption or fraud, or on a document that was obtained through a hack or a data leak. Where the illegal origin has been established, tribunals must carefully contemplate the interests involved by weighing the importance of the evidence against the violation of the aggrieved parties' rights.[457]

2.140 Closely linked to the question of illegality is the issue of data protection. As part of the 2021 revision of the IBA Rules, the task force included Article 2.2(e), stating that the tribunal shall consult the parties on 'the treatment of any issues of cybersecurity and data protection'.

(iv) Burden of Proof

2.141 In recent years, the question has arisen whether tribunals are required to consider the burden of proof, particularly with regard to the applicable substantive law.[458] From what was found to be a 'distinctly continental perspective',[459] *Derains* argued that only a party bearing the burden of proof for a specific issue should be granted a request for document production with respect to that issue:

> [W]hen a document production request is disputed, the arbitrators have the responsibility of determining whether the request party actually needs the documents to discharge its burden of proof. If not, the request should be denied.[460]

2.142 A party which did not bear the burden of proof was not obliged to bring evidence on the issue. This, in turn, rendered the request neither relevant nor material.[461]

2.143 On the other side of the spectrum, some commentators advocated considering the burden of proof particularly where German substantive law applied.[462] The result, however, is the opposite. Specifically, according to this view, the principle of *nemo tenetur* was an eminent feature of the burden of proof under German law, meaning that

455. 1999 IBA Working Party, 2010 Rules of Evidence Review Subcommittee and 2020 IBA Rules of Evidence Review Task Force (n. 188) 6.
456. *Ibid.*
457. *See* below, Chapter 3, C.III.2.
458. Varga (n. 386) 61.
459. ME Jaffe, JT Dulani and DJ Stute, 'Burden of Proof as a Prerequisite to Document Production Under the 2010 IBA Rules: An Obituary' (2017) 1 Transnational Dispute Management 1.
460. Yves Derains, 'Towards Greater Efficiency in Document Production before Arbitral Tribunals' (2006) Special Supplement ICC International Court of Arbitration Bulletin 83, 87.
461. *Ibid.*
462. Trittmann (n. 338) 14, 15; *See also* Varga (n. 386) 61, who raised the question of whether an interplay of US-based international (evidentiary) procedural law and German material law was compatible at all, but concludes that parties which consent to arbitration proceedings, also consent to any presumed modification which the procedural structure of arbitration proceedings might impose on the applicable substantive law.

a party which did not bear the burden of proof had the substantive right to withhold adverse information. This also meant that said party could not be ordered to produce documents to this effect, and any such order would violate the substantive law.[463]

2.144 Neither position finds support in the language of the IBA Rules, and they seem to mostly be inspired by domestic procedures. While it is true that there is a substantial need to expedite document production, considering the burden of proof does not appear to promise adequate results. As for the German approach, the principle of *nemo tenetur* is a procedural rather than a substantive issue.[464] It might have its merits within the context of German civil procedure[465] but does not bind international arbitration tribunals. Rather, the above survey confirms that, in modern arbitration, the parties are subject to rather comprehensive information duties that override any domestic standards.[466]

2.145 Similar objections apply to *Derains'* suggestion of performing an extended test of relevancy and materiality. Document production usually takes place at an early stage of the proceedings, where it serves not only to supply evidence but also to gather and clarify facts. At the point in time when documents are exchanged under IBA Rules, it is usually not possible to assess whether a specific document might bear on the outcome of the dispute simply by considering the (abstract) distribution of the burden of proof. If, for example, the burdened party submits evidence during the proceedings, the burden of production shifts to the other party. The other party will accordingly be required to rebut the evidence by submitting counterevidence. Documents that were discarded as immaterial may thus become material at a later stage of the proceeding.

2.146 The same was found in *Adel A Hamadi Al Tamiimi v Sultanate of Oman*:

> To the extent that it may be argued that in some of these requests the Claimant seeks material to enable it to attempt to rebut any defences raised by the Respondent, and that there is no reason to grant these requests as the Claimant can simply rely on the burden of proof which rests upon the Respondent in relation to defences, the Tribunal does not consider that this is a dispositive answer. This matter is discussed in Procedure and Evidence in International Arbitration by Jeffrey Waincymer where it is stated at paragraph 11.7.1.2 that 'It has also been suggested that a document needs to be material to an issue as to which the requesting party carries the burden of proof. There would be problems in applying this as a blanket rule [...] to deny the opposing party the opportunity to make targeted requests, removes an ability to easily identify selective presentation

463. Trittmann (n. 338) 14, 15.
464. Note that the discussion on the *nemo tenetur* principle in Germany revolves around the question of whether there is a procedural information duty or not ('prozessuale Aufklärungspflicht'). *BGH, Judgment of 11 June 1990* (n. 336) para. III with further references; *see also* Markus Benzing, *Das Beweisrecht vor internationalen Gerichten und Schiedsgerichten in zwischenstaatlichen Streitigkeiten* (Springer 2010) 308, 321; Gomille (n. 337) 31.
465. This proposition is, however, also questionable, *see* above, Chapter 2, B.II.1.
466. *See* above, Chapter 1, B.II.

where this has occurred. The opponent should not have to rely on the tribunal holding that the burden was not satisfied.[467]

2.147 Accordingly, the tribunal shall not consider the distribution of the burden of proof when deciding on document production requests.

f Consequences of Non-Compliance

2.148 As will be detailed below, a party which does not comply with a tribunal's orders to produce documents may be subject to adverse inferences[468]. Moreover, the tribunal is also entitled to consider the party's conduct when rendering adverse cost decisions.[469]

ii The Prague Rules: A Shift of Paradigm?

2.149 While the use of the IBA Rules can certainly be considered the best practice standard, their application nevertheless remains controversial. The Prague Rules provide an alternative. In fact, one of the main goals of the Prague Rules was to create a counter-balance to the procedures under the IBA Rules, which are frequently perceived as excessive.[470]

2.150 Article 4 of the Prague Rules, concerning 'documentary evidence', addresses the issues surrounding document production. The initial intention was to follow both a 'civil law' and an 'inquisitorial'[471] approach (*see* above) to the exchange of documents.[472] To a certain degree, the Prague Rules thus seem to perpetuate the stereotypical 'common law versus civil law' dichotomy[473] rather than dissolving it. Overall, they operate on a rather restrictive model of information exchange, leaving it the general responsibility of the parties to submit documents that they seek to rely upon (Article 4.1 Prague Rules).

2.151 The production of documents is governed by Articles 4.1–4.6 of the Prague Rules. Article 4.2 states that 'the parties are encouraged to avoid any form of document production, including e-discovery' (Article 4.2). This is a compromise formula, as in an earlier draft of Article 4.1, the rules stated that the arbitral tribunal 'shall' avoid any form of document production.[474] Interestingly, a similar wording is reflected in

467. *Adel A Hamadi Al Tamiimi v Sultanate of Oman, ICSID ARB/11/33* Rulings on Claimant's Requests for Production of Documents of 21 August 2013 [5, 6].
468. *See* below, Chapter 3, E.II.3.
469. *See* on inner-procedural measures to ensure compliance with transnational rules, Chapter 1, A.III.3.
470. Duggal and Rangachari (n. 189) 27 et seq.
471. For more details on adversarial and inquisitorial models of procedure, *see* below Chapter 2, C.
472. 'Prague Rules Draft: Inquisitorial Rules on the Taking of Evidence in International Arbitration (The Prague Rules)' 2, 3.
473. *See* above, Chapter 1, B.I.
474. 'Prague Rules Draft: Inquisitorial Rules on the Taking of Evidence in International Arbitration (The Prague Rules)' (n. 472).

Appendix IV (d) (iii) to both 2017 and 2021 ICC Rules, according to which the tribunal may consider 'avoiding requests for document production when appropriate in order to control time and cost'.

2.152 In any case, parties are expected to 'indicate' to the tribunal at the case management conference that they 'would need to request certain documents from the other party' while stating the respective reasons (Article 4.3). Requests at a later stage are only permitted under 'exceptional circumstances', especially where the party could not have made such a request at the time of the case management conference (Article 4.4). In case the tribunal is convinced that the production of documents is necessary, the parties' requests must relate to 'specific documents' which are 'relevant and material to the outcome of the case', 'not in the public domain' and 'in the possession of another party or within its power or control'. Particularly the requirements of specificity as well as relevance and materiality resemble the requirements of the IBA Rules.[475]

2.153 Furthermore, under Article 3(2)(a) of the Prague Rules, the arbitral tribunal may, after having heard the parties, at any stage of the arbitration and at its own initiative, request that any of the parties submit relevant documentary evidence. This is supplemented by the general clause under Article 3 of the Prague Rules, according to which, for the purposes of fact-finding, the tribunal may take any other actions which it deems appropriate. The interplay of Articles 3 and 4 of the Prague Rules confirms that, rather than leaving the gathering of facts entirely to the parties, the Prague Rules are based on a semi-inquisitorial model.[476]

2.154 It is questionable whether the approach to document production provided by the Prague Rules is adequate for default use in international arbitration proceedings. While in theory the general limitation of such procedures is to be welcomed, the approach of the Prague Rules seems to be overly restrictive, inflexible and contradictory with regard to the current legal framework in modern arbitration. In particular, the Prague Rules' approach is not fully compatible with the requirements of most modern arbitration rules, which, subject to few exceptions, grant the tribunal ample powers to order the production of documents (and other means of evidence).[477]

2.155 Also, it is debatable whether the case management conference is the most suitable forum to apply for the production of specific documents. Case management conferences take place at the very beginning of the proceeding and mainly serve to discuss the organization of the proceeding. At that stage of the procedure, the stakeholders usually do not yet have a sufficiently in-depth knowledge of the relevant factual and legal issues. A certain level of familiarity is nonetheless necessary to make informed party requests. The same is true for the tribunal's decision. In most cases, however, it is the tribunal in particular which lacks sufficient knowledge to properly decide on such applications at an early stage of the proceedings, when the parties have

475. *See* above, Chapter 1, A.III.3.1.a.iii.
476. For more details on adversarial and inquisitorial models of procedure, *see* below Chapter 2, C.
477. *See* above, Chapter 1, B.I.

only exchanged the first round of submissions, if that. In addition, the oral nature of the arbitration conference makes the decision-making process even more difficult and is no substitute for reasoned requests in writing.

2.156 Beyond that, although the Prague Rules aspire to cure the ills of adversarialism, allowing the parties to withhold potentially adverse facts may counteract the purpose.[478] In fact, the restrictive approach to document production seems to be inconsistent with the proclaimed objective of mostly 'inquisitorial' procedures.[479] Fact-finding becomes significantly more difficult and error-prone when the parties may conceal information, even when such information may be relevant to the outcome of the dispute.

2.157 Of course, the tribunal can and must ensure that the parties do not issue their requests for disclosure in an abusive manner. There are, however, less restrictive options than a blanket exclusion of document production requests, or limiting these requests to the case management conference.

2 *Depositions and Interrogatories*

2.158 While the practice of document production is widely accepted in international arbitration nowadays, this acceptance does not extend to other forms of mandatory information exchange.

2.159 An important feature of discovery (or, respectively, disclosure) is that litigants in the US[480] and England and Wales[481] may submit question forms on the facts to the other party, obliging these to disclose further information. Upon receipt, the other party is required to respond to these fully and completely under oath,[482] or, respectively, confirmed by a statement of truth.[483] In the US, these forms are referred to as 'interrogatories'.[484] In England and Wales, interrogatories have been replaced by 'requests for further information'[485] and written questions to experts.[486] Notwithstanding the terminological differences, the scope of the rights and obligations remains similar.[487]

2.160 As a further particularity of the US system, litigants are entitled to gather information by taking depositions before going to trial. Whereas interrogatories are

478. *See* above, Chapter 2, B.II.1.
479. *See* on the terminology below, Chapter 2, C.I.
480. *See* Rule 33 FRCP.
481. *See* CPR 18.
482. *See* Rule 33(b)(3) FRCP.
483. *See* CPR16 PD 3.
484. *See* Rule 33 FRCP.
485. *See* Rule CPR 18.
486. CPR 35.6; *see* Thomas Terrell, *Terrell on the Law of Patents* (19th edn, Sweet & Maxwell 2019) para. 19.419.
487. As far as practicable, English case law decided in relation to interrogatories is considered to remain applicable in determining the limits of requests for further information, *see ibid.*, 19.420.

directed at the other party, depositions can be taken from 'any person',[488] i.e., both parties and non-parties.[489] The right to take depositions is far-reaching and even allows a party to depose the opponent's attorney, for example, in order to identify potential witnesses or locate documents.[490]

2.161 While most laws and sets of rules do not contain any explicit provisions, under the English Arbitration Act, for example, it is for the tribunal to decide, subject to any party agreement, 'whether any and if so what questions should be put to and answered by the respective parties and when and in what form this should be done'.[491] Article 24.10 of the ICDR Rules, in turn, states that '[d]epositions, interrogatories, and requests to admit as developed for use in U.S. court procedures generally are not appropriate procedures for obtaining information in an arbitration under these Rules'.

2.162 In practice, depositions and interrogatories play, if any, a minor role. At times, however, parties represented by US counsel agree to the exchange thereof.[492] This was illustrated, for example, by the ICDR case of *Kaselitz et al. v Hisoft Technology International, Ltd.* The proceedings were based on an arbitration clause which made express reference to the California Code of Civil Procedure, adopting certain means of discovery, including interrogatories. During the procedure, the tribunal, therefore, ordered the parties to serve interrogatory responses.[493] Since the claimant failed to comply with these orders, the respondent sought discovery sanctions,[494] which the tribunal accordingly granted in the final award.[495]

2.163 That being said, despite the lack of a transnational rule to this effect, ordering the taking of interrogatories or depositions lies within the tribunal's powers to conduct the proceedings as it deems appropriate.[496] When doing so, the tribunal must always consider the parties' expectations in light of their legal background and the potential costs and benefits of such an undertaking. There is, however, no subjective right of the parties to request the taking of depositions or interrogatories in international arbitration. A Beirut Court, for example, denied an annulment request, stating that refusing to conduct an interrogatory did not violate a party's right to defence.[497]

---

488. *See* Rule 30 (a) (1) FRCP.
489. Esther Seitz, *Fact-Gathering in Patent Infringement Cases: Rule 34 Discovery and the Saisie-Contrefaçon* (Nomos 2009) 12.
490. Timothy Flynn, 'On "Borrowed Wits": A Proposed Rule for Attorney Depositions' (1993) 93 Columbia Law Review 1956, 1956.
491. Section 34 (2) (e) of the English Arbitration Act.
492. Born (n. 338) 2529.
493. *Kaselitz et al v Hisoft Technology International, Ltd (Final Award), ICDR Case No 15 2013 000 319, 23 October 2015* Arbitrator Intelligence Materials 37, 38.
494. *Ibid.*
495. *Ibid.*, 52.
496. Waincymer (n. 343) ch 10.5: 'While there are no such formal rules in international arbitration, a tribunal's broad discretion might allow it to draft lists of questions for the parties.'; Born (n. 338) 2530.
497. *First Civil Chamber of the Court of Appeals in Beirut, Court of Appeals of Beirut Governorate, Decision No 1605/2012 Case Date 19 November 2012* ITA Board of Reporters.

2.164 In view of the far-reaching acceptance of document production, the arbitral community's opposition to interrogatories and depositions is indeed peculiar. It is not evident why document production is generally accepted while other forms of discovery (or, respectively, disclosure) are considered unfit. In particular, the prevalent practice of document production seems to be neither a less invasive nor a more efficient and just feature than other forms of information exchange. Nevertheless, as the current developments seek to restrain the exchange of documents rather than extend it, and in light of the adverse attitude particularly of the ICDR Rules, it does not seem as though other discovery techniques will be adopted in international arbitration in the near future.

3 *Substantive Information Claims*

2.165 Beyond the above-outlined procedural mechanisms of exchanging information, some jurisdictions provide for information claims which are founded in substantive law. These are not part of the canon of transnational fact-finding law but apply only when the specific substantive law so allows.

2.166 Their substantive nature is owed to the overall structure of the proceedings. Civil litigation in Germany, for example, consists of two main phases, the pleading phase and the evidence phase, without any intermediate disclosure. The exchange of information takes place during the pleading phase, following a structure based on reciprocal pleading burdens, i.e., the interplay between the initial pleadings and the parties' respective burdens to contest, and/or further elaborate (substantiate) their pleadings of the facts.[498] In general, parties are not required to disclose any information that they do not seek to rely upon. This is especially true for adverse facts and evidence.[499]

2.167 In order to avoid unfair procedural outcomes in a particular case, German substantive law provides for information rights in specific (mostly contractual) constellations.[500] The general claim to information requires that the claimant (i) is likely to have a claim to performance (ii) within an existing special legal relationship, (iii) whereby the claimant is excusably uncertain about the existence and scope of its claim, (iv) whereas the respondent has knowledge of the facts on which the claimant depends in order to assert his right and (v) can disclose them without difficulty. These prerequisites must be fulfilled cumulatively.[501] If successful, the claiming party can demand disclosure of information or (preparation of) accounts which it needs to specify (i.e., usually quantify) its main claim (*see* section 259 BGB).

498. *See* above, Chapter 2, B.II.1.
499. *See* above, Chapter 2, B.II.1.
500. *See, e.g.*, sec. 666, 713 BGB and sec. 87c (3) or 384 (2) HGB, as well as a general claim to information under sec. 242 BGB, for a non-exhaustive enumeration of substantive claims to information, *see* Ulrich Foerste, 'ZPO § 254' in Hans-Joachim Musielak and Wolfgang Voit (eds), *Zivilprozessordnung* (17th edn, Franz Vahlen 2020).
501. *BGH, Judgment of 14 June 2016* [2016] NZG 983.

2.168 Procedurally, the information claim is commonly raised at the beginning of the proceeding and is combined with an unspecified payment claim, the specific amount of which then depends on the information sought ('*Stufenklage*'; action by stages, section 254 ZPO). Accordingly, in the first stage of the procedure, the parties litigate exclusively on the claim for information. Since the court will only deal with the main issue in a second phase of the proceeding,[502] actions by stages tend to be time-consuming.

2.169 To a certain degree, there is a structural incompatibility between these substantive information claims and the current best practices in international arbitration. A party initiating an arbitration by invoking such a claim may be understood to waive its right[503] to document production, or at least give the impression of not expecting any pre-hearing document disclosure. This may put the party at a disadvantage, as the requirements to be met under an information claim are substantially higher. Specifically, a party must provide full proof (i.e., a reasonable degree of conviction)[504] for all the above prerequisites. On a practical note, it is thus recommended to first test the tribunal's attitude towards document production (or select the arbitrators accordingly) before raising substantive information claims.[505]

IV Conclusion

2.170 The rules on document production serve as a stellar example of how transnationalization may occur and develop. Without ever having been sanctioned by any national or international legislator, document production according to the IBA Rules has become a standard procedure widely applied in arbitrations across the globe. While there are ongoing trends to contain and limit document production procedures, the requirements as set out by the IBA Rules – particularly those relating to the specification of the request, relevance, materiality and objections – can be considered consolidated best practice and showcase the emergence of transnational fact-finding law.

2.171 The principle that parties must disclose certain information and documents also affects the duty of truth: unlike in some domestic jurisdictions, the *nemo tenetur* principle (i.e., the right to withhold adverse information) does not apply in international arbitration. By the same token, overly extensive discovery proceedings, as known, *inter alia,* from US litigation, do not apply, as they fit neither the procedural structure nor the needs of international arbitration. Rather, the parties must always comply with their (subjective) duty of truth and disclose all information which can be reasonably expected.

502. Foerste (n. 500) paras 4 et seq.
503. Note, however, that it is submitted that there is no inherent subjective right to document production, *see* above, Chapter 2, B.III.1.a.(i).
504. *See* below, Chapter 3, D.I.1.a.
505. This may be different in German domestic proceedings where an adverse position to document is still prevalent, cf. Annex 3 lit. E DIS Rules, according to which the tribunals and parties shall discuss whether considerations of the burden of proof shall limit document production.

2.172 Other issues relating to disclosure duties are less settled. In particular, there is no best practice of ordering the parties to provide depositions and interrogatories. Lastly, where available, parties may invoke substantive information claims under the *lex causae*. In practice, however, their use is not recommended, as they clash with the general structure of information exchange in arbitration. Further, information claims under substantive German law in particular stipulate a rather high threshold to be met, which is in most cases more burdensome than applications for document disclosure under the IBA Rules.

C FACTUAL INVESTIGATIONS BY THE TRIBUNAL

2.173 According to the old Roman maxim *da mihi factum, dabo tibi ius,* it is the parties' burden to feed the relevant factual material into the dispute, based upon which the trier of facts (i.e., the tribunal or court) applies the law.[506] Nonetheless, both in domestic litigation and international arbitration, the paradigm of this traditional division of tasks is slowly shifting. It can be observed that in international arbitration proceedings, the tribunal is equipped – at least on paper – with increasingly far-reaching powers to engage in fact-finding procedures itself, e.g., by directly or indirectly investigating relevant facts.

2.174 The below shall outline the difference between adversarial and inquisitorial procedures (*I*), before applying the terminology to international arbitration, which is found to be semi-inquisitorial (*II* and *III*).

I Adversarial and Inquisitorial Procedures

2.175 Comparative procedural law operates with the concepts of adversarial and inquisitorial proceedings. While in purely adversarial proceedings, the parties control the initiation and the course of the dispute, including fact-finding, in purely inquisitorial proceedings, this is the task of the trier of fact.

2.176 The term 'adversarialism' (also referred to as adversarial legalism)[507] describes a system of 'lawyer-dominated' governance which nowadays is particularly prevalent in the United States.[508] The framework of adversarial legalism not only affects the organization of civil disputes but also extends to the creation and implementation of

506. Luc Imbrechts, 'Truth in Arbitration. What Instruments Do Parties Have in Search for the Truth?' in Luc Demeyere (ed.), *Do Arbitral Awards Reveal the Truth?: Reports from the Third Joint Cepani-Nai Colloquium Held on March 21, 2019* (2019) 9; note, however, that due to cultural differences, the question of whether the tribunal must know and apply the law on its own motion in an international environment remains disputed, *see* Gabrielle Kaufmann-Kohler, 'The Arbitrator and the Law: Does He/She Know It? Apply It? How? And a Few More Questions' 21 Arbitration International 2005, 634 et seq.; *see also*, Rodrigo Ramina de Lucca, 'Iura Novit Curia Nas Arbitragens' (2016) XIII Revista Brasileira de Arbitragem 54, 65 et seq. who suggests a difference between the principles 'iura novit curia' and 'iura novit arbiter'.
507. Robert A Kagan, *Adversarial Legalism: The American Way of Law* (Harvard University Press 2001) 3 et seq.
508. *Ibid.*, 3.

policies featuring a heavy reliance on 'lawyers, legal threats, and legal contestation in implementing public policies'.[509] This is effected through, for the most part, 'complicated' and 'prescriptive laws' containing severe 'legal penalties'.[510] According to more recent publications, the archetypal adversarial dispute is marked by three main elements, namely '(1) it glorifies jury deliberation, (2) informed by the competition of equally matched lawyer-representatives, (3) in service of a preference for the fragmentation[511] of power'.[512] Under *Andrews*' rather broad definition, in adversarial procedures, the parties 'dictate at all stages the form, content, and pace of the proceedings'.[513] Distinctive elements of adversarial-dispute resolution thus include little to no judicial interference with fact-finding, broad discovery, and the preparation as well as examination of evidence by the parties, especially through direct and cross-examination.[514]

2.177 Inquisitorial proceedings, however, are marked by a dominant trier of facts ('and expert decision-maker')[515] who proactively manages the case and is engaged in fact-finding.[516] An inquisitorial trier of facts may initiate proceedings, investigate facts, order the parties to produce information, documents or means of evidence, instruct and examine (expert) witnesses, all without being limited by the parties' submissions and requests.[517] In practice, most proceedings that are labelled as inquisitorial are rather adversarial at heart but are supplemented by certain inquisitorial features. Truly inquisitorial proceedings are very rare. They are only to be encountered where certain interests are at stake that are in need of protection, as in matters of family law, where

509. *Ibid.*
510. *Ibid.*
511. Fragmentalization in this context means decentralization, *see ibid.*, 15; Andrew E Taslitz, 'Temporal Adversarialism, Criminal Justice, and the Rehnquist Court: The Sluggish Life of Political Factfinding' (2005) 94 The Georgetown Law Review 1589, 1594.
512. Taslitz (n. 511) 1591; Thomas Scheffer, *Adversarial Case-Making: An Ethnography of English Crown Court Procedure* (Brill 2010) xvii.
513. *See* Neil Andrews, 'The Adversaral Principle: Fairness and Efficiency' in AAS Zuckerman and Ross Cranston (eds), *Reform of Civil Procedure: Essays on 'Access to Justice'* (Clarendon Press; Oxford University Press 1995) 169, 171, who lists the following matters which are generally under the parties' control in England: '(a) the initiation of the action; (b) the framing of an action, especially the drawing up of pleadings; (c) the decision whether to add additional parties; (d) selection of material facts; (e) the legal framework within which the cause of action is to be considered (for example, the framing of a cause of action in contract or tort, or both) as well as the selection of remedies; (f) pre-trial progress of the litigation; (g) the decision to apply for interim or summary (and final) relief, (i) the reception of evidence at trial (or in other hearings); (j) Submissions of law at trial; (k) the decision to seek enforcement of a judgement; (l) the decision to bring an appeal (sometimes subject to the court's permission).'
514. As a deliberate exaggeration, according to John Thibaut, Laurens Walker and E Allan Lind, 'Adversary Presentation and Bias in Legal Decisionmaking' (1972) 86 Harvard Law Review 386, 388, purely adversarial procedures are characterized by 'openly biased advocates' who 'urge their client's case before a passive decisionmaker'.
515. *Ibid.*
516. Ahmed Galal Zaki, 'Adversarial or Inquisitorial: Which Approach Is Closer to Arbitration?' [2006] Thesis Submitted to the The American University in Cairo 22.
517. *Ibid.*, 23; In the German terminology, the inquisitorial principle is referred to as Amtsermittlungsgrundsatz or Untersuchungsmaxime, *see* Thomas Rauscher, 'Einleitung' in Wolfgang Krüger and Thomas Rauscher (eds), *Münchener Kommentar zur Zivilprozessordnung* (6th edn, C.H. Beck 2020) para. 353.

the court's decisions might affect the well-being of children or other vulnerable persons.[518]

2.178 Against this background, common law procedures are at times perceived to be adversarial while civil law procedures are characterized as more inquisitorial in nature.[519] The classification of common law proceedings as 'adversarial' usually also entails that the trier of facts has no (or highly limited) inquisitorial powers.[520] While this may be largely true for US litigation,[521] such dogma has ceased to apply in England and Wales. The Woolf Reforms have, at least in theory, substantively changed the role of the courts within the architecture of civil proceedings[522] and bestowed upon the court's extensive powers to manage cases,[523] which may even exceed the powers of different civil law courts. In particular, the reforms introduced substantial inquisitorial elements into the English civil procedure.[524] It was found that 'a dramatic shift in the balance occurred when the managerial judge who came with the introduction of case management replaced the passive judge of the adversary system'.[525] Nowadays, in modern English civil litigation, the courts have the power and are required to, *inter alia*, encourage the parties to co-operate, identify and (if possible) decide or dispose of issues at an early stage, encourage the parties to use an alternative means of dispute resolution, help the parties to settle the whole or part of the case or give directions to ensure that the trial of a case proceeds quickly and efficiently.[526] While, in practice,

518. *See, e.g.*, for the underlying considerations in the ambit of German family law in cases of endangerment of a child's welfare, Lugani, 'BGB § 1666' in Franz Jürgen Säcker and others (eds), *Münchener Kommentar zum BGB* (8th edn, Beck 2020) para. 224.
519. Luc Demeyere, 'An Essay on Differing Approaches to Procedures Under Common Law and Civil Law' [2008] SchiedsVZ 279, 283.
520. *See* David Alan Sklansky, 'Anti-Inquisitorialism' 122 Harvard Law Review 1637, who states that 'anti-inquistorialism has long been thought a core commitment of [the US] legal heritage'.
521. Note, however, that Rule 16 FRCP provides different case management techniques that shall, *inter alia*, serve to limit 'wasteful pre-trial activities' and expedite 'the disposition of the action'.
522. As an immediate reaction to the changes, some judges seem to have had difficulties embracing the idea that a judge might 'render a service' to the party by managing the case. *See, e.g.*, JJ Spigelman, 'Judicial Accountability and Performance Indicators' (2002) 21(Jan) Civil Justice Quarterly 18, 26: 'The courts do not deliver a "service". The courts administer justice in accordance with law. They no more deliver a "service" in the form of judgments and decisions, than a parliament delivers a "service" in the form of debates and statutes. Courts serve the people but they do not provide services to litigants. The proposition that courts serve people must not be understood in any immediate populist sense. Courts serve the people understood as a historical continuum: with debts to prior generations and obligations to succeeding generations. The administration of justice does, in fact, resolve disputes. In doing so it serves the public as a whole, not merely the litigants.'
523. Rupert M Jackson, *Review of Civil Litigation Costs: Preliminary Report* (The Stationary Office 2010) 416, 417; *see also* David Oldham, 'Case Management – A Judge's Perspective' (2009) 3 Journal of Personal Injury Law 212, 217.
524. *See*, for an overview John Anthony Jolowicz, 'The Woolf Report and the Adversary System' (1996) 15 Civil Justice Quarterly 198.
525. John Anthony Jolowicz, 'Adversarial and Inquisitorial Models of Civil Procedure' [2003] International & Comparative Law Quarterly 281, 286.
526. *See*, for more examples, CPR 1.4 (2) (3).

courts still have the tendency to remain rather reserved and avoid any active engagement in fact-finding,[527] a true culture of adversarialism only prevails in US litigation. The uniqueness of this approach must be considered when identifying possible ways of reconciling the parties' interests in international arbitration.

II Semi-inquisitorial Nature of International Arbitration Proceedings

2.179 Arbitration proceedings are, due to their heavy reliance on party autonomy, commonly perceived to be mainly adversarial in nature.[528] The contradictory nature of arbitration proceedings and the principle of party autonomy suggest that it is primarily the parties' task and responsibility to feed information and evidence into the dispute.[529]

2.180 The above definition of adversarialism,[530] however, suggests that international arbitration is less adversarial than often assumed. At first glance, two of the three items reflected in the above definition apply to arbitration proceedings: even though there is no jury involvement, the proceedings are usually very lawyer driven. Apart from drafting submissions, counsel bears the main responsibility for preparing and examining evidence[531] and frequently cooperates to identify and solve procedural issues. Further, the non-hierarchical and non-state nature of tribunals leads to a certain 'fragmentation of power', thus limiting the state's influence and intervention.

2.181 Yet, in recent years one can observe the trend that different arbitral institutions have been seeking to contain overly adversarial proceedings. Different institutional rules, such as the ICC, DIS and LCIA have bestowed upon the tribunal substantial (but varying) powers to proactively participate and assist the parties in the gathering of facts.[532] Interestingly, as an expression of this development, an early draft of the Prague Rules was titled 'Inquisitorial Rules on the Taking of Evidence in International Arbitration'.[533]

2.182 As of now, it is evident that in practice, tribunals do not fully embrace their powers but tend to remain in a rather passive, observant and recipient position. The likely reason is that the scope of the tribunal's powers is still the subject of heated debate, especially due to the varying legal traditions in play. While, indeed, many proceedings could benefit from and be streamlined through robust case management

527. *See, e.g.*, *The Society of Lloyd's v Sir William Otho Jaffray BT* [2000] WL 989565 [6]: 'In civil proceedings, the trial judge has no power to dictate to a litigant what evidence he or she should tender.'
528. Cf. Robert Hunter, 'Arbitration in Germany – A Common Law Perspective' [2003] SchiedsVZ 155, 161, 162; VK Rajah, 'W(h)Ither Adversarial Commercial Dispute Resolution?' (2017) 33 Arbitration International 17, 17, 18.
529. *See* above, Chapter 2, A.I.
530. *See* above, Chapter 2, C.I: Adversarialism 'glorifies jury deliberation, (2) informed by the competition of equally matched lawyer-representatives, (3) in service of a preference for the fragmentation of power'.
531. *See, inter alia*, below, Chapter 3, B.I.2.a.
532. *See* for a survey of different arbitration laws and acts below, Chapter 2, C.I.
533. 'Prague Rules Draft: Inquisitorial Rules on the Taking of Evidence in International Arbitration (The Prague Rules)' (n. 472).

and proactive arbitrators, there is always the risk that tribunals may, particularly in the absence of an express party agreement, overstep boundaries and infringe on the parties' right to be heard.[534]

2.183 Even though some arbitration laws (such as the Swiss[535] and the Brazilian)[536] state that the tribunal must always heed the adversarial nature of arbitration, a survey of different arbitration laws and rules as well as modern sets of soft law confirms the trend towards proactive tribunals.

2.184 While the Model Law is silent as to the tribunal's powers to investigate, many arbitration acts operate according to a semi-inquisitorial approach. Notably, under the English Arbitration Act, and despite England's rather adversarial tradition, Article 34(1) and (2)(g) state that:

> [i]t shall be for the tribunal to decide (...), subject to the right of the parties to agree any matter (...) whether and to what extent the tribunal should itself take the initiative in ascertaining the facts and the law.

2.185 Article 25 (2) Second Sentence of the Spanish Arbitration Act (Lei de Arbitraje) states that:

> [t]he power conferred upon the arbitrators includes the power to determine the admissibility, relevance and usefulness of any evidence, the manner of taking evidence, including on the arbitrators' own motion, and its weight.

2.186 The German Arbitration Act is equally found to grant the tribunal semi-inquisitorial powers.[537] According to section 1042 (4) Second Sentence, the tribunal:

> is authorised to decide on the admissibility of the taking of evidence, to so take evidence, and to assess the results at its sole discretion.

2.187 The previous version of the German Arbitration Act actually went so far as to state that the tribunal was required (i.e., not only authorized) to investigate the factual

534. P Landolt, 'Arbitrators' Initiatives to Obtain Factual and Legal Evidence' (2012) 28 Arbitration International 173, 222 et seq.; Teresa Giovannini, 'Chapter 8: Ex Officio Powers to Investigate: When Do Arbitrators Cross the Line?' in Michael E Schneider, Bernd Ehle and Domitille Baizeau (eds), *Stories from the Hearing Room: Experience from Arbitral Practice: Essays in Honour of Michael E. Schneider* (Kluwer Law International 2015) 72, 73.

535. Article 182 (3) of the Swiss PIL: 'Regardless of the chosen procedure, the arbitral tribunal shall ensure equal treatment of the parties and their right to be heard in adversarial proceedings.'

536. Article 21 (2) of the Brazilian Arbitration Act: 'Serão, sempre, respeitados no procedimento arbitral os princípios do contraditório, da igualdade das partes, da imparcialidade do árbitro e de seu livre convencimento.' Note that in the English translation, the reference to the 'princípio do contraditório' has been translated as: 'The principles of due process of law, equal treatment of the parties, impartiality of the arbitrator and freedom of decision shall always be respected.' *See* further Selma M Ferreira Lemes, 'Arbitragem. Princípios Jurídicos Fundamentais. Direito Brasileiro E Comparado' (1991) VII Revista de la Corte Espanhola de Arbitraje 31, para. VI.2.

537. Vincent Fischer-Zernin and Abbo Junker, 'Between Scylla and Charybdis: Fact Gathering in German Arbitration' (1987) 4 Journal of International Arbitration 9, 13; Münch, 'ZPO § 1042' in Thomas Rauscher and Wolfgang Krüger (eds), *Münchener Kommentar zur ZPO* (5th edn, C.H. Beck 2017) para. 108.

issues underlying the dispute as far as it was necessary.[538] It has been argued that this requirement of the tribunals remained in force even after the reform of the arbitration laws.[539] However, it is submitted that no such obligation applies to tribunals in international arbitration, as this would frequently exceed the parties' legitimate expectations. Nonetheless, in any case, tribunals remain entitled to investigate the facts if they find it necessary.[540]

2.188 Other arbitration laws, although less explicit, also provide rather comprehensive inquisitorial features. Under Article 1467 (1) of the French Arbitration Law, the tribunal shall take 'all necessary steps' concerning evidentiary and procedural matters. While the Brazilian Arbitration Act emphasizes the principle of contradictory proceedings (*see* Article 21 (2)),[541] according to Article 22, the tribunal may at its own motion 'hear parties' and witnesses' testimony and rule on the production of expert evidence, and other evidence deemed necessary'. These far-reaching provisions on the taking of evidence imply that tribunals may also enquire into (or investigate) specific issues if this is deemed necessary, as long as the equal treatment of the parties is guaranteed (cf Article 21(2)).

2.189 To an even greater extent, nearly all of the analysed arbitration rules reflect (varying) inquisitorial features. Prominently, under Article 43.1 of the CIETAC Rules, the arbitral tribunal 'may undertake investigation and collect evidence as it considers necessary'. Likewise, the ICC Rules in their Article 25 state that the arbitral tribunal shall 'establish the facts of the case by all appropriate means' (Article 25.1). While the language ('appropriate') is rather vague, Article 25.2 of the ICC Rules clarifies that the tribunal may 'decide to hear witnesses, experts appointed by the parties or any other person, in the presence of the parties, or in their absence provided they have been duly summoned'. Further, the tribunal may, upon consultation with the parties, appoint experts (Article 25.3) and, 'at any time during the proceedings', 'summon any party to provide additional evidence' (Article 25.4).

2.190 The same applies to the DIS Rules, which notably sought inspiration from the ICC Rules. Under the DIS Rules, the tribunal may engage in and control the fact-finding procedures, although it may also leave this to the parties. As a central provision, Article 28.2 First Sentence of the DIS Rules says that, for the purpose of establishing the facts of the case, the arbitral tribunal may, *inter alia*, on its own initiative, appoint experts,

---

538. Section 1034 (1) ZPO (old version): 'Bevor der Schiedsspruch erlassen wird, haben die Schiedsrichter die Parteien zu hören und das dem Streit zugrunde liegende Sachverhältnis zu ermitteln, soweit sie die Ermittlung für erforderlich halten.' English translation by the author: 'Before making the award, the arbitrators shall hear the parties and investigate the factual circumstances underlying the dispute to the extent they deem the investigation necessary.'
539. Münch (n. 537) 114.
540. *See, inter alia, ibid.*, 114 with further references.
541. Article 21 (2) of the Brazilian Arbitration Act: 'Serão, sempre, respeitados no procedimento arbitral os princípios do contraditório, da igualdade das partes, da imparcialidade do árbitro e de seu livre convencimento.' Note that in the English translation, the reference to the 'princípio do contraditório' has been translated as: 'The principles of due process of law, equal treatment of the parties, impartiality of the arbitrator and freedom of decision shall always be respected.' *See* further Lemes (n. 536) para. VI.2.

examine witnesses other than those called by the parties, and order any party to produce or make available any document or electronically stored data. Moreover, the arbitral tribunal shall not be limited to admit only evidence offered by the parties (Article 28.2 Second Sentence DIS Rules), i.e., it may also take evidence ex officio. In contrast with the German arbitration law, the wording of Article 28.2 of the DIS Rules ('may') clarifies that the tribunal is not obliged but merely entitled to exercise its investigatory powers.[542]

2.191 As a further example of broad inquisitorial powers, according to Article 29.1 of the Vienna Rules:

> [i]f the arbitral tribunal considers it necessary, it may on its own initiative collect evidence, question parties or witnesses, request the parties to submit evidence, and call experts.

2.192 As under the DIS Rules, the tribunal is thus not confined to the evidence submitted by the parties but may gather any evidence which it deems relevant to its decision.[543] Naturally, the tribunal's powers are limited by the principles of fair treatment and the right to be heard.[544]

2.193 Another notable provision can be found in the LCIA Rules, which state in Article 15.7 that the tribunal can direct the parties to 'the service of written evidence from any fact or expert witness' and 'the service of any other form of written evidence'. According to Article 22.1.iii of the LCIA Rules, it may also, after having heard the parties:

> conduct such enquiries as may appear to the Arbitral Tribunal to be necessary or expedient, including whether and to what extent the Arbitral Tribunal should itself take the initiative in identifying relevant issues and ascertaining relevant facts and the law(s) or rules of law applicable to the Arbitration Agreement, the arbitration and the merits of the parties' dispute.

2.194 Furthermore, under Article 22.1.iv and v of the LCIA Rules, it is the tribunal's authority:

> to order any party to make any documents, goods, samples, property, site or thing under its control available for inspection by the Arbitral Tribunal, any other party, any expert to such party and any expert to the Tribunal
>
> and
>
> to order any party to produce to the Arbitral Tribunal and to other parties documents or copies of documents in their possession, custody or power which the Arbitral Tribunal decides to be relevant.

542. Nina Das Gupta, 'Kurzkommentare Zu Den Änderungen in Der 2018 DIS-Schiedsgerichtsordnung' (2018) 1 SchiedsVZ-Beilage 44, 68, 69.
543. Vienna International Arbitral Centre of the Austrian Federal Economic Chamber (ed.), 'Article 29 [Establishing the Facts of the Case]', *Handbook Vienna Rules: A Practitioner's Guide* (2014) 171.
544. *Ibid.*, 174.

2.195 A similar attitude in favour of proactive tribunals has also been adopted by the Prague Rules. In broad terms, they stipulate that, for the purposes of fact-finding, the tribunal may take any other actions which it deems appropriate (Article 3). At the same time, the provision emphasizes that this shall not release the parties from their burden of proof, i.e., the main responsibility to introduce evidence remains with the parties. Even the IBA Rules, which are commonly perceived as largely adversarial, state in Article 8.6 First Sentence:

> Subject to the provisions of Article 9.2 and 9.3, the Arbitral Tribunal may request any person to give oral or written evidence on any issue that the Arbitral Tribunal considers to be relevant to the case and material to its outcome.

2.196 The UNCITRAL Rules operate according to a hybrid approach with an emphasis on the adversarial tradition. Accordingly, it is generally the parties' responsibility to introduce facts and evidence (Article 27.3 UNCITRAL Rules). Yet, at any time during the arbitral proceedings, the arbitral tribunal may require the parties to produce documents, exhibits or other evidence within a timeframe determined by the arbitral tribunal (Article 27.3 UNCITRAL Rules). Similar-worded provisions can also be found under Article 22.3 of the HKIAC Rules,[545] Article 24.3 of the SCAI Rules,[546] and Article 27.3 of the PCA Rules.[547] A similar provision is found under Article 31.3 of the SCC Rules, which, however, limits such ex officio orders to 'exceptional circumstances'.[548]

2.197 The above provisions can be categorized into three different approaches. First, the rules of the CIETAC, ICC, DIS, VIAC, as well as the German and English arbitration acts, allow for a strongly inquisitorial nature of the tribunal, namely by allowing (though not obliging) the tribunal to assume the main responsibility for the fact-finding procedures. Under these rules, it is submitted that the tribunal may also actively investigate facts, as long as it safeguards the parties' right to be heard, in particular by informing the parties about the activity and the findings and allowing comment. The second category operates on a more adversarial approach but allows the tribunal to become selectively active and supplement the parties' efforts by ordering the production of specific documents or means of evidence. This applies to the UNCITRAL Rules and the Rules of the HKIAC, SCAI and PCA. The last category, in this study, represented by the SCC Rules, follows a similar approach but clarifies that the tribunal may only

545. Article 22.3 HKIAC Rules: 'At any time during the arbitration, the arbitral tribunal may allow or require a party to produce documents, exhibits or other evidence that the arbitral tribunal determines to be relevant to the case and material to its outcome. The arbitral tribunal shall have the power to admit or exclude any documents, exhibits or other evidence.'

546. Article 26.2 SCAI Rules: 'At any time during the arbitral proceedings, the arbitral tribunal may require the parties to produce documents, exhibits, or other evidence within a period of time determined by the arbitral tribunal.'

547. Article 27.3 PCA Rules: 'At any time during the arbitral proceedings the arbitral tribunal may require the parties to produce documents, exhibits or other evidence within such a period of time as the arbitral tribunal shall determine. The arbitral tribunal may also, after consultation with the parties, perform a site visit.'

548. Article 31.3 SCC Rules: 'At the request of a party, or exceptionally on its own motion, the Arbitral Tribunal may order a party to produce any documents or other evidence that may be relevant to the case and material to its outcome.'

become active under exceptional circumstances. Overall, however, a general tendency can be observed to move away from adversarialism and towards semi-inquisitorial procedures which allow the tribunal to become proactive where necessary.

III The Tribunal's Inquisitorial Powers in Practice

2.198 Should tribunals be encouraged to regularly exercise their inquisitorial powers, or should they leave issues of fact-finding and taking of evidence to the parties? While not always successful, the objective of adversarialism is to enhance legal efficiency by leaving the gathering of relevant facts to the parties, which have an inherently closer link to the matter in dispute.[549] Moreover, and especially relevant for arbitration proceedings, it aims at upholding the principle of party autonomy, thus inspiring 'flexible and creative' solutions.[550] Nevertheless, in practice, adversarial procedures are frequently found to be overly complex, punitive or unpredictable, and have even been described as 'thoroughly savaged'.[551] Pure adversarialism is apt to bring about 'unjust' results and impede 'socially constructive cooperation'.[552] Moreover, especially in combination with excessive discovery, it is found to be habitually ineffective,[553] thus forfeiting one of its main purported objectives.

2.199 By employing active case management techniques, tribunals may ensure that cases are handled more justly, fairly, expeditiously, and proportionally. Specifically, the tribunal's active case management as to facts and evidence can help to enhance the proceedings by focusing the dispute on what is relevant. It also may assist in evening out structural inequalities between the parties. Against this backdrop, arbitration usually benefits from tribunals which adopt certain inquisitorial techniques (or rather methods that soften adversarialism) while duly respecting party autonomy. This, of course, requires solid preparation and arbitrators who closely monitor the events and the parties' submissions from the very beginning in order to be able to react adequately.[554]

---

549. Zaki (n. 516) 22.
550. Kagan (n. 507) 3.
551. Geoffrey Hazard, *Ethics in the Practice of Law* (Yale University Press 1978) 122; cited after Monroe H Freedman, 'Our Constitutionalized Adversary System' (1998) 1 Chapman Law Review 57, 58.
552. Kagan (n. 507) 4.
553. Zaki (n. 516) 59.
554. *See* James M Turner, 'Prague Rules... or Does It?' (*Practical Law Arbitration Blog*, 23 April 2019): 'It also remains common, even now, for cases not to be handled as efficiently as in retrospect they might have been, so the problem is not that tribunals lack the tools required for efficient case management. Rather, the challenges to efficiency lie in time and understanding, and the hard edge of the requirement for a fair hearing. To unpack that a little: in many if not most cases, a case management hearing (or equivalent) is the tribunal's first real opportunity to grapple with the issues in the case. If a case is a mountain, then the tribunal is at this point still in the wooded foothills. Even the parties' lawyers may barely have broken through the tree line; added to that, the good arbitrator is also a busy arbitrator and so may lack the time needed to get even as well on top of the issues as the parties' lawyers. It should be no surprise, then, if tribunals are reluctant to make full use of the range of powers at their disposal, not least because to do so when their understanding of the case is undercooked is to invite challenge.'

2.200 That being said, in practice, tribunals remain rather hesitant to apply inquisitorial techniques. Nevertheless, under due consideration of all circumstances, it can be beneficial for the proceedings if the tribunal opts to independently investigate specific issues (1), have recourse to the public domain (2), order disclosure of facts or documents at its own motion (3), and define issues and give its preliminary views at an early stage (4).

1 Independent Investigations

2.201 Tribunals rarely engage in independent investigations. Despite the encouraging attitude of many of the above arbitration laws and rules, commentators thus far tend to take a rather opposing view, pointing out that the right to be heard may be infringed if the final award is not (solely) based on the parties' submissions.[555]

2.202 Prominently, however, it has been found that a tribunal can be required to investigate where suspicions of corruption and money laundering arise.[556] This is confirmed by the Toolkit for Arbitrators on Corruption and Money Laundering in International Arbitration (the '*Toolkit*'). The Toolkit relies primarily on the requirement that awards must be enforceable, which was not the case where they grossly contradicted considerations of international (or transnational) public policy – such as the fight against corruption:[557]

> While arbitrators are not state judges, they do fulfil a certain public function because – in general terms – arbitral awards are enforceable like court decisions. Furthermore, arbitrators have a duty to issue an enforceable award. If arbitrators ignore issues of corruption, there is a risk that their award will be challenged in front of state courts in set-aside proceedings or at the enforcement stage on the ground that it is contrary to the national or transnational public policy. While in ICSID arbitration, the possibilities to challenge an award are limited to the review procedures provided for in the ICSID Convention, parties may equally seek revision or annulment of an award before an annulment committee. Therefore, whether in the context of commercial or investor-state arbitration, if a party alleges or arbitrators suspect that corruption was involved in the underlying dispute, arbitrators should consider investigating (also on a *sua sponte* basis) those issues. Arbitrators should do so even if the allegations or suspicions arise only at the final stages of the proceedings.[558]

555. John Fellas, 'Arbitrators' Questions: Can They Cross a Line?' (2019) New York Law Journal 8.
556. Domitille Baizeau and Tessa Hayes, 'The Arbitral Tribunal's Duty and Power to Address Corruption Sua Sponte' (2017) 19 ICCA Congress Series 225; Raul Pereira de Souza Fleury, 'Do Arbitrators Have an Ex Officio Duty/Right to Self-Investigate Corruption?' (25 November 2015).
557. *See, inter alia, World Duty Free Co Ltd v The Republic of Kenya, ICSID ARB/00/7* (n. 140) paras 138–157; *Metal-Tech Ltd v Republic of Uzbekistan, ICSID ARB/10/3* Award of 4 October 2013 292.
558. Competence Centre Arbitration and Crime (Basel Institute on Governance) (ed.), *Corruption and Money Laundering in International Arbitration. A Toolkit for Arbitrators.* (2019) 12.

2.203 Aside from cases of fraud, corruption and comparable criminal conduct, independent arbitral investigations are appropriate where the institutional rules expressly allow such authority.[559] If this is the case, the parties' agreement on the use of the institution confirms the tribunal's powers. However, the use of these powers naturally always remains at the discretion of the tribunal.

2.204 The question remains whether a tribunal has the authority to make independent investigations if the applicable procedural rules do not contain any specific rule for or against it. One objection against such authority might be that the parties bear the main responsibility for putting forward their arguments, especially where 'both sides are represented by able counsel'.[560] Then again, it is not uncommon that there are structural inequalities between the parties and the quality of their representation. While choosing suitable and able representatives remains each parties' own responsibility, the right way to proceed in such situations may differ on a case-by-case basis. It is left to the tribunal's discretion, based on considerations of due process, procedural fairness and the right to be heard, weighed against the importance of the issue in question. Moreover, the tribunal must always consider the parties' expectations, which may differ due to different legal backgrounds and traditions.

2.205 In any case, there is no general legal principle or rule that would prevent the tribunal from addressing relevant and material issues that have not been previously introduced.[561] Rather, in the absence of any specific rule or party agreement to the contrary, tribunals have wide discretion to conduct the proceeding as they deem adequate. As highlighted above, many arbitration laws and rules confirm the tribunal's powers to either investigate the facts or order the parties to disclose further relevant material.[562] However, it must be emphasized that if a tribunal finds it necessary to consider material which the parties have not introduced, it must always grant the parties the right to review and comment on the material.[563]

2 *Recourse to Public Knowledge*

2.206 Unlike various domestic procedural rules,[564] international arbitration laws and other sets of procedural rules in arbitration do not provide any statement as to whether tribunals may have recourse to public knowledge. Taking into account the broad

559. *See* David E Wagoner, 'U.S. Court Demonstrates Pro-Enforcement Bias in a Comprehensive Review of a Cietac Award Under the New York Convention' (1998) 16 ASA Bulletin 289, 305 et seq., analysing a US court ruling upholding a CIETAC award which was presumably based on the tribunal's independent investigation.
560. Fellas (n. 555).
561. Giovannini (n. 534) 75 et seq.
562. *See* above, Chapter 2, C.I.
563. Giovannini (n. 534) 72.
564. Cf. sec. 292 ZPO: 'Facts that are common knowledge with the court need not be substantiated by evidence'; Rule 201 Federal Rules of Evidence: 'The court may judicially notice a fact that is not subject to reasonable dispute because it (...) is generally known within the trial court's territorial jurisdiction; or can be accurately and readily determined from sources whose accuracy cannot reasonably be questioned.'

inquisitorial powers, it is submitted that international tribunals may consider information which pertains to the public domain.[565] As has been shown, most modern arbitration rules are free from overly adversarial rules which would limit the factual basis of the award (or other decisions) to precisely the parties' pleadings. It may, for example, be acceptable for the tribunal to determine the applicable interest rate ex officio without consulting the parties.[566]

2.207 A problem that may arise, however, is the scope and definition of public domain. Difficulties particularly arise due to the ever-growing public access to information.[567] Issues may arise when a tribunal conducts an online search for specific facts or events, or visits relevant sites via online mapping services. A Polish Court, for example, found that it was reasonable for a tribunal to review websites when establishing evidentiary issues.[568] In this case, the court went so far as to find it acceptable for the tribunal to do this, even without consulting the parties beforehand.[569] Nonetheless, it is crucial that a tribunal that considers such information always bears in mind the right to be heard, i.e., grants the parties the right to submit a statement.

2.208 Moreover, in certain cases, parties may agree on a fact that evidently contradicts public knowledge. Here, too, the tribunal must be entitled to assess the factual situation independently, provided that it has granted the parties the right to be heard prior to making a decision.

3 Disclosure Orders

2.209 In international proceedings, the tribunal may order the parties to disclose documents or other information (including potential means of evidence) on its own motion. This is reflected by most of the examined arbitration rules, albeit to different degrees.[570]

2.210 The tribunal does not require express consent on the part of the parties. Rather, these powers derive from the specific arbitration rules, the tribunal's general procedural discretion and the international arbitration practice. While it may not amount to a transnational principle yet, the density of comparable rules certainly points toward the emergence of a transnational rule on the tribunal's authority.[571] However, despite

565. This is accepted, *inter alia*, in the ambit of the German arbitration law, *see* Münch (n. 537) para. 117.
566. Giovannini (n. 534) 73.
567. *See, e.g.*, Benedikt Windau, 'Das Googelnde Gericht – Ist Der Beibringungsgrundsatz Noch Zeitgemäß?' [2018] NJOZ 761, who raises the issue in the context of German civil procedure.
568. *Warsaw Appellate Court, Judgment of 16 April 2008* LexPolonica, No 2062236; cited after Łukasz Błaszczak and Joanna Kolber, 'Annulment and Enforcement of Arbitral Awards in Poland' (2012) 30 ASA Bulletin 564, 270.
569. *Warsaw Appellate Court, Judgment of 16 April 2008* (n. 568); cited after Błaszczak and Kolber (n. 568) 270.
570. *See* above, Chapter 2, C.1.
571. *See* above, Chapter 1.

the far-reaching powers, in practice, tribunals thus far seem to be hesitant to make such orders without proper party application.[572]

2.211 Controversies may also arise where a tribunal has ordered a party to produce documents (or other information or evidence) and the party fails to comply with such order. In some cases, tribunals have resorted to drawing adverse inferences in response.[573]

2.212 Importantly, when ordering a party to disclose a document or specific facts, the tribunal needs to exercise its discretion, under due consideration of its duty to neutrality as well as the presumed informational or probative value of the document or information in question. The subsequent disclosure of the party may be used both to clarify the facts and for the purpose of taking evidence.

4 Definition of Preliminary Issues

2.213 Finally, the tribunal may resort to procedural notifications regarding factual issues and orders as well as orders to produce specific means of evidence.

2.214 Both the IBA Rules[574] and the Prague Rules[575] affirm that the tribunal should define the issues in dispute, to help to focus the efforts on the relevant points. Some institutions also provide that the parties should agree upon the relevant issues as part of the terms of reference.[576] While the determination of preliminary issues may serve to expedite the proceedings, this is not always the case. The experience from civil litigation in England and Wales, for example, shows that in complex cases it may even delay the process, especially if it requires the conduction of separate hearings on the definition of issues.[577] The tribunal should, therefore, always assess the cost-benefit

572. There are, however, also practical examples of such orders. *See*, e.g., *Asian Agricultural Products Ltd v Republic of Sri Lanka, ICSID ARB/87/3* Final Award of 27 June 1990 [16] where the Tribunal 'requested the Parties to submit certain additional documents and information, together with their respective comments thereon'.

573. *See* below, Chapter 3, E.II.3.

574. Article 2.3 IBA Rules: 'The Arbitral Tribunal is encouraged to identify to the Parties, as soon as it considers it to be appropriate, any issues: (...) that the Arbitral Tribunal may regard as relevant to the case and material to its outcome; and/or (...) for which a preliminary determination may be appropriate.'

575. Article 2.5 Prague Rules: 'When establishing the procedural timetable, the arbitral tribunal may decide – after having heard the parties – to determine certain issues of fact or law as preliminary matters (...).'

576. Article 23.1 (d) ICC Rules: 'The terms of reference shall include, in particular, unless the arbitral tribunal considers it inappropriate, a list of issues to be determined.'

577. *Bond v Dunster Properties Ltd & Ors* [2011] EWCA Civ 455 [106–108]: '106. The first problem was that the parties agreed to the determination of preliminary issues. This appears to me to have been very unwise, given that the hearing was anticipated to last four days, and, it would seem, to involve oral evidence, much of it from parties or witnesses who could reasonably have been expected to give evidence at any subsequent hearing. By the time the preliminary issues hearing was intended to start, the proceedings would have already been on foot for nearly two years and the relevant events would have taken place nearly four years earlier. 107. While they have their value, it is notorious that preliminary issues often turn out to be misconceived, in that, while they are intended to short-circuit the proceedings, they actually increase the time

ratio of such an undertaking. In practice, tribunals frequently do not seem to feel comfortable with providing a detailed list of issues at an early stage, despite the preliminary character.

2.215 The Prague Rules further expressly stipulate that the tribunal should give its preliminary views on disputed issues (Article 2.4(e)). Doing so may both clarify the vital points of the dispute and allow the parties to supplement their submissions thus far. It may also facilitate an early settlement, rendering subsequent proceedings superfluous. Due to cultural differences, it is advisable to discuss the application of these techniques in a first case management conference, as the parties' attitudes towards preliminary views might be different.[578]

IV Conclusion

2.216 As the third key issue of fact-gathering, the above analysis has shown that most arbitration laws and rules as well as sets of soft law grant the tribunal rather substantial authority to pro-actively engage in fact-finding. Duly regarding basic procedural principles (in particular, due process and the right to be heard), the tribunal may, where appropriate, investigate specific issues on its own motion. This is particularly the case if there are allegations of corruption, fraud or other relevant criminal conduct.

2.217 Apart from that, and equally, under due consideration of the parties' procedural rights, the tribunal may consider issues of public domain, order the parties to disclose specific evidence (including documents) or information and give its preliminary views on the facts. In practice, tribunals have so far been rather reticent to employ these powers, mainly owing to the diverging legal cultures and understanding of practitioners. Nevertheless, it is to be expected that in the course of ongoing transnationalization, tribunals will continue to act more independently of domestic approaches in the future and will further explore their wide-ranging powers to this effect, provided that it contributes to procedural efficiency and procedural fairness.

D SUMMARY

2.218 The above analysis of the rules on the gathering of facts provides two key findings. It first corroborates the initial hypothesis, namely that there is a palpable trend towards the transnationalization of international arbitration law, in particular regarding the rules of fact-finding. The analysis of the legal framework reveals an extensive (albeit not complete) synchronization of the fact-gathering procedures,

and cost of resolving the underlying dispute. It would, in my judgment, require a very exceptional case, almost inevitably one where a subsequent multi-week trial was anticipated, before a preliminary issue hearing, involving witnesses and expected to last four days, could be justified. 108. (...) In my view, parties and their legal advisers should carefully consider the potential benefits and risks before proposing a preliminary issue hearing, and, before a judge orders such a hearing, he or she should normally test the soundness of the proposed course.'

578. Klaus Peter Berger and J Ole Jensen, 'The Arbitrator's Mandate to Facilitate Settlement' (2017) 40 Fordham International Law Journal 887, 908.

serving as the foundation of the transnational *Lex Evidentiae*. While also driven by the UNCITRAL Model Law and UNCITRAL Rules, the uniformization is largely based on self-developing best practices rather than specific efforts by national or international legislative bodies to uniformize the proceedings. As has been shown, many fact-finding rules are created and consolidated by re-enacting practices known to the stakeholders from prior proceedings rather than applying laws enacted by national or international legislators. As a matter of course, arbitration laws mostly stipulate basic requirements in broad terms, leaving the specific application to the institutional or ad hoc rules, the discretion of the tribunal and/or any agreements of the parties. However, since the arbitration rules often only provide vague guidelines, a significant part of the procedural organization is left to best practices, either consolidated by arbitral institutions and private codifying agencies (e.g., the IBA or the Prague Rules Working Group) or deriving from prior experiences of the stakeholders.

2.219 Closely linked to this, the second main finding is that the individual procedural steps in international arbitration (such as pleadings, document production and the tribunal's case management) are heavily intertwined and cannot be considered and analysed independently of each other. For example, in order to understand the scope of the applicable rules on pleadings, one must consider to what extent parties are required to disclose documents and evidence at a later stage of the proceedings and whether the tribunal has the power to interfere with the gathering of facts, e.g., by conducting independent investigations or having recourse to the public domain. As a result, domestic approaches, which must also be seen in their specific domestic procedural context, often do not fit in international arbitration. Accordingly, the main effect of the transnationalization of arbitration law is that the fact-finding rules are becoming increasingly independent of domestic (litigation) practices. Rather, international arbitration is developing a unique and continuously evolving fact-finding regime tailored to its specific needs.

CHAPTER 3
Proving Facts

3.1 As the second and final vital phase of fact-finding, the taking of evidence serves to determine relevant factual issues on which the parties disagree. The tribunal is only required to take evidence if (i) the particular issue or fact has been properly introduced into the dispute, (ii) the issue is disputed and (iii) relevant to its outcome, and finally, (iv) if the party bearing the burden of proof has submitted evidence which can be examined. If these requirements are fulfilled, the tribunal must resolve the issue and cannot leave it unresolved. A so-called *non liquet* (literally: 'it is not clear') decision is inadmissible as it violates the parties' access to justice. In such cases, the tribunal must make its decision based on the burden of proof.

3.2 The taking of evidence naturally revolves around the very evidence to be examined before the tribunal. Despite its prominence, the English term 'evidence' is less clear than it seems. In fact, it is rather ambiguous, in that its meaning is two-fold. The first meaning refers to the information (i.e., the testimony) itself, which helps to confirm the veracity of a disputed allegation.[579] A witness of fact, for example, gives 'evidence' on the course of events. The second meaning is the rather more common one; namely, it describes the means of evidence which contain such testimony.[580]

3.3 Rather than being prescribed by municipal or international laws, the rules on the taking of evidence have been largely developed and consolidated by the practice itself. That is, not only in regard to the gathering of facts[581] but also in the rules surrounding the taking of evidence there is an ongoing transnationalization of the arbitral law of evidence, i.e., the emergence and further consolidation of the *Lex Evidentiae*.

3.4 The below shall address the relevant steps in the procedure of the taking of evidence, starting with the submission of evidence (*A*). The subsequent sections analyse the different means of evidence (*B*) and matters relating to the admission of

579. *See* for the terminology in England and Wales: Keane and McKeown (n. 290) 2.
580. Pilkov (n. 422) n 1.
581. *See* above, Chapter 2.

evidence (*C*). The final sections (*E* and *F*) address the standard of proof applicable in international arbitration as well as issues surrounding the assessment of evidence.

A SUBMISSION OF EVIDENCE

3.5 Before the tribunal can determine the facts by taking evidence, the means of evidence that will be analysed must be introduced into the dispute.

3.6 While the legal framework stipulates only basic requirements for the submission of evidence (*I*), based on the burden of proof, it remains largely the parties' responsibility to introduce the evidence they seek to rely upon (*II*). Further, in light of the recent tendencies towards using more inquisitorial techniques, the tribunal may, under certain circumstances, be entitled to collect evidence on its own motion (*III*).

I Minimum Requirements under Arbitration Laws and Arbitration Rules

3.7 Similar to the common practice in civil litigation across various jurisdictions, in arbitration, it is primarily the parties' responsibility to introduce evidence into the dispute. This is confirmed by a survey of different arbitration laws and rules, which contain similar stipulations in slightly different wording. As pointed out, however, the generally adversarial approach to fact-finding is increasingly being softened, or rather, supplemented by the tribunal's powers to take evidence ex officio.[582]

3.8 Under Article 23 (1) Second Sentence of the Model Law, the parties 'may submit with their statements all documents they consider to be relevant or may add a reference to the documents or other evidence they will submit'. A nearly identical wording is reflected by section 1046 (1) of the ZPO[583] as well as section 597 (1) of the ÖZPO.[584] Article 21 (2) of the Brazilian Arbitration Act puts the same in more abstract terms, stating that the tribunal shall always uphold the 'principle of contradictory procedures'.[585] A similar wording can be found in Article 182 (3) of the Swiss PIL, according to which, '[i]rrespective of the procedure chosen, the arbitral tribunal shall accord

582. *See* above, Chapter 2, C.

583. Section 1046 (1) ZPO: 'Within the period determined by the parties or by the arbitral tribunal, the plaintiff is to present his claim and the facts on which this claim is based, and the defendant is to state his position in this regard. In this context, the parties may submit all documents that they deem significant, or they may designate any other evidence of which they intend to avail themselves.'

584. Section 597 (1) ÖZPO: 'Within the period of time agreed by the parties or determined by the arbitral tribunal, the claimant shall submit his claim and state the facts on which the claim is based on, and the respondent shall respond. The parties may present any evidence they consider to be relevant or indicate further evidence they wish to rely on.'

585. Article 21 (2) of the Brazilian Arbitration Act: 'Serão, sempre, respeitados no procedimento arbitral os princípios do contraditório, da igualdade das partes, da imparcialidade do árbitro e de seu livre convencimento.' Note that in the English translation, the reference to the 'princípio do contraditório' has been translated as: 'The principles of due process of law, equal treatment of the parties, impartiality of the arbitrator and freedom of decision shall always be respected.' *See* further Lemes (n. 536) para. VI.2.

equal treatment to the parties and their right to be heard in an adversarial proceeding'.[586]

3.9 Comparable provisions are stipulated by most arbitration rules. Articles 20.4 and 21.2. Second Sentence of the UNCITRAL Rules states that the statement of claim and the statement of defence 'should, as far as possible, be accompanied by all documents and other evidence relied upon' by the parties. Articles 18.3 and 19.2 of the SCAI Rules read that '[a]s a rule', the parties 'shall annex all documents and evidence' to their submissions. Similarly, other arbitration rules require the parties to submit 'all documents relied upon' (15.2[587] and 15.3 LCIA Rules[588]), 'any evidence' on which the parties rely (Article 29.1.(iii)[589]; 2.(v) SCC Rules[590]), 'all written evidence' (Article 9.2 Vienna Rules)[591] or 'all supporting materials' (Articles 16.3[592] and 17.3 HKIAC Rules[593]).

3.10 According to Appendix IV (d) (i) to the ICC Rules, the tribunal shall require the 'parties to produce with their submissions the documents on which they rely'. The DIS Rules make no express reference but merely stipulate that the tribunal is not 'limited by the evidence offered by the parties',[594] thus confirming the basic presumption that the parties must 'offer' evidence. Notably, the concept of 'offering evidence' (*Beweisantritt*) stems from German civil litigation where the parties usually do not submit evidence directly, but describe the evidence they seek to rely on, leaving it to the court's decision whether the production is necessary.[595]

---

586. It was held that '[u]nder the Swiss Private Law Act, the right to be heard in adversarial proceedings specifically guarantees each party's right to participate in the evidentiary proceedings, to rebut allegations made by the opposite party, to examine and criticize evidence adduced by the opposite party and to bring its own evidence in rebuttal before an award is rendered to its detriment', *CAS Case No 2000/A/274, Award of 19 October 2000* 2 Digest of CAS Awards II 1998-2000 [3 (Summary)].
587. Article 15.2 LCIA Rules: 'the Claimant shall deliver to the Arbitral Tribunal and all other (...) its written Statement of Case setting out in sufficient detail the relevant facts and legal submissions on which it relies, together with the relief claimed against all other parties, and all documents relied upon'.
588. Article 15.3 LCIA Rules: 'the Respondent shall deliver to the Arbitral Tribunal and all other parties (...) its written Statement of Defence and (if applicable) Statement of Counterclaim setting out in sufficient detail the relevant facts and legal submissions on which it relies, together with the relief claimed against all other parties, and all documents relied upon'.
589. Article 29.1.(iii) SCC Rules: 'Within the period determined by the Arbitral Tribunal, the Claimant shall submit a Statement of Claim which shall include, unless previously submitted: (...) any evidence the Claimant relies on.'
590. Article 29.2.(v) SCC Rules: 'Within the period determined by the Arbitral Tribunal, the Respondent shall submit a Statement of Defence which shall include, unless previously submitted: (...) any evidence the Claimant relies on.'
591. Article 9.1. Vienna Rules: 'The parties shall make all factual arguments in their written submissions and all written evidence shall be attached to the written submissions.'
592. Article 16.3 HKIAC Rules: 'The Claimant shall annex to its Statement of Claim all supporting materials on which it relies.'
593. Article 17.4 HKIAC Rules: 'The Respondent shall annex to its Statement of Defence all supporting materials on which it relies.'
594. Article 28 Second Sentence DIS Rules: 'The arbitral tribunal shall not be limited to admit only evidence offered by the parties.'
595. *See, e.g.*, sec. 373 ZPO: 'Evidence by hearing witnesses shall be offered by naming the witnesses and designating the facts regarding which the witnesses are to be examined.'

3.11 Similar provisions can be found under different sets of soft law as well. Article 3 (1) of the IBA Rules states that:

> [w]ithin the time ordered by the Arbitral Tribunal, each Party shall submit to the Arbitral Tribunal and to the other Parties all Documents available to it on which it relies, including public Documents and those in the public domain, except for any Documents that have already been submitted by another Party.

3.12 Article 4.1 of the Prague Rules reads that:

> [e]ach party shall submit documentary evidence upon which it intends to rely in support of its case as early as possible in the proceedings.

3.13 ALI/UNIDROIT Rule 21.1 stipulates that the parties:

> must identify to the court and other parties the evidence on which the party intends to rely, in addition to that provided in the pleading.

Specifically, this includes copies of documents and other records, summaries of expected witness testimonies (or, alternatively, written witness statements) (ALI/UNIDROIT Rule 21.1.1 and 21.1.2).

3.14 Accordingly, all of the above arbitration laws and rules as well as sets of soft law confirm that it remains the party's responsibility to submit the documents and other means of evidence upon which it seeks to rely. However, the analysed rules do not contain any elaborate dogmatic statements on the underlying burden to adduce evidence or the distribution of this burden.[596] Rather, similar to the above findings on pleading requirements,[597] they address the submission of documents and other forms of evidence on a formal level, for the most part stating that the parties are required to present the evidence they seek to rely on with their submissions. Thus, they do not deal with the burden of proof in a legal sense and do not provide the tribunal with any guidance on how to proceed if, by the end of the proceeding, material evidence has not been introduced. If the tribunal does not find it appropriate to order the production of specific evidence on its own motion, it must decide which party will bear the consequences of the omission to provide evidence, based on the burden of proof.

II The Parties' Burden of Proof

3.15 Upon closer examination, the seemingly simple term 'burden of proof' presents itself as a rather more complex issue. To begin with, the concept of 'burden of proof' is multi-layered and is comprised of separate individual issues and rules. Importantly, it exceeds its role as a mere means of risk distribution where the tribunal is convinced by neither version brought forward by the parties. It also guides the submission of

596. An exception, however, can be found, *inter alia*, in ALI/UNIDROIT Principle 21, which will be addressed below in Chapter 3, A.II.
597. *See* above, Chapter 2, A.I.

facts[598] and impacts the standard of proof.[599] Moreover, the burden of proof is neither fully procedural nor fully substantive in nature. Rather, it exists somewhere in the grey-zone of the substance-procedure dichotomy.[600] Owing to its different dimensions, some aspects of the burden of proof are found to be governed by substantive law, while others are mainly understood as procedural matters, which makes it increasingly challenging to define one uniformly applicable law.[601] Consequently, the burden of proof cannot be analysed as a separate issue outside of the procedural context. Rather, it is deeply embedded in the complex interplay between the parties' burdens and duties and the tribunal's powers which unfold throughout the fact-finding procedures and must be viewed in that context.

3.16 The below shall, therefore, first outline the different dimensions and meanings of the term 'burden of proof' (*1*), before examining the allocation and potential reversals of the burden of proof (*2*). This is followed by a brief analysis of the impact of the burden of proof on the tribunal's powers to collect evidence on its own motion (*3*).

1 Legal Burden and Evidential Burden

i Terminology

3.17 The term 'burden of proof' is comprised of two main components, namely first, the 'legal burden' (also referred to as the 'probative burden' or 'ultimate burden'[602]; in German: *objektive Beweislast* or *Feststellungslast)*[603] and second, the 'evidential burden' (also referred to as the 'burden of going forward' or 'burden of producing evidence'[604]; in German: *subjektive Beweislast* or *Beweisführungslast*).[605] This distinction can be found, *inter alia*, in England and Wales,[606] the US,[607] and Germany.[608]

598. *See* above, Chapter 2, A.III.
599. *See* below, Chapter 3, D.
600. *See* below, Chapter 3, A.II.1.
601. *See* below, Chapter 3, A.II.1; *see*, for instance, the discussion on considering the burden of proof during the exchange of document procedure, Chapter 2, C.III.1.a.v.(d).
602. Keane and McKeown (n. 290) 58.
603. Rosenberg (n. 282) 11–18; Hanns Prütting, *Gegenwartsprobleme Der Beweislast: Eine Untersuchung Moderner Beweislasttheorien Und Ihrer Anwendung Insbesondere Im Arbeitsrecht* (C.H. Beck 1983) 5, 6; Hans-Joachim Musielak and Max Stadler, *Grundfragen Des Beweisrechts: Beweisaufnahme, Beweiswürdigung, Beweislast* (C.H. Beck 1984) 129; Michael Henninger, *Die Frage der Beweislast im Rahmen des UN-Kaufrechts: zugleich eine rechtsvergleichende Grundlagenstudie zur Beweislast* (utzverlag 1995) 20; Gregory Benedicter, *Die Sachverhaltsermittlung Im Zivilprozess* (Hochschulschrift 2005) 15, 16; Prütting, 'ZPO § 286' (n. 239) para. 100; Bacher, 'ZPO § 284' in Vorwerk and Wolf (eds), *Beck'sche Online-Kommentar ZPO* (39th edn, C.H. Beck 2020) para. 64.
604. Fleming James, 'Burdens of Proof' (1961) 47 Virginia Law Review 51, 55.
605. Keane and McKeown (n. 290) 80; James (n. 604) 51.
606. Keane and McKeown (n. 290) 58 et seq., 80 et seq.
607. James (n. 604) 51 et seq.
608. Prütting, 'ZPO § 286' (n. 239) paras 100–106.

3.18 The 'legal burden' describes the burden to convince the trier of facts in case of *non liquet*, i.e., where neither party's position is more probable.[609] It thus only takes effect at the very end of the proceeding, namely after (i) the parties have pleaded all relevant issues (ii) the tribunal has taken evidence and (iii) it is not convinced of either of the parties' versions. Rather than being a real burden on the parties, it is thus a rule of risk distribution.

3.19 The 'evidential burden', however, describes the parties' burden to adduce evidence on specific factual issues.[610] The evidential burden thus determines which party must produce evidence for a contested factual allegation; failing to do so may lead to an adverse decision of the tribunal.[611] It takes effect after (or parallel to) the pleading of facts, namely when determining which issues are relevant, material and in dispute between the parties, and which accordingly require the taking of evidence. The parties mostly annex written evidence (such as documents, witness statements and expert reports) to their pleadings.[612] If necessary, these will be tested during a hearing, e.g., by examining the author(s) of the documents or other relevant witnesses and experts. In court proceedings, merely omitting to submit evidence may lead to a procedural loss.[613] In modern international arbitration, however, if evidence has not been submitted, the tribunal has far-reaching powers to order the parties to produce specific evidence or even engage in investigations on its own motion.[614] Nonetheless, experience thus far shows that tribunals seldom interfere with the procurement of evidence.

ii *Applicable Rules*

3.20 Despite the tendency to consider the burden of proof a procedural issue,[615] it is mostly understood to be substantive in nature.[616] While this may be partly true, the complexity of the concept of burden of proof demands a more specific distinction. The legal burden[617] is, in fact, closely linked to substantive law.[618] Likewise, the

609. Aimoré Carreteiro (n. 277); for England and Wales, *see* Keane and McKeown (n. 290) 58; for Germany, *see* Prütting, 'ZPO § 286' (n. 239) paras 103–105.
610. Aimoré Carreteiro (n. 277) 84, 85; for England and Wales, *see* Keane and McKeown (n. 290) 80 et seq.; for Germany, *see* Prütting, 'ZPO § 286' (n. 239) paras 101, 102.
611. Aimoré Carreteiro (n. 277) 84, 85; for England and Wales, *see* Keane and McKeown (n. 290) 80 et seq.; for Germany, *see* Prütting, 'ZPO § 286' (n. 239) paras 101, 102.
612. *See* above, Chapter 3, A.I.
613. *See, e.g.*, for Germany, Prütting, 'ZPO § 286' (n. 239) para. 101.
614. *See* above, Chapter 2, C and below, Chapter 3, A.III.
615. *See Fiona Trust & Holding Corporation Ors v Privalov Ors* [2010] EWHC (Comm) 3199 [93]: 'Generally, as a matter of English private international law, the burden of proof is probably a procedural matter determined by the lex fori (...).'
616. Redfern and others (n. 271) 331, 332, 342; Schlaepfer (n. 277) (at least for civil law jurisdictions).
617. *Fiona Trust & Holding Corporation Ors v Privalov Ors* (n. 615) para. 94.
618. Athanassios V Skontzos, 'The Burden and Standard of Proof in Model International Procedural Law: Dealing with the Burden and Standard of Proof in International Disputes' (2018) 23 Uniform Law Review 569, 577.

distribution and reversals[619] of the burden of proof are found to be governed by substantive law,[620] especially where the provision of the requirements which are in dispute is part of the substantive law.[621]

3.21 By contrast, the evidentiary burden, i.e., the burden to adduce evidence, is mostly considered to be a matter of procedural law,[622] since the particulars of the production and submission of evidence are closely linked to the structure and organization of the proceeding.[623] The question of whether a party must produce evidence for an issue is frequently not governed by the *lex arbitri* and/or the applicable (institutional or ad hoc) arbitration rules. Rather, as shown above, most arbitration laws and rules merely stipulate that parties shall submit the evidence they seek to rely upon. In the absence of specific rules or party agreements, the tribunal accordingly enjoys greater discretion in this regard. Nonetheless, in most cases, it is advisable to take the general distribution of the burden of proof into consideration, as is set out in more detail below.

3.22 However, there is a growing tendency to consider both the legal burden and the evidentiary burden to be in the grey zone between substantive and procedural law,[624] which allows to apply the transnational principle of *actori imcumbit*, rather than allowing recourse to (potential) specifics of the *lex causae*.[625] The principle of *actori imcumbit* also applies to the procedural burden of proof, as sets of procedural rules rarely reflect particulars of the legal burden. Such issues may arise if, for example, a party challenges the jurisdiction of the tribunal or an individual arbitrator, or if a party alleges that a document was falsified.[626]

2 *Allocation of the Burden of Proof*

3.23 As a general rule, the allocation of the burden of proof follows the principle of *actori incumbit onus probatio* (*a*). This rule is, however, subject to different modifications (*b*), such as legal presumptions (*c*).

619. Dagmar Coester-Waltjen, *Internationales Beweisrecht: Das Auf Den Beweis Anwendbare Recht in Rechtsstreitigkeiten Mit Auslandsbezug* (R Gremer 1983) 295.
620. *Ibid.*, 283 with futher references to French law, German law, English law and US-American law.
621. *Ibid.*
622. Skontzos (n. 618) 577, 578; Gidi (n. 213) 49; *see also* Coester-Waltjen (n. 619) 301, 302 on potential conflicts between civil law and common law notions of the burden to adduce evidence.
623. Coester-Waltjen (n. 619) 301.
624. Pauker (n. 19) 19 p.
625. *See* below, Chapter 1, A.II.2.
626. For example, where a party relies on a document while the other party alleges the document was falsified, *see* below Chapter 3, B.III.

i Actori Imcumbit Onus Probatio

3.24 The general and widely undisputed rule states that the burden of proof lies upon a party which substantially asserts the affirmative of an issue.[627] Accordingly, a party that invokes a right bears the burden of proof for its prerequisites. The distribution of the burden of proof is independent of the procedural roles of the parties.[628] A claiming party (*nota bene*: not the claimant) is thus required to prove the facts supporting its claim, and the defending party (*nota bene*: not the defendant) must prove the facts supporting its affirmative defence.

3.25 The above understanding derives from the Roman legal maxim: 'he who asserts, and not who denies it must prove' (*ei qui incumbit probatio qui dicit, non qui negat* or *actori incumbi*).[629] Rules to this effect can be found, *inter alia*, in England and Wales,[630] the USA,[631] Germany,[632] France,[633] Italy,[634] Spain,[635] Portugal[636] as well as under the CISG.[637] Due to its prevalence, there is thus a strong tendency to consider the rule on the distribution of the burden of proof as transnational law.[638]

627. Francisco Blavi and Gonzalo Vial, 'Burden of Proof in Internation Commercial Arbitration: Are We Allowed to Adjust the Scales' (2016) 39 Hastings International and Comparative Law Review 41, 47; Aimoré Carreteiro (n. 277) 91; Mojtaba Kazazi, *Burden of Proof and Related Issues: A Study on Evidence Before International Tribunals* (Kluwer Law International 1996) 369.
628. Aimoré Carreteiro (n. 277) 85.
629. Waincymer (n. 343) para. 10.4.1; Keane and McKeown (n. 290) 62; Djordjević, 'CISG Article 74' in Kröll, Mistelis and Perales Viscasillas (eds), *UN Convention on Contracts for the International Sales of Goods (CISG)* (2nd edn, 2018) para. 15.
630. Keane and McKeown (n. 290) 61, 62.
631. James (n. 604) 51; John J Barceló III, 'Burden of Proof, Prima Facie Case and Presumption in WTO Dispute Settlement' (2009) 42 Cornell International Law Journal 23, para. II.A.1.
632. *Rosenberg*, Die Beweislast, S. 98, 99.
633. Article 9 NCPC: 'Il incombe à chaque partie de prouver conformément à la loi les faits nécessaires au succès de sa prétention.' English translation (by the author): 'Each party has the burden of proving in accordance with the law the facts necessary for the success of its claim.'
634. Article 2697 Codice Civile: 'Chi vuol far valere un diritto in giudizio (Cod. Proc. Civ. 163) deve provare i fatti che ne costituiscono il fondamento (Cod. Proc. Civ. 115). Chi eccepisce l'inefficacia di tali fatti ovvero eccepisce che il diritto si è modificato o estinto deve provare i fatti su cui l'eccezione si fonda.' English translation (by the author): 'Whoever wishes to assert a right in court (Civil Code 163) must prove the facts on which it is based (Civil Code 115). Whoever objects to the ineffectiveness of these facts or objects that the right has been modified or extinguished must prove the facts on which the objection is based.'
635. Article 217 Ley de Enjuiciamiento Civil: 'Incumbe al demandado (...) de probar los hechos que, conforme a las normas que les sean aplicables, impidan, extingan o enerven la eficacia jurídica de los hechos a que se refiere el apartado anterior.' English translation (by the author): 'It is incumbent upon the defendant (...) to prove the facts which, in accordance with the rules applicable to them, prevent, extinguish or reinforce the legal effectiveness of the facts referred to in the preceding paragraph.'
636. Article 342.1 Código Civil: 'Àquele que invocar um direito cabe fazer a prova dos factos constitutivos do direito alegado.' English translation (by the author): 'The one who invokes a right is responsible for proving the facts constituting the alleged right.'
637. Djordjević (n. 629) para. 15.
638. 'Commentary to Trans-Lex Principle No. XII.1 – Distribution of Burden of Proof, https://Www.Trans-Lex.Org/966000'.

3.26 Confirming the *actori incumbit* principle, ALI/UNIDROIT Principle 21.1 reads that, '[o]rdinarily, each party has the burden to prove all the material facts that are the basis of that party's case'. The same is set out by Trans-Lex principle No. XII.1, according to which, 'the burden of proof rests on the party who advances a proposition affirmatively (*actori incumbit onus probandi*)'.[639]

3.27 The fact that the legal burden is considered a matter of substantive law may explain why, usually, arbitration rules do not contain any express provision on the distribution of the burden of proof.[640] There are, however, some exceptions. Article 27.1 of the UNCITRAL Rules, Article 27.1 of the PCA Rules and Article 22.1 of the HKIAC Rules, for example, state in identical language that '[e]ach party shall have the burden of proving the facts relied on to support its claim or defence'. During the drafting process, the responsible UNCITRAL Working Group discussed whether Article 27.1 UNCTIRAL Rules was in 'conflict with applicable law on evidence, since there were a variety of legislative approaches to that matter'.[641] The Working Group nevertheless maintained the wording, as it found that, rather than overriding the applicable law, the paragraph was meant to clarify that the parties were required to provide evidence for their allegations. Accordingly, it concluded that '[a]rbitrators would in any case have the ability to determine the applicable law, including to the question of evidence and burden of proof'.[642] That is, under the UNCITRAL Rules, tribunals are expected to consider potential deviating effects under the *lex causae*.[643] This is also in line with Article 18 (1) of the Rome I Regulation, according to which the law governing a contractual obligation under this Regulation shall apply if it contains rules which raise presumptions of law or determine the burden of proof.[644]

3.28 To the extent that arbitration awards are published, the burden of proof, and the distribution thereof, is a recurring issue. In the arbitral case law, there is a strong tendency to confirm the *actori incumbit* rule as a transnational principle. For instance, the ICSID tribunal in Asian *Agricultural Products Ltd. v Republic of Sri Lanka*, found that:

---

639. While the literal translation of the *actori incumbit* principle means that the claimant bears the burden of proof, as pointed out, the distribution of the burden of proof applies independent from the procedural role, *see also ibid.*
640. *Inter alia*, the DIS Rules, ICC Rules, LCIA Rules, Vienna Rules, ICDR Rules.
641. UNCITRAL, 'A/Cn.9/669 – Report of Working Group II (Arbitration and Conciliation) on the Work of Its Fiftieth Session' para. 96.
642. *Ibid.*, 97, 98; *see* further Paulsson and Petrochilos (n. 14) 237, 238; Kabir AN Duggal and Wendy W Cai, *Principles of Evidence in Public International Law as Applied by Investor-State Tribunals: Burden and Standards of Proof* (Brill 2018) 3; David D Caron and Lee Caplan, *The UNCITRAL Arbitration Rules: A Commentary: (With an Integrated and Comparative Discussion of the 2010 and 1976 UNCITRAL Arbitration Rules)* (2nd edn, Oxford University Press 2013) 561.
643. Paulsson and Petrochilos (n. 14) 237, 238, *see* further below Chapter 3, A.2.c on the effect of legal presumptions.
644. For the sake of clarity it must be emphasized that arbitral tribunals are not required to apply the Rome I convention, *see* Franco Ferrari (ed.), 'The Rome I and Rome II Regulations in International Commercial Arbitration', *The Impact of EU Law on International Commercial Arbitration* (Juris 2017) paras II.B and II.C.

> [a] Party having the burden of proof must not only bring evidence in support of his allegations, but must also convince the Tribunal of their truth, lest they be disregarded for want, or insufficiency, of proof.[645]

3.29 This was subsequently confirmed in *Tokios v Ukraine* and *Alpha Projektholding GmbH v Ukraine*. Here, the tribunals noted:

> The principle of onus probandi actori incumbit – that a claimant bears the burden of proving its claims – is widely recognized in practice before international tribunals. The significance of this burden was stated effectively by the tribunal in Asian Agricultural Products, Ltd. v. Sri Lanka (ARB/87/3) (...).[646]
>
> The Tribunal agrees with the standard (...) that, with regard to 'proof of individual allegations advanced by the parties in the course of proceedings, the burden of proof rests upon the party alleging the fact'. The Tribunal notes that other ICSID tribunals have reaffirmed this principle, including (...). [*Tokios v Ukraine*] (...).[647]

3.30 The same approach can be found in commercial arbitration, where, for example, a sole arbitrator in an ICC Award held:

> Th[e] principle, also known as the maxim 'actori incumbit probatio' has been applied consistently in ICC international practice and it is regarded as a fundamental concept of the international legal community.[648]

3.31 The application of *actori incumbit* requires a determination to be made whether a specific rule relied upon is an affirmative claim, an affirmative defence, or a mere negation of such affirmative.[649] In most cases, the determination follows from the inherent nature of the matter at hand.[650] If a party demands performance, repayment or compensation, it relies on an affirmative claim. If the other party seeks to set off or counterclaim or relies on a statute of limitations, i.e., evokes a right of its own, this is an affirmative defence. If, however, the other party argues to have already performed the duty, paid the claimed sum, or simply not to have committed a breach of duty, it merely negates the requirements of the claim and is not burdened to provide evidence. In other cases, the differentiation is somewhat more difficult, for example, when it comes to proving negatives. If a party claims to have made a payment without legal grounds (e.g., where a contract is void) and demands repayment, the question may

645. *Asian Agricultural Products Ltd. v Republic of Sri Lanka, ICSID ARB/87/3* (n. 572) para. 56 with further references.
646. *Tokios Tokelés v Ukraine, ICSID ARB/02/18* Award of 26 July 2007 [121].
647. *Alpha Projektholding GmbH v Ukraine, ICSID ARB/07/16* Award of 8 November 2010 [236].
648. *ICC Case No 18728, Final Award of 2007* [2018] XLIII Ybk Comm Arb 108 [32].
649. *See* for English law, Keane and McKeown (n. 290) 78 et seq.; *See* for German law, Prütting, 'ZPO § 286' (n. 239) paras 113–116.
650. *See* for English law, Keane and McKeown (n. 290) 78, 79.

arise whether the lack of legal ground is affirmative of the claim, or the (positive) existence of a legal ground is an affirmative defence.[651]

3.32 Moreover, while it does not amount to a general principle,[652] in some instances, the very language of rule orders is the distribution of the burden of proof (the so-called rule-exception principle).[653] According to this doctrine, in particular, under German law, each legal sentence contains specific statements on the distribution of the burden of proof by defining requirements and, at times, exceptions.[654] While a claiming party bears the burden of proof for all requirements which are expressly spelt out, the opposing party must bear the burden of proof for the exceptions. The latter are identified as such through expressions like 'unless' (*es sei denn*) or 'if not' (*wenn nicht*).[655] Nevertheless, the 'rule-exception' principle is applied where specific rules were drafted under due consideration of the distribution of the burden of proof. This is, however, frequently not the case for doctrines of common law or international law, where the grammatical form of such rules may vary.

3.33 The above shows that, as a general principle, the distribution of the burden of proof in international arbitration follows the rule of *actori incumbit*. The specific application of the said rule, however, makes it necessary to consult the substantive law in order to determine which party pleads affirmative claims or defences in a legal sense. In dubious cases, the tribunal should, therefore, also consider case law and commentary on the respective (substantive) cause of action, in order to enhance legal certainty. If, however, in individual cases, there are reasons for a different approach, the tribunal may of course deviate, since classifying an issue as affirmative is a matter of applying the law - which is incumbent on the tribunal and not subject to judicial review.

ii *Reversals of the Burden of Proof*

3.34 While there seems to be a global consensus regarding the allocation of the burden of proof, the question of under which circumstances a reversal may be appropriate remains controversial. As a rule, the distribution of the legal burden (*nota bene*: not the

651. In these cases of unjust enrichment, under German law, for example, the claiming party bears the burden of proof for the lack of a legal grounds, *see* Schwab, 'BGB § 812' in Franz Jürgen Säcker and others (eds), *Münchener Kommentar zum BGB* (8th edn, C.H. Beck 2020) para. 552.
652. Benzing (n. 464) 605, 606.
653. In Germany, this is referred to as theory of syntax ('Satzbaulehre'), *see* Prütting, *Gegenwartsprobleme Der Beweislast* (n. 603) 283 et seqq., 302 et seqq.
654. Rules of law are designed as general conditional normative statements. These conditional normative statements are the exact linguistic expression of a legal norm and verbalize the relation between and legal requirements and the legal consequence. The so-called Satzbaulehre connects the linguistic and syntactic structure of normative statement with the distribution of the burden of proof. Ota Weinberger, *Rechtslogik* (2nd edn, Duncker & Humblot 1989) 199, 229.
655. *See, e.g.*, sec. 24 BGB: 'The seat of an association, unless otherwise provided, is the place where the management is conducted.'; sec. 139 BGB: 'If a part of a legal transaction is void, then the entire legal transaction is void, unless it is to be assumed that it would have been undertaken even without the void part.' *See* further Prütting, *Gegenwartsprobleme Der Beweislast* (n. 603) 283.

'evidential burden', which may in fact shift) for a particular issue is abstract and independent of the specific procedural situation.[656] This means that it can be determined prior to the beginning of the proceeding based on the distinction between affirmative claims and defences. Importantly, the abstract character also means that the distribution of the legal burden does not shift in the course of the proceeding but lies with the same party throughout the dispute. There are, however, exceptions.

3.35 In Brazil, for instance, the 2015 reform of the procedural code (Novo Código de Processo Civil) introduced a novel element. According to the theory of dynamic distribution (*distribuição dinamica*), the trier of fact may modify the distribution of the burden of proof in individual cases where it deems this to be appropriate.[657] Assuming that the distribution of the burden of proof was a matter of substantive law, tribunals could accordingly apply the burden of proof dynamically in cases where Brazilian substantive law governs the dispute.

3.36 Likewise, for example, under American[658] and German[659] law, the legal burden of proof, despite its abstract character, may be shifted if this is necessary to balance a party's structural difficulty in providing evidence. A similar approach is taken by the ALI/UNIDROIT Principles, which state in Principle 21.2 that '[o]rdinarily, each party has the burden to prove all the material facts that are the basis of that party's case'. Their language ('ordinarily') suggests a certain flexibility which may allow for shifts of the burden of proof throughout the proceedings. *Inter alia*, the commentary remarks to Principle 21.3 suggest that when it appears that a party has possession or control of relevant evidence that it declines – without justification – to produce, the court may shift the burden of proof to the declining party.[660]

3.37 In a similar vein, Article 26 SCAI Rules states:

> The arbitral tribunal shall determine (...) the burden of proof.

---

656. *See*, e.g. Waincymer (n. 343) para. 10.4.1: 'The burden of proof never shifts (...)'; Barceló III (n. 631) para. III.C.2; note that the terminology derives from German law. The German approach to this issue is rather complicated and based on a distinction between the 'abstract' and 'concrete' subjective burden of proof. The party bearing the legal burden always bears the subjective burden of proof in an abstract sense. That is, throughout the proceeding, it remains its duty to produce evidence which is convincing. In a concrete sense, the burden to produce may shift to the opponent after the claiming party has offered convincing evidence. It is then up to the opponent to produce evidence that is suitable to shake the court's conviction. Thus, the concrete burden to produce evidence parallels the distinction between main evidence (Hauptbeweis) and counterevidence (Gegenbeweis). The main evidence is provided when the court is convinced of the existence of a fact to be proved. In order to produce evidence to the contrary, it is sufficient to shake this conviction, i.e., to bring about a non liquet, *see* Hans-W Laumen, 'Die "Beweiserleichterung Bis Zur Beweislastumkehr" – Ein Beweisrechtliches Phänomen' [2002] NJW 3739, 3740, 3741; *see* for English law, Keane and McKeown (n. 290) 59.
657. Adriano Ribeiro Caldas and Marco Félix Jobim, 'A Distribuição Dinâmica Do Ônus Da Prova No Sistema Processual Brasileiro E O Projeto De Novo Código De Processo Civil' (2015) 42 Revista da Associação dos Juízes do Rio Grande do Sul 32.
658. James (n. 604) 62, 63.
659. Prütting, 'ZPO § 286' (n. 239) paras 126–131.
660. American Law Institute (ALI) and UNIDROIT (n. 203) para. P-21C.

3.38 A similar view is taken by *Born*, particularly in view of international arbitration proceedings, who maintains that:

> the tribunal should allocate the burden of proof in the light of its assessment of the substantive law and procedures adopted in the arbitration. In so doing, the tribunal need not apply the burden of proof rules of any specific jurisdiction, but can instead fashion specialised rules in light of the particular substantive issues and procedures at issue in a specific instance.[661]

3.39 Other commentators have noted that:

> in practice, arbitral tribunals have broad powers to determine which party has the burden of proof, or to shift that burden by applying abstract principles that are generally accepted in all jurisdictions with absolute independence from what the applicable national law provides.[662]

3.40 For reasons of legal certainty, it is submitted that tribunals should be rather careful when modifying the general distribution of the legal proof. In any case, the question of whether, under exceptional conditions, reversals of the burden of proof are appropriate is a question of law, thus fully determinable by tribunals and not subject to judicial review. Accordingly, the arbitral tribunal has a certain degree of freedom in this regard.

3.41 Unlike the legal burden, the burden to adduce evidence (evidentiary burden) may, by its very nature, shift throughout the proceedings.[663] After the party bearing the burden of proof has adduced sufficient evidence to convince the tribunal, the other party will be required to rebut such evidence by adducing counterevidence:

> It goes without saying that it is the Claimant who carries the initial burden of proving the facts upon which he relies. There is a point, however, at which the Claimant may be considered to have made a sufficient showing to shift the burden of proof to the Respondent.[664]

3.42 If the counterevidence is sufficient to shake[665] the tribunal's conviction, the evidential burden shifts back again.[666] This demonstrates that the burden of proof and its distribution is closely linked with the standard of proof.[667] Moreover, the issue of

661. Born (n. 338) 2488, 2489; *see also* Aimoré Carreteiro (n. 277) 91, 92.
662. Blavi and Vial (n. 627) 75.
663. Redfern and others (n. 271) 362.
664. *Reza Said Malek v The Government of the Islamic Republic of Iran, IUSCT Case No 193* Final Award of 11 August 1992 [111].
665. As such, as will be explained in more detail below, it is also linked to the standard of proof. Commonly, the party bearing the burden of proof for an issue in dispute must produce evidence that is sufficient to convince the trier of facts to the necessary degree. The opponent, in turn, may limit its efforts to shake the conviction of the court. That means that the threshold which the quality of the opponent's evidence must meet is, in theory, lower. In practice, of course, the parties seek to produce the best evidence possible in order to support their case, *see* below Chapter 3, D.
666. Redfern and others (n. 271) 362.
667. *See* below, Chapter 3, D.

shifting the evidentiary burden is also discussed in connection with the doctrine of *prima facie evidence*, which will be addressed below.[668]

3.43 Accordingly, it follows from the above that the legal burden, despite its abstract character, may be modified in particular cases. Likewise, the burden to adduce evidence shifts throughout the proceeding if one party submits evidence which, in the absence of a rebuttal, is apt to convince the tribunal.

iii Presumptions

3.44 These case-specific modifications aside, presumptions are frequently named as examples of a reversal of the burden of proof. In particular, one can distinguish between 'legal presumptions' and 'judicial presumptions' (the latter are also referred to as 'factual presumptions').

a Legal Presumptions

3.45 Legal presumptions are stipulated as such by the applicable law and expressly assign the burden of proof to one of the parties to convince the tribunal of the contrary.[669] They are generally rebuttable unless otherwise stated.[670] As they derive from the *lex causae*, the tribunal must consider these when deciding the case, particularly in cases where the parties have agreed on the application of a specific substantive law to govern the contract. The same applies in investor-state proceedings if municipal law is relevant to determine an issue in dispute and such municipal law stipulates legal presumptions.[671] Usually, the law provides legal presumptions on issues which may be difficult to prove otherwise, and/or where the application of a legal presumption is needed to facilitate legal relations. A typical example is the probative value of public registers, such as commercial registers and land registers.

3.46 In *Vestey Group v Venezuela*, it was undisputed between the parties that Venezuela had taken over the control of the supposedly expropriated land. While the defendant, *inter alia*, argued that the claimant had never been the legal owner of the land, the claimant brought forward that its title to the land had been publicly registered, thereby relying on a presumption of ownership under Venezuelan land law.[672] The tribunal concurred with the claimant to find that:

> Unless it is invalidated through the means established by law, the registration obliges any third party, including this Tribunal, to presume that the property right

668. Redfern and others (n. 271) 362.
669. Dr Aristidis Tsatsos, 'Burden of Proof in Investment Treaty Arbitration: Shifting?' [2009] Humboldt Forum Recht 91, 6; Sourgens, Duggal and Laird (n. 442) para. 6.29.
670. Sourgens, Duggal and Laird (n. 442) para. 6.35.
671. *Ibid.*, 6.32.
672. *Vestey Group Ltd v Bolivarian Republic of Venezuela, ICSID ARB/06/4* Award of 15 April 2016 [251, 252].

has been validly transferred by operation of the registered property transfer agreement.[673]

b Judicial Presumptions

3.47 Unlike legal presumptions, judicial presumptions 'rely upon the existence of some general practice or habit' and are usually based on 'specific protocols' in business or other 'widespread practices'.[674] They are accordingly premised on (at times empirical) principles identified by case law and scholarly writing and are not declared as such by the applicable substantive statutory law. It follows that they are not binding upon the tribunal but may be considered when analysing the evidence presented before it. Unlike legal presumptions, judicial presumptions do not cause a full reversal of the burden of proof. Rather, they give rise to 'reasonable inferences' rebuttable by the counterparty.[675]

3.48 Judicial presumptions are manifold and may arise in different contexts. In a case between a German buyer (claimant) and a Thai seller (defendant), the tribunal applied a legal presumption on representation without specifying the applicable substantive law. In said proceeding, the defendant raised the defence that the contract in dispute was invalid, as the claimant had not been properly represented during its negotiation and conclusion. Nonetheless, it was undisputed between the parties that the presumed agent had repeatedly acted on behalf of the defendant and had used the defendant's letterhead and company stamp in correspondence with the claimant. The tribunal found:

> In a company of such importance [as the defendant], one may expect the presence of, and the compliance with an established division of responsibilities regulating the employees' authority and at least preventing their repeated abuse of this authority.
>
> (...)
>
> It ensues from these facts that there exists a 'factual presumption' that Mr. P, at least during the period from 15 to 19 January, was validly authorized by defendant to conclude export contracts. Defendant has not validly challenged this presumption and, in particular, did not answer (...) how it could be possible that P negotiated – unnoticed and without authorization – for the conclusion of a contract.
>
> The arbitral tribunal, therefore, concludes that defendant granted to Mr. P the legal authority to make the offer of 15 January. It needs not be decided whether defendant gave Mr. P a special authorization for the contract at issue or a general authorization.[676]

3.49 As another example, in sports arbitration, there is a legal presumption that an elevated testosterone/epitestosterone ratio ('*T/E ratio*') may indicate the exogenous

673. *Ibid.*, 268.
674. Sourgens, Duggal and Laird (n. 442) para. 6.17.
675. *Ibid.*, 6.26.
676. *WVHB Case No 23/1982, Award of 12 March 1984* [1991] XVI Ybk Comm Arb 11, 12.

administration of testosterone, thus violating anti-doping rules (*'T/E rule'*). In *S. v Fédération Internationale de Natation* (*'FINA'*), the tribunal dealt with the T/E rule and explained its character as a rebuttable legal presumption, as opposed to the more accurate isotope ratio mass spectrometry (*IRMS*). The latter, according to the tribunal, is able to positively verify allegations of exogenous administration. With reference to the FINA Doping Protocol (*DP*) the tribunal found:

> FINA introduced the T/E Rule under which a *T/E ratio greater than six (6) to one (1) constitutes presumptive evidence of an exogenous administration of testosterone.* Under the express wording of the T/E Rule, this presumption may be rebutted with evidence that the elevated T/E ratio is 'due to a physiological or pathological condition. *The provision creates a rebuttable factual presumption; it is thus fundamentally evidentiary in nature.* By contrast, *IRMS analysis provides direct evidence of the exogenous administration of testosterone and, accordingly, there is no place for such a defence under the IRMS Rule.*[677]

3.50 Legal presumptions are also acknowledged in the ambit of investment arbitration.[678] Similar to the issue in *Vestey Group v Venezuela*, in *Quiborax v Bolivia*, the question arose whether the registration of shares in the name of the claimants positively confirmed their ownership. Here, the tribunal decided differently. Agreeing with the defendant's expert, the tribunal found that said registration merely created a 'rebuttable presumption [...] in favour of the person therein registered' but did not 'exhaust the discussion over who really is the shareholder of the corporation'. Thus, the claimants were 'wrong to argue that the shareholders registry gives rise to an irrebuttable presumption (*presumptio iuris et de iure*)'.[679]

3.51 In the ambit of German law, a prominent example is the judicial presumption of profitability (*Rentabilitätsvermutung*).[680] It applies in case of a (failed) sales contract, where a buyer has incurred expenses on the good before the transfer of the title, e.g., if a buyer makes investments in the planned installation site of a purchased machine. It is then presumed that the expenses would have been profitable, and the buyer may claim the loss as damages.[681] The seller, in turn, does not bear the burden of proof for its defence that the expenses would not have been profitable, i.e., it is not required to positively convince them of the contrary. Rather, it is sufficient to shake the conviction of the court. Moreover, German law operates with the doctrine of *Anscheinsbeweise* (evidence of first appearance), which will be examined in more detail below.[682]

677. *CAS Case No. 2000/A/274, Award of 19 October 2000* (n. 586) paras 60, 61, 76.
678. Sourgens, Duggal and Laird (n. 442) paras 6.29–6.36.
679. *Quiborax SA, Non Metallic Minerals SA and Allan Fosk Kaplún v Plurinational State of Bolivia, ICSID ARB/06/2* Decision on Jurisdiction of 27 September 2012 [161].
680. Patrick Meier and Felix Jocham, 'Die Rentabilitätsvermutung – Aufwendung Als Schaden?' [2018] JuS 1168.
681. *BGH, Judgment of 19 April 1991* [1991] NJW 2277 [3.a)].
682. *See* below, Chapter 2, E.II.2.

3.52 Under English law, different factual presumptions apply to evidentiary matters. For example, all persons are presumed to be competent to give evidence.[683] However, a witness may be incompetent if they are cognitively unable to understand the nature of the oath they might be required to give, or if they are unable to understand the questions asked and reply accordingly.[684] There are also different factual presumptions as to the formal requirements of documents. *Inter alia*, it is presumed that a document which dates back more than twenty years was duly executed, or that the date of issue of a document corresponds to the date it reflects.[685]

3.53 As pointed out, tribunals may decide to consider these factual presumptions, but are not obliged to do so, particularly as they are not covered by the parties' choice of substantive law (where applicable). Rather, such presumptions can be referred to in order to facilitate the evidence procedure ('*facilitation of evidence*'). In an ICC proceeding, the tribunal rejected the application of the presumption of a causal link between a breach of contract and the damage suffered as developed by French case law.[686] The Tribunal, *inter alia*, found that the Cour de cassation was 'not fully constant in its rulings' on the presumption[687] and that 'several commentators' had 'criticized the rule'.[688] It, therefore, concluded that the causal link between the breach of duty and the actual losses was not to be presumed in that specific case.[689]

3.54 Accordingly, although legal presumptions apply as part of the substantive law, the tribunal has the authority to decide whether to resort to factual presumptions. Beyond that, as will be further detailed below, it may also be appropriate to apply other similar facilitations of evidence that do not amount to a full reversal of the burden of proof. While, in this case, the claiming party still bears the risk of non-persuading, it may benefit from the recourse to circumstantial evidence, *prima facie evidence* or adverse inferences.[690]

III The Tribunal's Powers to Take Evidence Ex Officio

3.55 As has been shown, there is a strong tendency in international arbitration to allow for and encourage the tribunal to proactively engage in fact-finding, thus adding 'inquisitorial' elements to the otherwise rather adversarial structure of the

683. In former times, under common law, different categories of incompetent people existed, such as non-Christians and atheists, as they were considered to be unable to take give the religious oath. Keane and McKeown (n. 290) 118.
684. *Ibid.*, 140 et seq.
685. *Ibid.*, 313.
686. *ICC Case No 12745, Final Award* [2010] XXXV Ybk Comm Arb 40 [193].
687. *Ibid.*, 195.
688. *Ibid.*, 196.
689. *Ibid.*, 200.
690. *See* below, Chapter 3, E.II.

proceeding.[691] These powers, as provided by different arbitration laws, rules and soft law,[692] are not limited to the fact-gathering phase but also apply during the taking of evidence.

3.56 In particular, under many (though not all) of these sets of rules, the tribunal has the power to order the parties on its own motion to produce evidentiary documents and witnesses on specific issues. Moreover, under nearly all sets of rules, the tribunal may appoint an expert upon proper consultation with the parties.[693] These rather extensive powers are, *inter alia*, confirmed by:

- Article 3.1 (i) IBA Rules, according to which the tribunal may 'request any Party to produce Documents';
- Article 8.5 IBA Rules, according to which, 'the Arbitral Tribunal may request any person to give oral or written evidence on any issue that the Arbitral Tribunal considers to be relevant to the case and material to its outcome'; and
- finally, Article 6.1 IBA Rules, which states that the tribunal 'after consulting with the Parties, may appoint one or more independent Tribunal-Appointed Experts to report to it on specific issues designated by the Arbitral Tribunal' (first sentence).

3.57 Other sets of rules additionally stipulate in broad and general terms that the tribunal may opt to take evidence ex officio, if deemed appropriate. As, for example, foreseen by Article 29 (1) First Sentence of the Vienna Rules, '[i]f the arbitral tribunal considers it necessary, it may on its own initiative collect evidence, question parties or witnesses, request the parties to submit evidence, and call experts'. Similarly, under Article 28 (2) of the DIS Rules, the tribunal 'may, *inter alia*, on its own initiative, appoint experts, examine fact witnesses other than those called by the parties, and order any party to produce or make available any documents or electronically stored data' (first sentence). Further, it shall 'not be limited to admit only evidence offered by the parties' (second sentence).

3.58 The same applies under the ICSID Convention. Specifically, Article 43 of the Convention states:

> Except as the parties otherwise agree, the Tribunal may, if it deems it necessary at any stage of the proceedings,
>
> (a) call upon the parties to produce documents or other evidence, and
> (b) visit the scene connected with the dispute, and conduct such inquiries there as it may deem appropriate.

3.59 There are several decisions that confirm that these powers not only exist in theory but are also used in practice. In *Maffezini v Spain*, for example, the tribunal 'called

691. *See* above, Chapter 2, C.
692. For a more extensive survey of the legal provisions, *see* above Chapter 2, C.I.
693. For a more extensive survey of the legal provisions, *see* above Chapter 2, C.I.

upon' the parties 'to produce' various 'witnesses to be available for examination at the hearing on the merits'.[694] Similarly, in *Champion Trading v Arab Republic of Egypt*, the tribunal ordered the respondent to produce 'one or several' (unspecified) witnesses, subsequent to which the parties agreed on the hearing of two specific testimonies.[695] The case thus provides an illustrative example of how the tribunal's inquisitorial powers and the parties' right to party autonomy can complement each other in favour of thorough but efficient fact-finding.

3.60 Nonetheless, as has been pointed out, tribunals remain rather reluctant to embrace their powers.[696] In any case, the tribunal is not required to engage in fact-finding and it might equally choose to leave the responsibility of producing, preparing and presenting evidence entirely to the parties.

IV Conclusion

3.61 The submission of evidence is governed by transnational rules. While most arbitration laws and rules contain only very vague provisions on the submission of evidence, the transnational principle of *actori incumbit* stipulates that the party submitting an affirmative claim or defence must bring forward the required evidence.

3.62 The principle may, however, be subject to legal presumptions under the applicable substantive law. Where appropriate, the tribunal may also shift the burden of proof in individual cases.

3.63 There is a growing tendency for the general rule that parties must introduce their evidence to be supplemented by the tribunal's powers to take evidence ex officio where this is necessary and under due consideration of the parties' procedural rights. Even though the legal framework grants broad authority in this regard, in practice, tribunals remain rather reticent to proactively engage in fact-finding.

B MEANS OF EVIDENCE

3.64 Over the past decade, certain common practices have emerged on how to prepare, introduce and present the means of evidence in international arbitration. The arbitral law of evidence is marked by comprehensive liberty and flexibility. There is neither a *numerus clausus* of evidence nor are the parties or the tribunal bound to apply domestic laws of evidence that would restrict the taking of evidence. Rather, parties enjoy broad freedom as to the submission of evidence, while decisions of admissibility are ultimately the authority of the tribunal.

---

694. *Emilio Agustín Maffezini v The Kingdom of Spain, ICSID ARB/97/7* Award of 13 November 2000 [26, 27].
695. *Champion Trading Company, Ameritrade International, Inc v Arab Republic of Egypt, ICSID ARB/02/9* Award of 27 October 2006 [15, 16].
696. *See* above, Chapter 2, C.

3.65 In order to uniformize and expedite proceedings, current arbitration practice has developed certain standards and best practices regarding the different types of evidence, specifically regarding fact witnesses (*I*), expert witnesses (*II*), documentary evidence (*III*) and real evidence (*IV*), each of which will be addressed below.

I Fact Witnesses

3.66 In nearly every dispute, but especially in fact-heavy ones, parties rely on witnesses of facts to support their allegations. Despite their inherent unreliability,[697] witnesses (alongside documents) are thus the most common form of evidence encountered in international arbitration. Apart from their testimony on specific disputed facts,[698] parties regularly rely on witness statements to give background to documents,[699] or even to provide technical explanations.[700] Beyond that, one can observe that, in practice, witnesses of fact frequently help to 'tell the story'. This use of witnesses is, however, being met with increasing frustration,[701] as it exceeds their traditional and immanent task.

3.67 Unlike domestic procedural codes,[702] arbitration acts and rules are largely silent as to the specifics of witness evidence. Despite the lack of explicit rules in international arbitration, there is a strong tendency to introduce witness evidence by submitting written witness statements (*1*) and presenting their testimony during the oral hearing in a party-controlled procedure (*2*). Moreover, while counsel are not allowed to coach their witnesses, certain forms of witness familiarization are considered permissible (*3*).

1 Written Witness Statements

3.68 Witnesses are usually introduced by submitting written witness statements, based upon which witnesses are liable to stand for examination during the hearing.[703] Contrary to what one might expect, the practice of written witness statements does not stem from a presumed 'Americanization' of international arbitration, but rather from English litigation. In contrast to US litigation, where witness statements are required mainly in bench trials,[704] they are in fact highly common practice in England and Wales. Under this system, if a party seeks to rely on witness evidence at trial, it is required to serve a witness statement beforehand.[705]

697. *See* above, Chapter 2, B.II.2.
698. ICC Commission on Arbitration and ADR, *Report on the Accuracy of Fact Witness Memory in International Arbitration* (2020) 17.
699. *Ibid.*
700. *Ibid.*, 19.
701. *Ibid.*, 18.
702. *See, e.g.*, for German procedural law, secs 373 et seq. BGB; for English law, CPR 34.
703. *See* below, Chapter 3, B.2.
704. John Fellas, 'Cross-Examination in International Arbitration' (2015) 254 New York Law Journal.
705. CPR 32.4: '(1) A witness statement is a written statement signed by a person which contains the evidence which that person would be allowed to give orally. (2) The court will order a party to

3.69 Witness statements offer the advantage that both the parties and the tribunal are able to properly prepare for the hearing, as all stakeholders know the expected scope of the testimony beforehand and may tailor the questions to fit their specific needs. Yet, since counsel frequently assists witnesses in drafting their statements[706] (or actually drafts the statements themselves), the statements do not always match the witnesses' direct perception of the events, rendering them more susceptible to manipulation. Moreover, due to the involvement of counsel, the preparation of witness statements can generate considerable costs, especially where the parties submit a large number of statements. Therefore, as suggested, *inter alia,* by the Commentary to the IBA Rules, the tribunal, 'in consultation with the parties, should determine whether or not to require such witness statements, depending on the circumstances of each case'.[707]

3.70 If the submission of written statements is ordered, as, for example, demanded by Article 4.5 of the IBA Rules, witness statements shall contain a statement regarding the identity and background of the witness and their relationship with any of the parties, and state all the relevant facts and the source of information. Further, the statements must be signed and annexed with an affirmation of truth. It is vital that these formal requirements are fulfilled, since the tribunal may reject witness statements which fail to do so. In *Cessna Finance Corporation v Gulf Jet LLC* (an ICC proceeding), for example, the tribunal found that:

> [the Witnesses'] statement was not signed and he did not appear at the merits hearing to be cross-examined on his ambiguous statement about the lack of notice. Therefore, this Tribunal attaches no weight or significance to the [Witnesses'] unsiged [sic] statement and also finds that an adverse inference can be drawn against [the Witness] on the issue.[708]

3.71 Many rules are silent as to the submission of witness evidence. There are, however, exceptions. Article 26.4 of the ICDR Rules, for example, states that '[u]nless otherwise agreed by the parties or directed by the tribunal, evidence of witnesses may be presented in the form of written statements signed by them'. Similar provisions are contained in Article 33.2 of the SCC Rules,[709] and notably, Article 27.2 Second Sentence of the UNCITRAL Rules.[710] The Prague Rules, however, suggest an approach that resembles the practice in (*inter alia*) German litigation.[711] Rather than disclosing

---

serve on the other parties any witness statement of the oral evidence which the party serving the statement intends to rely on in relation to any issues of fact to be decided at the trial.'

706. *See, e.g.*, Art. 4.3 IBA Rules: 'It shall not be improper for a Party, its officers, employees, legal advisors or other representatives to interview its witnesses or potential witnesses and to discuss their prospective testimony with them.'
707. 1999 IBA Working Party, 2010 Rules of Evidence Review Subcommittee and 2020 IBA Rules of Evidence Review Task Force (n. 188) 18.
708. *ICC Case No 18769/VRO/AGF, Final Award of 2014* Arbitrator Intelligence Materials [151].
709. Article 33 (2) SCC Rules: 'The testimony of witnesses or party-appointed experts may be submitted in the form of signed statements.'
710. Article 27.2 Model Law: 'Unless otherwise directed by the arbitral tribunal, statements by witnesses, including expert witnesses, may be presented in writing and signed by them.'
711. *See* sec. 373 ZPO: 'Evidence by hearing witnesses shall be offered by naming the witnesses and designating the facts regarding which the witnesses are to be examined.'

written witness statements, under Article 5.3. Prague Rules, a party shall identify in its submissions:

> each fact witness (if any), on whose testimony the party intends to rely in support of its position; the factual circumstances on which the respective fact witness intends to testify; and the relevance and materiality of the testimony for the outcome of the case.

3.72 It is then the responsibility of the tribunal to decide whether a written witness statement must be submitted (*see* Articles 5.4 and 5.5 Prague Rules). Alternatively, the tribunal may directly call the witness to testify during the hearing.

3.73 Similarly, some modern arbitration rules, such as the ICC Rules,[712] LCIA Rules[713] and DIS Rules[714] suggest that the tribunal shall, upon hearing the parties, consider limiting the use of written witness statements. Nonetheless, despite these tendencies to limit their use, their submission remains a standard practice in international arbitration.[715]

2 *Presentation of Oral Testimony*

3.74 Closely linked to the modalities of submitting witness evidence is the question of how the testimony shall be presented and tested during the hearing. Again, an examination of different jurisdictions reveals a certain cultural divide.[716] In some countries, such as Germany, the court has a rather comprehensive mandate to question the witness before opening the floor to the parties (section 396, 397 ZPO).[717] However,

712. *See* Appendix 4 (e) to the ICC Rules: '(…) Limiting the length and scope of written submissions and written and oral witness evidence (both fact witnesses and experts) so as to avoid repetition and maintain a focus on key issues.'
713. Article 14.6 LCIA Rules 2020: 'The Arbitral Tribunal's power under Article 14.5 includes the making of any procedural order with a view to expediting the procedure to be adopted in the arbitration by:

    > (…) limiting the length or content of, or dispensing with, any written statement to be delivered under Article 15.'

714. *See* Annex 3 A to the DIS Rules: 'During the case management conference, the arbitral tribunal shall discuss with the parties the following measures for increasing procedural efficiency: (…) Limiting the length or the number of Submissions, of any written fact witness statements, and of any expert reports provided by the parties.'
715. Christian Oetiker, 'Witnesses before the International Arbitral Tribunal' (2007) 25 ASA Bulletin 253, 255.
716. American Law Institute (ALI) and UNIDROIT (n. 203) R-29C: 'The traditional distinction between common-law systems, which are based upon direct and cross-examination, and civil-law systems, which are based upon examination by the court, is well known and widely discussed in the comparative legal literature. Equally well known are also the limits and defects of both methods.'
717. *See* sec. 396 ZPO; Jürgen Damrau and Alexander Weinland, 'ZPO § 396' in Thomas Rauscher and Wolfgang Krüger (eds), *Münchener Kommentar zur ZPO* (6th edn, C.H. Beck 2020) paras 3, 4.

the adversarial tradition[718] of the United States, as well as England and Wales, suggests that it is mainly the parties' right and responsibility to adequately present evidence.[719] Consequently, and tellingly, the English CPR thus speaks of 'giving' rather than 'taking' evidence.[720] The underlying system of proving facts is thus one where a party actively hands over evidence to the court, i.e., prepares and presents evidence to the trier of facts, who receives it passively.[721]

3.75 Nevertheless, as a consequence of the ongoing transnationalization of fact-finding rules, these cultural differences are becoming less important in international arbitration. In fact, Article 8.3 First Sentence of the IBA Rules – which are commonly perceived to reflect a certain bias towards common law practices – states that '[t]he Arbitral Tribunal shall at all times have complete control over the Evidentiary Hearing'. In exercising its control and discretion, the tribunal has three different options regarding the examination of witnesses. Namely, it may opt for a party-controlled presentation of evidence (*a*), a tribunal-controlled presentation of evidence (*b*) or a hybrid form, such as witness conferencing (*c*). In the absence of specific party agreements and/or relevant provisions, the determination of an appropriate method of witness examination lies within the tribunal's discretion.

i *Party-Led Presentation of Evidence (Direct, Cross- and Re-Examination)*

3.76 In international arbitration, as a main feature of the party-led presentation of evidence, it is the party's (rather than the tribunal's) right to introduce its witness evidence and guide the witness through the testimony by open questioning during the hearing. This is famously supplemented by the opposing party's right to rebut the testimony by cross-examining the witness, which is undeniably rooted in the common law tradition.

3.77 Most arbitration laws and rules do not provide any specifics as to the examination of witnesses,[722] with most merely stating that the tribunal may decide to hear witnesses.[723] Some arbitration laws only mention the parties' right to question witnesses, without specifying the format of the questioning. Such provisions can be

718. *See* above, Chapter 2, C.
719. For an outline of the history of cross-examination, which can be traced back to Athenian law, *see* Richard H Underwood, 'The Limits of Cross-Examination' (1997) 21 American Journal of Trial Advocacy 113, 114 et seq.
720. *See, e.g.*, CPR 32.11: 'Where a witness is called to give evidence at trial, he may be cross-examined on his witness statement whether or not the statement or any part of it was referred to during the witness's evidence in chief.'
721. Demeyere (n. 519) 283.
722. This is true, for example, for the DIS Rules, ICC Rules, SCC Rules and Vienna Rules.
723. *See, e.g.*, Art. 25.2 ICC Rules: 'The arbitral tribunal may decide to hear witnesses, experts appointed by the parties or any other person, in the presence of the parties, or in their absence provided they have been duly summoned.' *See also* Art. 33.3 SCC Rules: 'Any witness or expert, on whose testimony a party seeks to rely, shall attend a hearing for examination, unless otherwise agreed by the parties.'

found, *inter alia*, under the Model Law[724] as well as German[725] and Spanish[726] Arbitration Law.

3.78 Article 28.2 of the UNCITRAL Rules and Article 28.2 of the PCA Rules stipulate, quite vaguely, that:

> [w]itnesses, including expert witnesses, may be heard under the conditions and examined in the manner set by the arbitral tribunal.

Likewise, without going into any detail, the ICDR Rules[727] as well as the HKIAC Rules[728] state in broad terms that:

> [t]he tribunal shall determine the manner in which witnesses are examined and who shall be present during witness examination.

A similar provision is stipulated by Article 27 of the SCAI Rules.[729] In slightly more specific terms, Article 20.5 of the LCIA Rules allows that the:

> Tribunal and any party may request that a witness, on whose written testimony another party relies, should attend for oral questioning at a hearing before the Arbitral Tribunal.

Furthermore, according to Article 20.9 of the LCIA Rules:

> [a]ny witness who gives oral testimony at a hearing before the Arbitral Tribunal may be questioned by each of the parties under the control of the Arbitral Tribunal. The Arbitral Tribunal may put questions at any stage of such testimony.

3.79 Particularly in investment arbitration, party-led witness examination is the absolute standard. Article 35.1 of the ICSID Rules states that:

> [w]itnesses and experts shall be examined before the Tribunal by the parties under the control of its President.

---

724. Article 26 (2) Model Law: 'Unless otherwise agreed by the parties, if a party so requests or if the arbitral tribunal considers it necessary, the expert shall, after delivery of his written or oral report, participate in a hearing where the parties have the opportunity to put questions to him and to present expert witnesses in order to testify on the points at issue.'
725. Section 1049 (2) ZPO: 'Unless otherwise agreed by the parties to the dispute, the expert is to attend a hearing for oral argument should a party file a corresponding petition, or should the arbitral tribunal believe this to be required, after he has submitted his written or oral report. At the hearing, the parties to the dispute may ask questions of the expert and may have experts they have themselves retained state their position regarding the matters at issue.'
726. Article 32 (2) Spanish Arbitration Law: 'If requested by a party or deemed necessary by the arbitrators, and subject to any contrary agreement by the parties, after delivery of their reports, experts will participate in a hearing to enable the arbitrators and the parties, themselves or assisted by experts, to put questions to them.'
727. Article 26.3 ICDR Rules.
728. Article 22.2 HKIAC Rules.
729. Article 27.5 First Sentence SCAI Rules: 'At the hearing, witnesses and expert witnesses may be heard and examined in the manner set by the arbitral tribunal.' *See* further Art. 27.1 First Sentence SCAI Rules: 'At any stage of the proceedings, the arbitral tribunal may hold hearings for the presentation of evidence by witnesses, including expert witnesses, or for oral argument.'

3.80 More guidance is provided by the IBA Rules, which in Article 8.4 address the course of the witness examination, based on a party-led model:

> (a) the Claimant shall ordinarily first present the testimony of its witnesses, followed by the Respondent presenting the testimony of its witnesses;
> (b) following direct testimony, any other Party may question such witness, in an order to be determined by the Arbitral Tribunal. The Party who initially presented the witness shall subsequently have the opportunity to ask additional questions on the matters raised in the other Parties' questioning;

The same applies to party-appointed experts (*see* lit c).

3.81 Frequently, tribunals set out the specifics of the examination of witnesses in a pre-hearing procedural order. In *Philip Morris v Australia*, for example, the tribunal ordered the following agenda for the presentation of witness evidence:

> Examination of the Respondent's witnesses and experts. Each witness shall be examined in the following manner and sequence:
>
> a. Affirmation of witness as to the truth of his or her evidence;
> b. Short introduction by Respondent (this may include short direct examination on new developments after the last written statement of the witness);
> c. Cross-examination by the Claimant;
> d. Re-direct examination by the Respondent, but only on issues raised in cross-examination;
> e. Re-cross examination by the Claimant, but only on issues raised in re-direct examination;
> f. Re-re-direct examination by the Respondent, but only on issues raised in the re-cross examination;
> g. Remaining questions by Members of the Tribunal.[730]

3.82 As reflected by the language of both the IBA Rules and the above procedural order, they follow the mechanics of witness examination in common law litigation, subject to certain modifications. Parties usually have the choice whether or not to call a witness for examination, while, importantly, the failure to do so generally does not amount to an admission of the correctness of the written witness statement.[731] If a witness is then called and is liable for examination, the party relying on the witness may question the witness first, as part of direct examination.[732] The purpose is to introduce the general topic by asking open questions that allow the witness to display his or her observations relating to the fact or facts in issue. One option that is frequently

---

730. *Philip Morris Asia Limited v The Commonwealth of Australia, UNCITRAL, PCA Case No 2012-12* Procedural Order No 15 of 17 December 2015.
731. Fellas (n. 704) 254, *see also* Art. 4.8 IBA Rules: 'If the appearance of a witness has not been requested pursuant to Article 8.1, none of the other Parties shall be deemed to have agreed to the correctness of the content of the Witness Statement.'
732. Rolf Trittmann and Ramona Schardt, '§2.05' in Gustav Flecke-Giammarco (ed.), *The DIS Arbitration Rules – An Article-by-Article Commentary* (Kluwer Law International 2020) para. 66.

employed,[733] as provided for by Article 8.4 Third Sentence of the IBA Rules, is that the parties may agree – or the arbitral tribunal may order – that the witness statement or expert report shall serve as that witness's direct testimony.[734] If direct examination is permitted, the tribunal may limit the questioning to a short period of ten to fifteen minutes.[735] In litigation practice, subject to certain minor exceptions, the use of leading questions, i.e., questions which require the witness to either respond with 'yes' or 'no', is prohibited.[736] In arbitration, there is no hard and fast rule. However, if a counsel is leading his or her party's witness through the direct testimony, this may 'obviously [undermine] the probative value of the oral evidence'.[737] This is confirmed by Article 8.2 of the IBA Rules which states that '[q]uestions to a witness during direct and re-direct testimony may not be unreasonably leading', which nevertheless does not completely exclude the use of leading questions.

3.83 After the direct examination, opposing counsel may cross-examine, i.e., question the witness. In contrast to direct examination, cross-examination is not limited to open questions. In fact, in the traditional approach, counsel mainly rely on closed or leading questions in order to control the witness and limit the issues that the witness may address.[738] This technique is also frequently used in arbitration and is considered to be its 'defining feature'.[739] It helps to serve the traditional purpose of cross-examination, which is to show that the evidence is unreliable by either damaging the credibility of the testimony (*ad rem*) or the witness itself (*ad hominem*).[740] Further, during cross-examination, the counsel may elicit further statements from the witness which are favourable to its own case.[741] These techniques may explain the perception of cross-examination as abusive rather than helpful in uncovering the truth.[742]

3.84 There is no general rule as to the scope of cross-examination. Commonly, in litigation, the cross-examination may exceed the scope of the direct examination, but it is limited to questions that relate to the facts in issue, or the credibility of the witness.[743] Similarly, in international arbitration, tribunals usually allow questions as to issues that have not been mentioned during direct examination but may only allow inferences to be drawn on facts that are in issue and that bear on the outcome, i.e., that

733. Fellas (n. 555).
734. A similar provision can be found under the English CPR. According to CPR 32.5(2), where a witness is called to give oral evidence, his witness statement shall stand as his evidence in chief unless the court orders otherwise.
735. Fellas (n. 704).
736. Keane and McKeown (n. 290) 181, 182.
737. O'Malley (n. 407) para. 8.43.
738. Michael J Walter, 'Controlling the Witness on Cross-Examination' in John G Koeltl and John Kiernan (eds), *The Litigation Manual – Trial* (American Bar Association (Section of Litigation) 1999); *see* further Keane and McKeown (n. 290) 217, 218.
739. Harbst (n. 373) 111.
740. *Ibid.*, 115 et seq.
741. *Ibid.*, 98; with respect to English litigation, cf. Keane and McKeown (n. 290) 194; for a practical describtion of the expected course of the cross-examination *see* Walter (n. 738).
742. *See* for an overview Todd A Berger, 'The Ethical Limits of Discrediting the Truthful Witness: How Modern Ethics Rules Fail to Prevent Truthful Witnesses from Being Discredited Through Unethical Means' (2015) 99 Marquette Law Review 285; Jolowicz (n. 525) 283, 284.
743. Keane and McKeown (n. 290) 218, 219.

are both relevant and material.[744] There are, however, restrictions based on considerations of procedural fairness. For example, witnesses should not be unexpectedly confronted with issues or exhibits that have not been submitted thus far.[745] In any case, the tribunal frequently defines the scope of the witness examination in a specific preparatory order prior to the hearing.

3.85 After the cross-examination, the party that has called the witness may apply for a re-examination if it finds it necessary to clarify certain facts and issues that were raised during cross-examination. In some cases, this can even be followed by a re-cross examination. Re-direct and re-cross examination follow the general rules on direct and cross-examination set out above.[746] It is usually confined to the scope of the cross-examination, i.e., no new issues may be raised.[747] That does, however, mean that, in certain cases, evidence which was held to be inadmissible during the direct may become admissible during re-examination, if the opposing party has addressed this evidence during cross.[748]

3.86 The above procedure is supplemented by the tribunal's general power to question witnesses at any time (e.g., as provided for under Article 8.4 (g) IBA Rules). Consequently, usually after the parties have presented and examined the witnesses, it is the tribunal's turn to ask any further questions which it finds relevant.

ii *Tribunal-Led Presentation of Evidence*

3.87 In light of the overall trend towards robust case management and more proactive tribunals,[749] the practice of party-led witness examination does not stand uncontested. Even within the common law tradition, the views are divided. According to *Wigmore*, one of the most eminent American scholars on evidence, for example, cross-examination is 'beyond any doubt the greatest legal engine ever invented for the discovery of truth'.[750] *Jolowicz*, by contrast, finds this statement 'difficult to accept'. In his view, cross-examination is apt to reveal 'untruth', while it is doubtful whether cross-examination serves to reveal the 'hitherto unrevealed truth'.[751] In a similar spirit, other commentators suggest that cross-examination is largely abused for the purpose of

744. O'Malley (n. 407) paras 8.34 et seq.
745. *Ibid.*, 8.38, n. 57.
746. *Ibid.*, 8.59, *see* further Art. 8.3 (b) IBA Rules; Trittmann and Schardt (n. 732) para. 61.
747. Trittmann and Schardt (n. 732) paras 61, 62.
748. For a concise description of re-examination in English litigation *see* Keane and McKeown (n. 290) 249, the same logic however also applies in arbitration.
749. *See* above, Chapter 2, C.
750. John H Wigmore, *A Treatise on the System of Evidence in Trials at Common Law* (3rd edn, Little, Brown 1940) 1367.
751. Jolowicz (n. 525) 283, 284.

discrediting truthful witnesses.[752] The criticism is owed to the usual style of questioning, which is designed to minimize the witnesses' opportunities to explain themselves, seeking to control the testimony through leading questions.

3.88 In arbitration, there is accordingly a certain tendency towards excluding cross-examination, instead leaving the primary responsibility and control over the examination of witnesses to the tribunal. To give a recent example, Article 5.9 First Sentence of the Prague Rules expressly stipulates that '[a]t the hearing, the examination of any fact witness shall be conducted under the direction and control of the arbitral tribunal'. In that case, the witness may first be questioned by the tribunal, after which all parties must be given sufficient opportunity to ask supplemental questions.[753]

3.89 In any case, the tribunal must have due regard for the parties' expectations and consider the overall conduct of the proceeding. Particularly where the parties have produced written witness statements, it might be appropriate to leave the witness examination to the parties, as suggested, *inter alia,* by the IBA Rules. As has been pointed out, the practices of submitting witness statements and subsequently allowing for cross-examination are complementary, allowing all parties to properly prepare for the witness examination, make their case and challenge the opposing party's evidence.[754] If, however, no written statements are to be submitted, it might be more efficient to first allow the tribunal to examine the witness, addressing those issues it deems relevant and material, thus focusing the examination on the vital points. As a matter of due process, the parties must of course have the right to subsequently challenge the witness as well.

iii Witness Conferencing and 'Hot-Tubbing'

3.90 In recent years there has been a growing tendency to conduct the examination of two (or more) contradictory witnesses simultaneously.[755] This applies both to expert witnesses and witnesses of fact. Rather than hearing these one by one, where appropriate, the tribunal may order that the witnesses shall attend the hearing concurrently and give their evidence together. This practice is figuratively known as 'hot-tubbing' and can help to identify common ground and contradictions as well as the reasons for each.[756] The procedure originally stems from the Australian litigation

752. *See* with comparable observation on cross-examination in criminal proceedings, Berger, 'The Ethical Limits of Discrediting the Truthful Witness: How Modern Ethics Rules Fail to Prevent Truthful Witnesses from Being Discredited Through Unethical Means' (n. 742) 287 et seq.
753. As allowed, for example by ALI/UNIDROIT Rule 29.4 First Alternative; the Second Alternative suggests that the party seeking the testimony may commence with the questioning.
754. *See* above, Chapter 3, B.I.1.
755. O'Malley (n. 407) para. 8.68.
756. Alasdair McAlpine, 'Hot-Tubbing in International Arbitration: Do We Need a Protocol?' (*Practical Law Arbitration Blog*, 1 May 2018); CIArb, *Guidelines for Witness Conferencing in International Arbitration* (2019) Preamble 2.

practice[757] and has successfully been adopted in England and Wales.[758] A similar rule can, however, also be found in German civil litigation in section 394 (2) ZPO, according to which '[w]itnesses whose statements contradict each other may be brought face to face'.

3.91 As a relatively new phenomenon, arbitration laws and rules are largely silent on the issue. Article 5.9 of the Prague Rules states quite vaguely that, upon consultation of the parties, the arbitral tribunal 'may hold witness conferences' as it 'deems appropriate'. After calls for more uniformization of the proceedings,[759] in 2019, the CIArb proposed new guidelines on the issue.[760] These contain both a checklist that can help to determine whether witness conferencing should be ordered and specific procedural directions that may be included in a procedural order (CIArb Guidelines for Witness Conferencing in International Arbitration, '*CIArb Guidelines*'). Their main goal is to 'further the efficient and effective taking of evidence',[761] while recognizing the 'diversity of approaches that can be adopted without seeking to restrict the ability and imagination of tribunals and parties to shape a conference most suited to any given dispute'.[762] Importantly, the CIArb Guidelines offer three different options, namely a Tribunal-led Conference (Option A), a Party-led Conference (Option B) and a Witness-led Conference (Option C). Moreover, the CIArb Guidelines not only address the examination during the hearing but also suggest the use of a joint report to reflect the agreed and disagreed issues, stating both (or all) witnesses' positions.[763]

3.92 There are other hybrid forms that can be observed in practice. At times, tribunals might first conduct a traditional form of witness examination and then order the hot-tubbing as a subsequent measure in an effort to eliminate disagreements.[764] Usually, however, the tribunal is in charge of examining the conferenced witnesses, leaving counsel the right to subsequently ask questions.[765] It follows that the general practice of hot-tubbing is another expression of the shift towards a more tribunal-centred taking of evidence.

3 Witness Familiarization and Coaching

3.93 Closely linked to the matter of presenting and examining witnesses during hearings, it is still under debate whether counsel in international arbitration are bound by domestic codes of professional ethics that forbid or highly restrict the preparation of

757. McAlpine (n. 756).
758. *See* CPR 35.12 (1).
759. McAlpine (n. 756).
760. Peter Yuen and Matthew Townsend, 'New CIArb Guidelines on Witness Conferencing' (*Kluwer Arbitration Blog*, 25 April 2019).
761. CIArb (n. 756) Foreword.
762. *Ibid.*, Preamble para. 1.
763. *Ibid.*, 38.
764. O'Malley (n. 407) para. 8.69.
765. McAlpine (n. 756).

witnesses.[766] Across jurisdictions, the matter is handled differently in domestic litigation.[767] In Germany, for example, while there are no express rules to this effect, there is a generally adverse attitude towards contacts between lawyers and witnesses, leading to tremendous uncertainties as to the permissible scope of witness preparation.[768] Nonetheless, the legislation leaves room for certain preparatory and coordinative measures.[769] In England and Wales, counsel 'must not rehearse, practice with or coach a witness in respect of their evidence'.[770] While it is accepted that counsel may draft the witness statement, counsel may not include any statement of fact other than the evidence which one reasonably believes the witness would give if the witness were giving evidence orally.[771] Further, counsel must not encourage witnesses to give statements which are untruthful or misleading.[772] Yet, a certain degree of 'witness familiarization'[773] is considered appropriate or even necessary to properly present a case. As part of the witness familiarization process, counsel may take witnesses through a mock cross-examination.[774] As pointed out above, these cultural differences are directly connected to the mode of presenting evidence. Since in Germany, for example, it is the court's primary responsibility to examine and question witnesses, less interaction between the counsel and the witnesses is necessary before the hearing. Other jurisdictions leave this responsibility to the parties, thus allowing for a more thorough and extensive preparatory interaction.[775]

3.94 Despite diverging approaches across jurisdictions, in international arbitration, counsel may interview and prepare their witnesses prior to the hearing.[776] Especially in party-driven proceedings where the responsibility for organizing and presenting witness evidence mainly lies with the parties, a certain degree of collaboration, in the sense of familiarization, is necessary. In practice, witness statements are frequently drafted by counsel based on the information given by the witnesses.

3.95 The legal framework of international arbitration provides several rules on witness familiarization. Rule 25 of the ICCA Congress 2010 International Code of Ethics for Lawyers, for example, states that:

---

766. Iris Ng, 'Rethinking Counsel Ethics in International Arbitration' (*Kluwer Arbitration Blog*, 12 December 2019); Gary Born, 'A Code of Conduct for Counsel in International Arbitration' (*Kluwer Arbitration Blog*, 16 November 2010); Trittmann and Schardt (n. 732) paras 51–53.
767. For an overview, *see* Miguel Angel Fernandez-Ballester and David Arias Lozano (eds), 'Interviewing and Preparing Witnesses for Testimony in International Arbitration Proceedings: The Quest for Developing Transnational Standards of Lawyers' Conduct', *Liber Amicorum Bernardo Cremades* (Wolters Kluwer España; La Ley 2010) 1164–1175.
768. Helmut Hoffmann and Frank Maurer, 'Voraussetzungen Und Grenzen Anwaltlicher Zeugenvorbereitung' [2018] NJW 257, 257, 258.
769. *Ibid.*
770. Bar Standards Board, *The BSB Handbook* (Version 46, 2020) para. rC9.4.
771. Geoffrey Vos (ed.), *Civil Procedure ('White Book')* (Sweet & Maxwell; Thomson Reuters 2019) 32.4.5.
772. Bar Council – Ethics Committee of The General Council of the Bar, *Witness Preparation* (21) para. 2.
773. *Ibid.*, 11.
774. *Ibid.*
775. *See* above, Chapter 3, B.I.
776. Blackaby and others (n. 14) paras 391 et seq.

> [l]awyers may communicate with a witness about facts and documents within the knowledge of that witness and about the witness' potential testimony, but lawyers may not directly or indirectly seek to influence witnesses to give testimony that is not accurate or true.

3.96 This is confirmed by the LCIA Rules[777] and IBA Rules,[778] as well as by the IBA Guidelines on Party Representation. The latter stipulate a quite detailed regime that stakeholders in international arbitration are encouraged to consider in order to maintain procedural fairness. Apart from allowing communication between counsel and the party (Guideline 24), the IBA Guidelines expressly state that counsel may assist witnesses in the preparation of their statements (*see* Guideline 20). In doing so, counsel shall 'seek to ensure' that the statement reflects the witness's 'own account of relevant facts, events and circumstances' (*see* Guideline 21). In any case, counsel 'should not invite or encourage a Witness to give false evidence' (Guideline 23).

3.97 A different approach is taken by ALI/UNIDROIT Rule 21.3. The provision states that 'a lawyer for a party may have a voluntary interview with a potential non-party witness. The interview may be on reasonable notice to other parties, who may be permitted to attend the interview'. Against the backdrop of the common practice in international arbitration, it is, however, submitted that it is a party's right to convene with a witness prior to the hearing without the presence of potential opponents. The principle of equality of arms and procedural fairness is sufficiently taken into account by the other restrictions described here.

3.98 While the topic is not frequently addressed in arbitral case law, individual decisions indicate that there is a general acceptance of witness familiarization. In an ICC proceeding, for example, the ICC tribunal found it reasonable to employ 'witness familiarisation services' and ordered that the respondent bear their costs.[779] Similarly, in *Bossart, LLC v James Howden & Company LTD*, another ICC case, the tribunal expressly acknowledged expenses of witness familiarization as a recoverable item.[780]

3.99 For the sake of fairness and equality of arms, it is vital to establish a common approach in international arbitration that may be applied across the jurisdictions, independent of domestic codes of conduct. A party represented by counsel who is allowed to familiarize a witness necessarily holds an advantage over a party whose counsel communicates with its witnesses for the first time during the hearing. Since, in international arbitration, the general tendency is in favour of a party-controlled

---

777. Article 20.6 LCIA Rules: 'Subject to the mandatory provisions of any applicable law, rules of law and any order of the Arbitral Tribunal otherwise, it shall not be improper for any party or its authorised representatives to interview any potential witness for the purpose of presenting his or her testimony in written form to the Arbitral Tribunal or producing such person as an oral witness at any hearing.'
778. Article 4.3 IBA Rules: 'It shall not be improper for a Party, its officers, employees, legal advisors or other representatives to interview its witnesses or potential witnesses and to discuss their prospective testimony with them.'
779. *ICC Case No 17195/MLK/ARP, Partial Award and Final Award on Costs of 2014* Arbitrator Intelligence Materials [25].
780. *ICC Case No 19667/TO, Final Award of 2015* Arbitration Intelligence Materials [290, 295].

presentation of evidence through direct and cross-examination,[781] it is submitted that it is necessary to allow for a certain degree of witness familiarization as well. However, counsel must always carefully assess ethical boundaries, i.e., bear in mind their duty to truth and good faith. In this regard, the IBA Guidelines on Party Representation in International Arbitration contain an elaborate framework which may provide guidance in defining the scope and limits.

II Party Experts and Tribunal Experts

3.100 The more technical the issue in dispute, the higher the chance that either a party or the tribunal will seek the opinion of experts in the form of expert witnesses. In the adversarial tradition, experts are selected, instructed and presented by the parties.[782] The terminology of 'expert witness' derives from the common law classification that differentiates between a witness of fact and a witness of opinion – the expert witness falls under the latter category. This differentiation also means that, in traditional common law litigation, witnesses of fact may not testify to their assessment or opinion of issues of expertise. The witness of fact's opinions or evaluations are not admissible as evidence.[783] Rather, as a general rule, only experts are eligible to give opinion evidence in specialized areas.[784]

3.101 In proceedings that are usually perceived as being more 'inquisitorial', it is the trier of fact's task to select, instruct and examine the expert. In Germany, for example, experts are not considered witnesses but fall into a separate category of evidence (*see* section 403 et seq. ZPO).[785] Moreover, and importantly, it is the court's responsibility to select and instruct experts (section 404a, 405 ZPO). Expert reports submitted by the parties do not qualify as a proper means of evidence but are considered to form part of the pleadings.[786]

3.102 As with many other aspects, in recent years, this classic 'common law versus civil law' divide is slowly fading. Relevantly, during the Reform of CPR in England and Wales, the understanding of the duty of the expert witness has undergone a substantial change. Even though experts are generally instructed by the parties, it is the expert's main duty to assist the court, and this duty overrides any obligation to the person from

781. *See* above, Chapter 3, B.I.1.a.
782. Jolowicz (n. 524) 209.
783. Keane and McKeown (n. 290) 634.
784. *Ibid.*
785. Note, however, that according to sec. 402 ZPO, the rules on witness examination apply *mutatis mutandis* if the rules on expert evidence are silent.
786. Walter Zimmermann, 'ZPO § 402' in Thomas Rauscher and Wolfgang Krüger (eds), *Münchener Kommentar zur ZPO* (6th edn, C.H. Beck 2020) para. 9: '(qualifiziertes) substantiiertes Parteivorbringen', i.e., 'qualified substantiated party pleading'; Walter Zimmermann, 'ZPO § 412' in Thomas Rauscher and Wolfgang Krüger (eds), *Münchener Kommentar zur ZPO* (6th edn, C.H. Beck 2020) para. 5 further, a German court required to instruct an expert in case of two contradicting party experts. Rather, it may explore other means to resolve these contradictions. If this is not sucessful, the court may render a decision on the merits to the detriment of the party which has failed to fulfil its burden of proof.

whom the expert has received instructions or by whom they are being paid (*see* CPR 35.3).

3.103 In international arbitration proceedings, it is common to have both party and tribunal experts. While it is generally the parties' right to submit expert reports into evidence,[787] most arbitration laws[788] and rules[789] expressly stipulate the tribunal's authority to appoint experts as well. Such authority can, in fact, be considered a general principle and transnational rule.[790] The tribunal's right to control the taking of expert evidence goes hand-in-hand with several specific powers and duties, which are largely (albeit to a varying degree) reflected by all of the above sets of rules. In particular, the tribunal must consult with the parties before appointing an expert. Designating an expert without consulting the parties beforehand may, in fact, amount to an excess of the tribunal's powers and/or a violation of due process, thus creating grounds for non-recognition of the award.[791]

3.104 Once the tribunal has appointed an impartial and independent expert, and in the absence of an agreement to the contrary, the parties may be required to make available all relevant information, documents and other means of evidence.[792] At the same time, the parties' interests are safeguarded through the right to receive and review the reports thus prepared as well as the right to apply for examination of the expert during the hearing. In practice, it can sometimes be observed that the parties put specific questions to the expert which are to be resolved within the report. This may be organized by using a table resembling the Redfern schedule. This allows for a party's question and its explanation as to its relevance, the opposing party's response, the tribunal's decision, and finally, the expert's answer.[793]

3.105 As a compromise between tribunal-appointed and party-appointed experts, tribunals at times refer to the so-called Sachs Protocol. The Sachs Protocol involves the parties exchanging a list of potential experts at an early stage of the proceedings and then commenting on each other's suggestions. Based on the parties' proposals and comments, the tribunal then selects two experts to jointly act as an expert team.[794] The purpose of this procedure is to strike a balance between the parties' right to make their case and the tribunal's control of the evidentiary proceedings. Also, instructing two

787. References to or rules on party experts can be found, *inter alia*, Art. 27.2 UNCITRAL Rules; Art. 33.1 SCC Rules; Art. 27.2 PCA Rules; Art. 5 IBA Rules; Art. 6.5 Prague Rules,
788. Article 26 Model Law; sec. 1049 ZPO; Art. 37 English Arbitration Act; Art. 32 Spanish Arbitration Act; sec. 601 Austrian ZPO; Art. 816 Italian Code of Civil Procedure.
789. Article 29 UNCITRAL Rules; Art. 28.2 DIS Rules; Art. 25 (4) ICC Rules; Art. 21 LCIA Rules; Art. 34 SCC Rules: Art- 29 (1) Vienna Rules; Art. 25 ICDR Rules; Art. 25 HKIAC Rules; Art. 28 SCAI Rules; Art. 29 PCA Rules; Art. 6 IBA Rules; Art. 6 Prague Rules.
790. *See also* ALI/UNIDROIT Principle 22.4 and Rule 26.
791. Giovannini (n. 534) 73.
792. *See, inter alia*, Art. 26 (1) (b) Model Law: 'Unless otherwise agreed by the parties, the arbitral tribunal (...) may require a party to give the expert any relevant information or to produce, or to provide access to, any relevant documents, goods or other property for his inspection.' *See* further Art. 6.3 IBA Rules.
793. *ICC Case No 22796/ASM/JPA/GSS, Procedural Order No 4 of 2019 (unreported)* [3].
794. Klaus Sachs and Nils Schmidt-Ahrendts, 'Protocol on Expert Teaming: A New Approach to Expert Evidence' [2011] ICCA Congress Series No 15 135.

experts, rather than only one, may be beneficial especially in complex matters, as the experts may review each other's approaches and develop arguments based on their joint experience and knowledge. One may object that this procedure generates more costs than a single joint expert and restricts the cooperation between parties and their experts during the preparation of the report.[795] Nonetheless, the Sachs Protocol offers a reasonable course of action, particularly in complex and high-value disputes.

3.106 In *Abaclat and Others v Argentina*, a dispute between the members of the tribunal arose regarding the appointment of a single expert, despite one arbitrator's suggestion to instruct two experts to jointly analyse the issue.[796] After the presiding arbitrator had issued a procedural order in which he appointed an expert on behalf of the tribunal, the arbitrator who disagreed felt compelled to issue a dissenting view. In his dissent, he objected to the procedural order, stating that:

> the applicable ICSID law allows an arbitral tribunal (or a dissenting member thereof) to submit a proposal or proposals to the Parties on the appointment of a given tribunal's expert or experts in connection with the taking or assessing of evidence. But, this does not mean that the arbitral tribunal in question be entitled to appoint for that purpose one or more of the proposed given expert or experts, unless the Parties empower by their mutual agreement the Arbitral Tribunal to do so.
>
> 27. In other words, ICSID law knows the figure of 'expert(s) of the tribunal' in the context of the taking or assessing evidence, but by leave of both Parties to the case, not as of right of the arbitral tribunal.[797]

3.107 It should be noted that said objection had no impact on the final decision which the tribunal rendered as a consent award.[798]

3.108 During the hearing, the examination of the experts follows the framework of the examination of witnesses. Experts can therefore be questioned in a tribunal-controlled or party-controlled manner. Moreover, if two (or more) expert reports contradict each other, tribunals frequently employ witness conferencing techniques.

III Documents

3.109 Alongside witnesses, documents are the most common form of evidence in international arbitration. As has been shown, the term 'documents' is understood in a

795. New Developments in International Commercial Arbitration and Sebastiano Nessi, 'Expert Witness: Role and Independence' in Christoph Müller, Sébastien Besson and Antonio Rigozzi (eds), *New Developments in International Commercial Arbitration 2016* (Schulthess 2016) 90, 91.
796. *Abaclat and Others v Argentine Republic, ICSID ARB/07/5 (formerly Giovanna a Beccara and Others v The Argentine Republic)* Dissenting Opinion to Procedural Order No 15 of 20 November 2012 [12].
797. *Ibid.*, 26, 27.
798. *Abaclat and Others v Argentine Republic, ICSID ARB/07/5 (formerly Giovanna a Beccara and Others v The Argentine Republic)* Consent Award of 29 December 2016.

broad sense, comprising all physically and digitally stored data.[799] The definition of international arbitration is, therefore, broader than in some civil law jurisdictions and rather resembles the common law approach.[800] In German civil litigation, for example, the legal definition of documents only includes physical and original documents, thus excluding digital files.[801] According to section 371a ZPO, electronic documents may only serve as evidence if they reflect a 'qualified electronic signature'.[802] These electronic signatures, however, are practically never used in business transactions, rendering electronic documents generally inadmissible as evidence before German courts. However, as domestic laws of evidence do not apply in international arbitration, the tribunal is not limited by such domestic restrictions.

3.110 In practice, one can observe that lawyers with a common law background tend to consider oral testimony available for examination to be the gold standard for evidence, while lawyers from other jurisdictions may consider documents to be the most reliable form,[803] mainly due to the apparent and known shortcomings of witnesses. Especially where the authenticity is not in dispute, documents speak for themselves. Likewise, in international arbitration, contemporaneous documents, i.e., those that were prepared before the dispute was known, are considered particularly reliable.[804]

3.111 Usually, parties annex the documents they seek to rely upon to their submissions. Especially in fact-heavy proceedings, parties usually submit hundreds of documents with their initial pleadings.[805] Moreover, as has been analysed in more detail above, parties frequently exchange further documents upon the request of the tribunal.[806] Beyond that, under certain circumstances, the tribunal may order the parties to produce certain documents on their own motion.[807]

3.112 In the event that neither party denies the veracity, simple copies or printouts of the original document are sufficient.[808] Documents are generally presumed to be

799. *See* above, Chapter 2, B.III.1.a.ii.
800. *See* above, Chapter 2, B.III.1.a.ii.
801. Klaus Schreiber, 'ZPO § 415' in Thomas Rauscher and Wolfgang Krüger (eds), *Münchener Kommentar zur ZPO* (6th edn, C.H. Beck 2020) para. 5.
802. *See* sec. 126a (1) BGB: 'If electronic form is to replace the written form prescribed by statute, the issuer of the declaration must add his name to it and provide the electronic document with a qualified electronic signature in accordance with the Electronic Signature Act [Signaturgesetz].'
803. Roman Khodykin, Carol Mulcahy and Nicholas Fletcher, *A Guide to the IBA Rules on the Taking of Evidence in International Arbitration* (Oxford University Press 2019) para. 7.142; Philipp Groz, 'Chapter 16, Part II: Commentary on the WIPO Arbitration and WIPO Expedited Arbitration Rules, WIPO Arbitration Rules, Article 56 / WIPO Expedited Arbitration Rules, Article 50 [Witnesses]' in Manuel Arroyo (ed.), *Arbitration in Switzerland: The Practitioner's Guide* (2nd edn, Kluwer Law International 2018).
804. As stated in the first edition of Nathan D O'Malley, *Rules of Evidence in International Arbitration: An Annotated Guide* (Informa 2012) para. 7.11.
805. *See* for the legal basis in different arbitration laws and rules above, Chapter 3, A.I.
806. *See* above, Chapter 2, B.III.
807. *See* above, Chapter 2, C.II.2.
808. Waincymer (n. 342) para. 11.3.

authentic,[809] which lays the burden of proof on the challenging party. Said party will then be required to present evidence to support its allegation of forgery, such as witnesses on the authorship or graphological reports.[810] Explicit provisions to this effect are frequently contained in the first procedural order. The Draft Procedural Order No. 1, as proposed by ICSID, for example, stipulates the following:

> 16.5.6 Copies of documentary evidence shall be assumed to be authentic unless specifically objected to by a party, in which case the Tribunal will determine whether authentication is necessary.

3.113 Generally, however, most documents will not be examined in formal evidence procedures, as their content frequently remains undisputed.

IV Real Evidence and Site Inspections

3.114 As a final category of evidence, the term 'real evidence' (also referred to as 'physical evidence')[811] summarizes all types of evidence that fall into none of the above categories, i.e., which does not pertain to the categories of fact witnesses, expert witnesses or documentary evidence. It includes everything 'from which the tribunal must use its own senses to draw conclusions or inferences in relation to the alleged facts'.[812] A typical example is the production of a real thing related to the issue which can be analysed and examined during the hearing by the tribunal and the parties. Unlike in criminal proceedings, the production of real evidence like machines or other technical devices is rare, as the parties frequently and habitually prefer to rely on documents and witnesses.[813] Nonetheless, where physical evidence becomes relevant, the tribunal must ensure that all stakeholders have sufficient opportunity to analyse and comment on the evidence. As suggested by the UNCITRAL Notes on Organizing Arbitral Proceedings (2016), the tribunal shall 'fix the time schedule and the manner for presenting such evidence, [and] make arrangements for the other party or parties to prepare for the presentation of the evidence'. It is also necessary to 'take measures for safekeeping the items of evidence'.[814]

3.115 Especially in technical disputes, as well as in investment proceedings, site inspections (as a form of real evidence) frequently assist in the analysis of the complex issues underlying the dispute. Only a few sets of rules contain specifics as to the proceedings of site visits. The ICSID Convention, for instance, stipulates in Article 43 that:

---

809. O'Malley (n. 407) para. 3.139.
810. For an indicative and extensive discussion on allegations of forgery *see ICC Case (No unreported), Preliminary Award of 2008* 29 [2011] 29 ASA Bulletin 4 860 [100–181].
811. 'UNCITRAL Notes on Organizing Arbitral Proceedings' para. 109.
812. John Cook, 'Factual and Expert Evidence in Arbitration' (2014) 16 Asian Dispute Review 30, 31.
813. Bernd Ehle and Courtney Furner, 'Eyeopeners – The Enlightening Effect of Site Visits in Construction Disputes' (2018) 12 Dispute Resolution International 176.
814. 'UNCITRAL Notes on Organizing Arbitral Proceedings' (n. 811) para. 109.

> [e]xcept as the parties otherwise agree, the Tribunal may, if it deems it necessary at any stage of the proceedings,
>
> (a) (...)
> (b) visit the scene connected with the dispute, and conduct such inquiries there as it may deem appropriate.

3.116 Similarly, according to Article 7 of the IBA Rules:

> [s]ubject to the provisions of Articles 9.2 and 9.3, the Arbitral Tribunal may, at the request of a Party or on its own motion, inspect or require the inspection by a Tribunal-Appointed Expert or a Party-Appointed Expert of any site, property, machinery or any other goods, samples, systems, processes or Documents, as it deems appropriate. The Arbitral Tribunal shall, in consultation with the Parties, determine the timing and arrangements for the inspection. The Parties and their representatives shall have the right to attend any such inspection.

3.117 According to the above stipulations, unless otherwise agreed by the parties, the tribunal, therefore, has the authority to order the inspection of a site, together with the party-appointed or tribunal-appointed experts, as required. Even without an explicit rule, such authority derives from the tribunal's power and mandate to conduct the proceedings as it deems fit. If an inspection is ordered, the tribunal shall make the necessary arrangements beforehand via procedural order[815] and allow the parties to attend the inspection. These arrangements include 'timing, cost allocation, arrangements necessary to ensure that all parties are able to be present or represented at the inspection and an indication of who will guide the inspection and provide explanations'.[816]

3.118 Relevantly, as further suggested by the UNCITRAL Notes on Organizing Arbitral Proceedings, the tribunal may also consider whether it is more appropriate to conduct the inspection physically or virtually.[817] Moreover, it may also consider whether to grant the parties the right to visit the site beforehand, in order to allow all stakeholders to get acquainted with the 'state and condition'.[818]

V Conclusion

3.119 Common means of evidence in international arbitration include witness testimonies, expert evidence, documentary evidence and different forms of real evidence.

3.120 Parties usually introduce their witnesses into the dispute by submitting written witness statements. Based on these, the testimonies are examined during the hearing

815. *See, e.g., Adel A Hamadi Al Tamimi v Sultanate of Oman, ICSID ARB/11/33* Procedural Order No 2 of 29 September 2012.
816. 'UNCITRAL Notes on Organizing Arbitral Proceedings' (n. 811) para. 111.
817. *Ibid.*, 110.
818. *Ibid.*, 112.

through a party-controlled procedure, specifically through direct, cross- and re-examination. As the parties bear the main responsibility for preparing and examining the evidence, a certain degree of witness familiarization is acceptable. An alternative model, which is less popular but not entirely uncommon, involves the parties being asked to introduce their witnesses by merely stating their names and their expected testimony in their submissions. The witnesses so introduced are then subject to tribunal-controlled examination, during which the tribunal begins the questioning of the witnesses and then allows the parties to continue. Moreover, where the parties have submitted contradicting witness testimonies, the tribunal may also order the examination of two (or more) contradicting witnesses to be conducted simultaneously ('hot-tubbing').

3.121 Similarly, expert witnesses can be either controlled by the parties or by the tribunal. In the first case, the parties instruct their experts to prepare reports on the issues in question. This practice mainly derives from common law litigation, where the essentially adversarial nature of the proceedings requires the parties to interact and work closely with their experts. In the second case, the tribunal may, upon consultation with the parties, select an expert to assist in determining technical issues. This practice is known, for example, in German litigation, where the court's involvement in the taking of evidence is traditionally stronger. As a compromise, the Sachs Protocol suggests that the tribunal may instruct a team of two experts based on the parties' suggestions. During the hearing, the experts are examined analogously to witnesses, i.e., either under the control of the parties or tribunals or, in the case of contradictory experts' reports, simultaneously.

3.122 Alongside witness evidence, documents usually have a decisive impact on the outcome. Importantly, the definition of the term is broad and includes not only physical but also all types of digital documents. Since parties generally do not challenge the authenticity of documents, tribunals usually do not have to take evidence but acknowledge the documents' scope and content as authentic.

3.123 Finally, as a less common form of evidence, parties may also present real evidence, i.e., real things from which the tribunal may draw inferences. This category also encompasses site visits, which can help to clarify the facts, especially in technical disputes and investment disputes.

C ADMISSION OF EVIDENCE

3.124 Based on what seems to be a profound cultural and legal misconception, the German legislature explained why, in its view, it was important to include an explicit rule on the tribunal's power to decide on the admission of evidence. In its understanding, such a provision was vital since in 'common law jurisdictions', the parties produced and examined evidence before the courts without the court's interference and without any prior decision on admissibility:

> The fact that the powers of the arbitral tribunal also include the decision on the admissibility of evidence and the free assessment of evidence is a commonplace in German law. However, the draft emphasizes this power (...) because in common law jurisdictions, a different practice prevails. There [in common law], it is customary in litigation and thus also in arbitration proceedings that the parties bring witnesses and experts to the hearing and examine them themselves, without the trier of fact conducting a test of relevance and materiality beforehand.[819]

3.125 Contrary to the understanding of the German legislature, and as a matter of course, both courts and arbitral tribunals in common law do have the power, duty and discretion to decide on the admission of evidence. Rather than being a German particularity, the tribunal's power to decide on the admission of evidence in modern international arbitration is undisputedly and fully recognized, amounting to a transnational principle (*I*). The widely recognized standard of admissibility is the one of relevance and materiality (*II*). Under certain circumstances, exclusionary rules may urge the tribunal to reject evidence even though it might have been born on the outcome of the case (*III*).

I Broad Arbitral Discretion

3.126 In modern international arbitration, the tribunal's power to decide on the admissibility of evidence amounts to a general and transnational principle.[820] It is reflected by many arbitration laws and rules. Article 19 (2) Second Sentence of the Model Law, for example, states that:

> [t]he power conferred upon the arbitral tribunal includes the power to determine the admissibility, relevance, materiality and weight of any evidence.

3.127 Similar wording can be found in other arbitration laws, such as the German[821], Spanish Arbitration Acts.[822] Under Article 34 (1), (2) (f) of the English Arbitration Act, it is for the tribunal to decide:

---

819. 'Official Records of Parliament (Bundestag Drucksache) 13/5274' 46: ' Daß zu den Befugnissen des Schiedsgerichts auch die Entscheidung über die Zulässigkeit von Beweismitteln und die freie Beweiswürdigung gehört, ist zwar für das deutsche Recht eine Selbstverständlichkeit. Der Entwurf stellt dies jedoch in Absatz 4 Satz 2 (der Artikel 19 Abs. 2 Satz 2 ModG entspricht) deshalb ausdrücklich klar, weil in den Staaten des common law eine andere Praxis herrscht. Hier ist es in Verfahren vor den staatlichen Gerichten und dementsprechend auch in Schiedsverfahren üblich, daß die Parteien Zeugen und Sachverständige zur Verhandlung mitbringen und selbst befragen, ohne daß der (Schieds-)Richter vorher eine Schlüssigkeitsprüfung zum Beweisthema vornimmt.' (Translation by the author).
820. *See* on the emergence of transnational rules in international arbitration above Chapter 1, in particular Chapter 1, B.
821. Section 1042 (4) Second Sentence of the German Arbitration Act: 'Absent an agreement by the parties, and in those cases regarding which the present Book does not make any provisions, the procedural rules shall be determined by the arbitral tribunal at its sole discretion. The arbitral tribunal is authorised to decide on the admissibility of the taking of evidence, to so take evidence, and to assess the results at its sole discretion.'
822. Article 25 (2) Second Sentence of the Spanish Arbitration Act: 'Failing [a party] agreement, the arbitrators may, subject to the provisions of this act, conduct the arbitration in such manner as

whether to apply strict rules of evidence (or any other rules) as to the admissibility, relevance or weight of any material (oral, written or other) sought to be tendered on any matters of fact or opinion.

3.128 Subject to a few exceptions,[823] comparable provisions granting extensive liberties to the tribunal can be found in nearly all the analysed arbitration rules.[824] The same is confirmed by both the Trans-Lex Principles[825] and the ALI/UNIDROIT Principles[826] - two of the most eminent collections of transnational principles.

3.129 The broad discretion does not mean that the tribunal is entirely free in assessing the admissibility. Due consideration must always be given to the parties' right to be heard, due process and procedural fairness. In particular, the right to be heard guarantees that the parties have the utmost opportunity to bring their case, which also includes the presentation of evidence that potentially influences the tribunal's decision on the case.[827] This must be fully considered when deciding on admissibility and is reflected by the commonly applied test of admissibility, namely the relevance and materiality test.

II Standards of Admissibility (Relevance and Materiality)

3.130 While the above sets of rules provide little guidance on how to determine the admissibility of evidence in detail,[828] they frequently cite the test of relevance and

they deem appropriate. The power vested in the arbitrators includes the power to determine the admissibility, relevance, materiality, taking (even ex officio) and evaluation of the evidence.'

823. There are, for example, no specific provisions under the ICC Rules or Vienna Rules.
824. *See* Art. 27.4 UNCITRAL Rules; Art. 28.2 DIS Rules; Art. 22.1 (vi) LCIA Rules (with a wording resembling Art. 34 (1), (2) (f) English Arbitration Act; Art. 31.1 SCC Rules; Art. 22.7 ICDR Rules; Art. 22.2 HKIAC Rules; Art. 26.2 SCAI Rules; Art. 27.4 PCA Rules.
825. 'Trans-Lex Principle XIII.3.2 – Determination of Rules of Procedure, https://www.Trans-Lex.Org/969030' No. XIII.3.2 – Determination of rules of procedure: '(a) Subject to the mandatory provisions of the arbitration law in force at the seat of the arbitration, the parties are free to agree on the procedure to be followed by the arbitral tribunal in conducting the proceedings, either by reference to a set of arbitration rules or by agreeing on specific rules for the conduct of the proceedings prior to or during the arbitration. (b) Failing such agreement, the arbitral tribunal may conduct the arbitration in such manner as it considers appropriate, taking into account the parties' due process rights under Principle XIII.3.1. The power conferred upon the arbitral tribunal includes the power to determine the admissibility, relevance, materiality and weight of any evidence.'
826. ALI/UNIDROIT Rule 18.3.4: 'In giving direction to the proceeding, the court, after discussion with the parties, may: (...) [m]ake decisions concerning admissibility and exclusion of evidence; the sequence, dates, and times of hearing evidence; and other matters to simplify or expedite the proceeding.'
827. Pilkov (n. 422) 147, 149; Ferrari, Rosenfeld and Czernich (n. 49) 27, 28.
828. Under the prevalent definition of the law of evidence in common law, evidence is admissible if it is relevant and of such quality that a jury, properly warned about any defects it might have, can place some weight on it Keane and McKeown (n. 290) 21. This again reflects the exclusive nature of the law of evidence, the purpose of which is, *inter alia*, to protect laypersons (i.e., jurors) from evidence which they might over- or undervalue. Thus, it is of little help in arbitration proceedings which function without a jury.

materiality. This standard is mentioned, *inter alia*, in Article 19 (2) Second Sentence of the Model Law:

> The power conferred upon the arbitral tribunal includes the power to determine the admissibility, relevance, materiality and weight of any evidence.

3.131 Provisions with an identical or similar wording can be found in Article 25 (2) of the Spanish Arbitration Act,[829] Article 27.4 UNCITRAL Rules,[830] Article 31 SCC Rules,[831] Article 22.7 ICDR Rules,[832] Article 21.1 (vi) LCIA Rules,[833] Article 22.2 HKIAC Rules,[834] Article 26.1 SCAI Rules and Article 27.4 PCA Rules[835].

3.132 As in the context of document production under the IBA Rules, evidence is 'relevant' if it renders a contention to be either more or less likely.[836] As a simple example, the contract (in the sense of the document) is relevant to determine whether the defendant has taken upon the duties which the claimant seeks to have fulfilled. By the same token, it is 'material' – the means of evidence in question might bear upon the final award.[837] Relevant evidence may, for example, be deemed not material if there is sufficient other evidence on record to determine the issue or if the issue in question is no longer contentious between the parties.

3.133 The same standard of relevance and materiality is also suggested under Article 9.1 of the IBA Rules[838] as well as the commentary to the ALI/UNIDROIT Principles, which states that:

829. Article 25 (2) Spanish Arbitration Act: 'Failing such agreement, the arbitrators may, subject to the provisions of this act, conduct the arbitration in such manner as they deem appropriate. The power vested in the arbitrators includes the power to determine the admissibility, relevance, materiality, taking (even ex officio) and evaluation of the evidence.'
830. Article 27.4 UNCITRAL Rules: 'The arbitral tribunal shall determine the admissibility, relevance, materiality and weight of the evidence offered.'
831. Article 31.3 SCC Rules: 'At the request of a party, or exceptionally on its own motion, the Arbitral Tribunal may order a party to produce any documents or other evidence that may be relevant to the case and material to its outcome.'
832. Article 21.1 (vi) ICDR Rules: 'The tribunal may, upon application, require a party to make available to another party documents in that party's possession not otherwise available to the party seeking the documents, that are reasonably believed to exist and to be relevant and material to the outcome of the case. Requests for documents shall contain a description of specific documents or classes of documents, along with an explanation of their relevance and materiality to the outcome of the case.'
833. Article 21.1 (vi) LCIA Rules: 'the tribunal may (...) decide whether or not to apply any strict rules of evidence (or any other rules) as to the admissibility, relevance or weight of any material tendered by a party on any issue of fact or expert opinion (...).'.
834. Article 22.2 HKIAC Rules: 'At any time during the arbitration, the arbitral tribunal may allow or require a party to produce documents, exhibits or other evidence that the arbitral tribunal determines to be relevant to the case and material to its outcome. The arbitral tribunal shall have the power to admit or exclude any documents, exhibits or other evidence.'
835. Article 27.4 PCA Rules: 'The arbitral tribunal shall determine the admissibility, relevance, materiality and weight of the evidence offered.'
836. *See* above, Chapter 2, C.III.1.a.iii.
837. *See* above, Chapter 2, C.III.1.a.iv.
838. Article 9.1 IBA Rules: 'The Arbitral Tribunal shall determine the admissibility, relevance, materiality and weight of evidence.' Note that, as shown above, under the IBA Rules,

> any factual information that is rationally useful in reaching judgment on the relevant facts of the case should be admissible as evidence.[839]

3.134 In its wording, the above definition also emphasizes the materiality of evidence ('useful in reaching judgment') and leaves the determination of relevance to the trier of fact ('rationally'). Other rules which are silent on the standard of admissibility leave it to the tribunal to apply the appropriate criteria. Reference to this general principle is, however, recommended for reasons of legal certainty, efficiency and practicability. Especially in light of the right to be heard, the parties must have the opportunity to fully present their case, i.e., to present all evidence from which material inferences may be drawn.[840] As a matter of course, evidence that does not bear on the decision may be disregarded. The test of relevance and materiality, therefore, serves an important exclusionary function, as there is no need to take evidence which is irrelevant (i.e., does not allow conclusions to be drawn on an issue in dispute) or not material (i.e., does not bear on the outcome of the case). Rather, such evidence must be rejected based on considerations of efficiency and cost reduction.

3.135 As this standard not only applies to the admission of evidence but also during the document production phase, the application of the same rule may lead to different outcomes throughout the proceeding.[841] In the early stages of the proceedings, when parties exchange documents, it is frequently difficult to determine whether or not a specific document will bear on the outcome of the case. When deciding on the admission of evidence, however, the perspective of the tribunal is usually more advanced and informed as the parties have further clarified their positions.[842] Since sufficient data is now available, the tribunal is able to make a more accurate assessment of whether it requires the analysis of the specific means in order to take its decision based on the facts, i.e., whether the evidence is relevant and material.

III Exclusionary Rules

3.136 The right to be heard demands that a party must be granted the opportunity to make its case fully.[843] This includes the right to present evidence before the tribunal, allowing for proper examination by all stakeholders. Under specific circumstances, however, a tribunal might have valid grounds to exclude relevant material evidence. Against the backdrop of the right to be heard, the threshold for excluding evidence is high. In general, the considerations laid out in the ambit of objections to the production of documents apply.[844]

---

discussions regarding the test of relevance and materiality usually arise during the document production phase, which is subject to a similar standard, *see* Art. 3.3 (b) IBA Rules.

839. American Law Institute (ALI) and UNIDROIT (n. 203) para. R-25A.
840. Pilkov (n. 422) 147, 149; Ferrari, Rosenfeld and Czernich (n. 49) 27, 28.
841. *See* above, Chapter 2, C.III.1.a.iii and iv.
842. *See* above, Chapter 2, C.III.1.a.iii and iv.
843. Pilkov (n. 422) 147, 149; Ferrari, Rosenfeld and Czernich (n. 49) 27, 28.
844. *See* above, Chapter 2, B.1.i.e.

1 *Privilege*

3.137 Some exclusionary rules aim at protecting the overwhelming public or private interests. As analysed above, especially those jurisdictions with far-reaching procedural rules on discovery and disclosure of documents usually stipulate detailed regimes of privilege. The purpose is to duly protect the parties' rights if they are ordered to extensively disclose information against their will. Likewise, in international arbitration, the tribunal must have regard for the applicable heads of privilege, in particular the attorney-client privilege, in-house privilege, work-product privilege (referring to documents produced in anticipation of a dispute) and cabinet privilege (especially in proceedings involving states and public entities).[845]

2 *Illegality*

3.138 There is also no general rule that would render illegally obtained evidence inadmissible.[846] Where the illegal origin has been established, tribunals must carefully contemplate the interests involved by weighing the importance of the evidence against the violation of the aggrieved parties' rights.[847]

3.139 Moreover, constitutional considerations may limit the discretionary powers of the arbitral tribunal. In *W. v International Equestrian Federation (FEI)*, a CAS dispute governed by substantive Swiss law,[848] the tribunal found that the use of a 'lie detector, of narco-examination or of a truth serum as a method to establish the truth' was not 'admissible on a constitutional basis'.[849] In light of the finding, the tribunal concluded that:

> [a]s a result, the Panel does not deem admissible as evidence in the present arbitration a deposition based on a lie detector test.[850]

3.140 Nonetheless, while it is understandable that the tribunal felt compelled to consider Swiss constitutional law, this way of proceeding might not be indicative of best practices in international arbitration. In particular, tribunals are required to carefully analyse whether the specific constitutional rules may apply as part of the *lex*

845. *See* above, Chapter 2, B.III.1.a.v.(a) with further references.
846. Waincymer (n. 343) 789–791; no general principle applies in common law litigation, *see* Andrew LT Choo and Susan Nash, 'Improperly Obtained Evidence in the Commonwealth: Lessons for England and Wales?' (2007) 11 The International Journal of Evidence & Proof 75, 77, 78.
847. O'Malley (n. 407) para. 9.119.
848. *CAS Case No 1999/A/246, Award of 11 May 2000* 2 Digest of CAS Awards II 1998-2000, Digest of CAS Awards Series Set 505 [3].
849. *Ibid.*, 6.
850. *Ibid.*, 9.

causae or bear an influence thereon, or whether the rules in question are part of the international or transnational public policy.[851]

3 *Other Domestic Rules*

3.141 Moreover, there is no room for the application of domestic,[852] and specifically of common law exclusionary rules, which are designed to protect lay jurors.[853] Under common law, evidence may be held inadmissible where it is considered to be inherently unreliable or likely to be misleading. In former times, this led to the exclusion of hearsay evidence.[854] Moreover, under the 'best evidence' rule, the parties were expected to only submit the 'best evidence available that a party to litigation could produce'.[855] The application of these exclusionary rules stems from the traditional procedural context, where it was found that a lay juror might attribute more importance to these issues than a professional judge.[856] Unlike laypersons, arbitrators in international proceedings are expected to be able to reasonably exercise their powers to analyse the evidence, which is why a recourse to any domestic law of evidence is not appropriate.

3.142 In *BQP v BQQ*, the High Court of Singapore dismissed BQP's challenge of an arbitral award, confirming the tribunal's discretion to freely decide on the admission of evidence without taking recourse to the traditional common law of evidence. In particular, the tribunal had been within its rights to consider evidence on the course of the negotiation rather than solely focusing on the language of the contract. The court found that in Singapore:

> the characterisation of admissibility of evidence as a rule of evidence or procedural law as compared to substantive law, has been made clear, and in that sense settled.[857]

The court then turned to the analysis of the applicable arbitration rules and highlighted Article 16.2 of the SIAC Rules 2013, which was also in line with the provisions under the LCIA Rules 2014, UNCITRAL Arbitration Rules 2010, HKIAC Rules, ICDR Rules and the Korean Arbitration Act,[858] and according to which:

---

851. *See* for a short overview on potential rules of transnational public policy, Born (n. 338) 2926–2930 Note, however, that a detailed discussion of these questions goes beyond the scope of this study.
852. Note, however, that under Art. 34 (1), (2) (f) English Arbitration Act and Art. 22.1 (vi) LCIA Rules, the tribunal may consider applying strict rules of evidence and admission in arbitration proceedings.
853. Keane and McKeown (n. 290) 3 et seq.
854. Note that in civil proceedings, the hearsay rule has been virtually abolished, *see, inter alia, Post Office Counters Ltd v Mahida* [2003] EWCA Civ 1583 [24].
855. Keane and McKeown (n. 290) 31.
856. *Ibid.*, 3.
857. *BQP v BQQ* [2018] SGHC 55 [122].
858. *Ibid.*, 128.

> [t]he Tribunal shall determine the relevance, materiality, and admissibility of all evidence. Evidence need not be admissible in law.[859]

The court, therefore, found that:

> admissibility clearly lies within the sole province of the tribunal, as do relevance and materiality.[860]

3.143 In *Azpetrol et al. v Republic of Azerbaijan*, the court took a different stance. As in *BQP v BQQ*, the question was whether the tribunal could take into consideration the parties' negotiations leading to the conclusion of the contract and their subsequent conduct, i.e., whether the claimant's evidence regarding these issues was admissible. The tribunal concluded that while, under international law, it would have the authority to admit said evidence, under English law, the tribunal was barred from considering the negotiations:

> While [evidence of the prior negotiations or subsequent practice of the parties] would be admissible under international law, the parties have agreed that the Tribunal should apply English law to determine whether or not there was a binding settlement agreement and the Tribunal is therefore bound to apply English law in good faith. There is little doubt that the present position under English law is that recourse to the negotiations and the subsequent conduct of the parties is not admissible as an aid to the interpretation of their agreement. While that approach has been subjected to some telling criticism, the Tribunal's duty is to apply in good faith English law as it is, not as it ought to be or might become.[861]

3.144 Nonetheless, in the end, the tribunal found that it did not matter whether or not it was entitled to admit the evidence in question as it did not 'sustain the Claimants' argument'.[862]

3.145 In light of the ongoing transnationalization of fact-finding rules as described in this study, it is submitted the tribunal was, in fact, allowed to consider extraneous evidence on the negotiations and the subsequent conduct. While it is true that the tribunal was required to 'apply in good faith English law as it is, not as it ought to be or might become', the analysis and specific application of English law is the very task of the tribunal. Had the tribunal concluded, along with other commentators on international law, that the four-corners-rule was a matter of procedural law, or perhaps in the grey zone between substantive and procedural law,[863] it could have had recourse to the standing practice in international law to duly consider the *travaux préparatoires*.[864]

859. *Ibid.*, 127.
860. *Ibid.*
861. *Azpetrol International Holdings BV, Azpetrol Group BV and Azpetrol Oil Services Group BV v The Republic of Azerbaijan, ICSID ARB/06/15* Award of 8 September 2009 [90].
862. *Ibid.*, 92.
863. *See also* the discussion in *BQP v BQQ* (n. 857) paras 118 et seqq.
864. Cf. *Azpetrol International Holdings B.V., Azpetrol Group B.V. and Azpetrol Oil Services Group B.V. v The Republic of Azerbaijan, ICSID ARB/06/15* (n. 861) para. 63 with further references.

3.146 As a further indicative example, in *Lummus Global Amazonas SA v Aguaytia Energy del Peru*, a US District Court decided a challenge of an ICC Award. In the award, the tribunal had rejected witness evidence as inadmissible to prove the meaning of a contractual term,[865] thereby contradicting the common practice in international arbitration analysed above. The US District Court upheld the award, stating that:

> [the] arbitrator is the judge of the relevance and admissibility of the evidence presented in an arbitration proceeding.[866]

In this particular case, there was no indication that:

> exclusion of the evidence as to the parties' intent (...) prevented [the challenging party] from receiving a fundamentally fair hearing.[867]

3.147 Although the tribunal chose to apply a domestic standard - which is not recommended in international arbitration – the court's ruling confirms the power of the tribunal to control the admission of evidence as it deems appropriate.

3.148 Importantly, one must consider that the traditional purpose of the English law of evidence is to protect jurors (i.e., laypersons) from drawing false inferences from misleading evidence. Conflicts between the wording of the contract and alleged statements before or after the conclusion of the contract may be difficult to classify, especially for laypersons. Arbitrators in international proceedings, however, are commonly highly skilled and experienced practitioners and well-trained in the analysis of evidence. The protection aim of the rule, therefore, does not apply to international arbitrations.

3.149 It follows that, subject to the above exceptions, tribunals are generally free to reject domestic approaches and adopt the standards of admissibility as developed by international arbitral jurisprudence.

IV Conclusion

3.150 As a general and transnational principle, the tribunal may freely, under due consideration of the parties' right to be heard, decide on the admission of evidence.

3.151 In practice, tribunals usually apply the standard of relevance and materiality, i.e., they review whether the evidence renders a contention to be more or less likely (relevant) and whether it bears on the outcome of the dispute.

3.152 Further, different exclusionary rules, such as privilege and, in individual cases, illegality, may require the tribunal to reject evidence in spite of its materiality. Nonetheless, in light of the parties' right to fully present their case, the threshold is high.

865. *Lummus Global Amazonas v Aguaytia Energy Del Peru* 256 F Supp 2d 594 (SD Tex 2002) 617.
866. *Ibid.*
867. *Ibid.*, 618.

D STANDARD OF PROOF

3.153 In recent years, the standard of proof in international arbitration has received wide attention in various articles and monographs,[868] and its application before international tribunals is a recurring issue.[869] Accordingly, the below shall be limited to an outline of the basic principles and an identification of the issues that remain disputed.

3.154 Before going into further detail, it is necessary to first establish the terminology. In particular, a distinction must be made between the applicable 'standard of proof' and the 'assessment of evidence'. The term 'assessment of evidence' describes the procedure of evaluating a specific means of evidence by analysing its content, relevance and credibility. The assessment of evidence (also referred to as 'evaluation of evidence' or 'weighing of evidence') is necessary to determine whether the evidence has sufficient probative value.[870] The term 'standard of proof' (in German *Beweismaß*, sometimes referred to as *Beweiskriterium*[871]), however, describes the threshold that has to be met in order to consider a factual assertion to be true, i.e., the threshold that the evidence must be assessed against.[872] As will be shown in further detail below, there are certain differences (if only terminological) between jurisdictions regarding the formulation of this threshold. Broadly speaking, while in civil law jurisdictions, the standard of proof requires a certain degree of conviction of the trier of facts, in common law jurisdiction, the relevant threshold is a balance (or preponderance) of probability. That means that a judge or an arbitrator, when assessing evidence, must analyse whether the evidence is convincing or, respectively, whether the evidence makes an allegation sufficiently probable.

3.155 Assessing the evidence against the backdrop of the standard of proof thus describes the inner, inherently subjective process of forming a certain persuasion. The challenge lies in the necessity of determining an objective threshold as to when a trier

868. Pauker (n. 19). *See, inter alia*; Luboš Tichý, 'Standard of Proof' in Luboš Tichý (ed.), *Standard of Proof in Europe* (Mohr Siebeck 2019); Philipp Alfter, *Das Beweismaß in der internationalen Handelsschiedsgerichtsbarkeit* (Springer 2019); Skontzos (n. 618); Duggal and Cai (n. 642); Jennifer M Smith and Sara Nadeau-Séguin, 'The Illusive Standard of Proof in International Commercial Arbitration' (2015) Volume 18 Legitimacy: Myths, Realities, Challenges, ICCA Congress Series 134; Mark Schweizer, *Beweiswürdigung und Beweismaß: Rationalität und Intuition* (Mohr Siebeck 2015); Brinkmann (n. 366); Brinkmann (n. 360); Redfern and others (n. 271).
869. *See, e.g.*, the following decisions which will be addressed in more detail in this study: *OLG Frankfurt a. M., Order of 2 February 2017* (n. 255) 51; *Fiona Trust & Holding Corporation Ors v Privalov Ors* (n. 615); *Karkey Karadeniz Elektrik Uretim AS v Islamic Republic of Pakistan, ICSID ARB/13/1* Award of 22 August 2017 [492]; *Republic of Croatia v MOL Hungarian Oil and Gas Company Plc, PCA Case No 2014-15* Award of 23 December 2016 [115 et seq., 119]; *VIAC Case No SCH-5196, Final Award 17 October 2013* Arbitrator Intelligence Materials [119].
870. Pilkov (n. 422) 153 et seq.; *see* for the weight of evidence under English law Keane and McKeown (n. 290) 33 et seq.; *see* for German law Prütting, *Gegenwartsprobleme Der Beweislast* (n. 603) 58; Reinhard Greger, *Beweis Und Wahrscheinlichkeit: D. Beweiskriterium Im Allgemeinen u. Bei d. Sogen. Beweiserleichterungen* (Heymann 1978) 8.
871. Greger (n. 870) 8.
872. Brinkmann (n. 366) 875, 876.

of fact may consider that it has formed said persuasion to the necessary degree of certainty.

3.156 In order to determine which threshold applies, it is necessary to bear in mind the applicable substantive law (*I*). There is, however, a strong tendency to apply a transnational standard of proof in international arbitration (*II*).

I The Standard of Proof under Substantive Law

3.157 While, in some jurisdictions, the standard of proof is considered a matter of procedural law,[873] it is usually understood to be governed by substantive law.[874] This may explain why none of the analysed arbitration laws and rules contain any specific provisions on the applicable standard of proof.[875] The same is true for best practice standards on the taking of evidence, especially the IBA Rules and the Prague Rules. Only the ALI/UNIDROIT Principles contain a particular provision which will be examined in more detail below.[876]

3.158 In the international arbitration practice, there is, however, a growing trend in which the standard of proof – alongside other fact-finding matters – is found to oscillate in the 'grey-zone of the substance-procedure dichotomy',[877] a position which allows a transnational standard of proof to be applied rather than having recourse to the substantive law of specific jurisdictions. As will be shown below, there are good reasons to consider such transnational approach in particular in international arbitrations.

3.159 Consequently, the below shall first outline the fundamentals of the standard of proof across different jurisdictions (*1* and *2*) and their comparability (*3*), before exploring the current trends towards a transnational principle (*II*).

1 Standard of Proof in Civil Law

3.160 It may not come as a surprise that there is no uniform 'civil law' standard of proof. Rather, due to diverging legal traditions,[878] the standard of proof across civil law jurisdictions varies. There are, however, common elements that can be identified,

873. *See, e.g.*, *Fiona Trust & Holding Corporation Ors v Privalov Ors* (n. 615) para. 138: 'It is a matter for the lex fori, in this case English law, to determine how the relevant facts are proved and the standard of proof.'
874. Tichý (n. 868) 298 et seq.; Skontzos (n. 618) 577; Klaus Sachs and Tillman Niedermaier, 'Die Rechtsfigur Der "Adverse Inferences" in Der Internationalen Schiedsgerichtsbarkeit' in Walter Eberl (ed.), *Beweis im Schiedsverfahren* (Nomos 2015) 133; Smith and Nadeau-Séguin (n. 868) 145.
875. *See, e.g.*, the Model Law, the German Arbitration Act, the English Arbitration Act as well as different analysed rules of arbitral institutions, such as the ICC Rules, LCIA Rules, Vienna Rules, SCC Rules, ICDR Rules, HKIAC Rules, SCAI Rules, and PCA Rules.
876. *See* below, D.II.
877. Mavromati (n. 19) 195; Pauker (n. 19) 19.
878. *See* above, Chapter 1, B.I.

namely that at the heart of different civil law standards of proof lies the conviction of the judge (or arbitrator), rather than a balance of probabilities (*a*). Moreover, the general threshold may be subject to modifications in particular cases (*b*).

i *Reasonable Degree of Conviction*

3.161 The German standard of proof revolves around the reasonable conviction of the trier of fact. Following decades of academic dispute on the threshold to be applied, *Anastasia*[879] finally settled the relevant general standard of proof ('full evidence'; *Vollbeweis*),[880] and found its way into legal history due to its rather peculiar factual background. At the beginning of the twentieth century, substantial financial assets belonging to the Tsarist family of Russia were distributed all over Germany. Subsequent to the Russian Revolution of 1917 and the execution of nearly all members of the Tsarist family, the distribution of the goods was subject to ongoing disputes which went on for decades. In *Anastasia*, the plaintiff to the principal dispute was registered in Germany under the name of *Anna Anderson*. Ms Anderson, however, alleged that she was not Ms Anderson but in fact the youngest daughter of the Russian Tsar, Anastasia Romanov and, as such, the last surviving family member. On this basis, she asserted her alleged right to the inheritance of the Tsarist family's remaining assets. Due to the technical and factual difficulties of proving this allegation and determining the plaintiff's true heritage, in 1970, the Federal Court of Justice felt compelled to clarify the applicable standard of proof, i.e., when the court may deem a fact to be established:

> it is wrong to state that in cases of that kind, the civil judge may be content with a mere probability. (...). The judge may and must be content, in truly doubtful cases, with a degree of conviction which is suitable for practical life and which commands silence to all doubts without completely excluding them.[881]

3.162 In short, according to *Anastasia*, the general standard of proof is met when the trier of fact is convinced of the veracity of an assertion, without being entirely free of doubt. With this definition, the Federal Court of Justice emphasizes the subjective component of the inner conviction, instead of relying on the presumably more objective standard of the preponderance of probability. This largely subjective standard is accompanied by the (procedural) requirement to provide reasons for the assessment of evidence, which shall serve the purpose of intersubjectivity.[882]

---

879. *BGH, Judgment of 17 February 1970* [1970] NJW 946.
880. Hanns Prütting, 'ZPO § 284' in Thomas Rauscher and Wolfgang Krüger (eds), *Münchener Kommentar zur ZPO* (6th edn, C.H. Beck 2020) paras 32-34.
881. *BGH, Judgment of 17 February 1970* (n. 879) para. II.2.a: ' Irrig ist jedoch der Vortrag, der Zivilprozßrichter dürfe sich in Fällen dieser Art mit einer bloßen Wahrscheinlichkeit begnügen. (...) Der Richter darf und muß sich aber in tatsächlich zweifelhaften Fällen mit einem für das praktische Leben brauchbaren Grad von Gewißheit begnügen, der den Zweifeln Schweigen gebietet, ohne sie völlig auszuschließen.' (Translation by the author).
882. *See* sec. 286 (1) Second Sentence ZPO: 'The judgment is to set out the reasons informing the conviction of the judges.'

3.163 The standard of proof is intertwined with the burden of proof.[883] The party bearing the burden of proof must submit 'full evidence' (*Vollbeweis*)[884] to meet the standard of proof. The opposing party, in turn, is merely required to submit evidence which may not be fully persuasive, but which is sufficient to shake the court's conviction (so-called counter evidence; *Gegenbeweis*).[885] If, however, a legal presumption[886] applies, the opposing party is required to positively convince the court or tribunal of the contrary. This means that the party needs to present full evidence for its assertion.[887]

3.164 The standard of a reasonable conviction of the trier of facts is also 'at the core of the Romanic approach to the standard of proof'.[888] While French civil law, for example, does not expressly stipulate a definition of the applicable standard of proof, many authors advocate that the result of the taking of evidence must be to convince the trier of facts,[889] rather than to balance probabilities.[890] Similarly, Italian law operates with the 'free conviction of the judge'.[891]

ii *Modifications*

3.165 German law provides several optional modifications of this general standard of proof. To begin with, in certain procedural circumstances, the trier of fact must be satisfied with a lowered standard of proof, especially where the nature of the matter does not allow for the extensive taking of evidence (so-called *Glaubhaftmachung*, 'to the satisfaction of the court').[892] The standard is fulfilled if the trier deems the truth of the alleged fact to be predominantly probable,[893] which resembles the common law balance of probabilities.[894] The lowered threshold applies particularly in cases where a party files for interim measures, i.e., where the urgency of the matter calls for a swift

883. *See* on the burden of proof, above Chapter 2, A.II.
884. Prütting, 'ZPO § 284' (n. 880) para. 20.
885. *Ibid.*, 21.
886. Section 292 ZPO: 'Should the law make a presumption as to a certain fact being given, its opposite may admissibly be proven unless otherwise provided for by the law. This proof may also be established by petitioning the examination of a party pursuant to section 445.'
887. Prütting, 'ZPO § 284' (n. 880) para. 22.
888. Brinkmann (n. 366) 881.
889. *Ibid.*, 880.
890. *See*, Emmanuel Jeuland, 'Standard of Proof in France' in Luboš Tichý (ed.), *Standard of Proof in Europe* (Mohr Siebeck 2019) 183 et seq., 187 et seq. who however in a recent study has advocated that no abstract rule on the standard of proof existed in France.
891. Roberto Poli, 'Standard of Proof in Italy' in Luboš Tichý (ed.), *Standard of Proof in Europe* (Mohr Siebeck 2019) 197 et seq.
892. Section 294 ZPO: '(1) Anyone who is to demonstrate an allegation as to fact to the satisfaction of the court may use all evidence and may also be permitted to make a statutory declaration in lieu of an oath.
(2) Evidence that cannot be taken immediately shall not be admitted.'
893. Hanns Prütting, 'ZPO § 294' in Thomas Rauscher and Wolfgang Krüger (eds), *Münchener Kommentar zur ZPO* (6th edn, C.H. Beck 2020) para. 24.
894. *See* below, Chapter 3, D.I.2; *see* for the difficulties of defining probability below, Chapter 3, D.I.3.

decision.[895] The fact that this modification is usually (but not exclusively) applied in certain procedural situations, independent of the substantive law,[896] raises doubts about whether the standard of proof, including modifications, is, in fact, a matter of substantive law. Rather, this seems to support the classification of the standard of proof as within the 'grey-zone of the substance-procedure dichotomy'.[897]

3.166 Moreover, German law[898] applies a lowered standard of proof to the calculation of damages. This is necessary since it is the inherent nature of damages to compensate for losses that would not have been incurred, had the defendant duly fulfilled its duties.[899] This means that to quantify damages, it is necessary to compare the situation on a hypothetical basis with and without a breach of duty. In other words: since a party invoking damages must be able to quantify an appropriate amount, it is required to 'prove' a hypothetical state of affairs (i.e., the state of satisfactory performance) that did not occur. This naturally imposes certain difficulties. Therefore, under German law, the trier of fact shall decide on the amount of damages at its discretion and conviction, based on its evaluation of all circumstances and under the consideration of a 'normal course of events'.[900] In doing so, the trier of fact is required to rely on circumstantial facts which the claiming party must submit and, in case of doubt, prove.[901]

3.167 Apart from these modifications, there are further mechanisms in place under German law that can help a party to prove its allegations in case of structural

895. *See* sec. 920 (2) ZPO: 'The claim and the grounds for a writ of seizure to be issued are to be demonstrated to the satisfaction of the court.'
896. Prütting, 'ZPO § 294' (n. 893) paras 4–11.
897. *See* above, Chapter 3, D.
898. Hanns Prütting, 'ZPO § 287' in Thomas Rauscher and Wolfgang Krüger (eds), *Münchener Kommentar zur ZPO* (6th edn, C.H. Beck 2020) para. 3; *See*, however, Brinkmann (n. 360) 52, who argues that this does not amount to an actual reduction of the burden of proof. The standard of proof prescribes when the trier of fact may deem an assertion to be true. The term 'truth', however, can also apply to past or present circumstances, but not to hypothetical causalities. Thus, the better view is that secs 287 and 252 BGB do not affect the standard of proof as a material question, but rather the assessment of evidence as a procedural question, regarding which arbitral tribunals enjoy comprehensive liberties.
899. *See* for a comparison of the damage calculation in German and France in practice Redfern and others (n. 271) 330: 'While French judges for instance take a generous or rather pragmatic and realistic approach towards the measure of commercial damages for the global disruption of a party's business in case of breach of a contract by the other party, Austrian and German judges would be particularly meticulous such as, for example, requiring precise proof that the members of the accounting department had to spend 12 hours overtime this or that day.'
900. *See* sec. 287 (1): 'Should the issue of whether or not damages have occurred, and the amount of the damage or of the equivalent in money to be reimbursed, be in dispute among the parties, the court shall rule on this issue at its discretion and conviction, based on its evaluation of all circumstances. The court may decide at its discretion whether or not – and if so, in which scope – any taking of evidence should be ordered as applied for, or whether or not any experts should be involved to prepare a report. (...)'; *See* further sec. 252 BGB: 'The damage to be compensated for also comprises the lost profits. Those profits are considered lost that in the normal course of events or in the special circumstances, particularly due to the measures and precautions taken, could probably be expected.'
901. *BGH, Judgment of 23 November 2006* [2007] NJW-RR 569 [21].

difficulties. A prominent example is the so-called evidence of first appearance (*Anscheinsbeweis*). As will be demonstrated in more detail below, *Anscheinsbeweise* stipulate that courts or tribunals may have recourse to certain empirical principles (*Erfahrungssätze*) when determining the veracity of an assertion.[902] The application of an *Anscheinsbeweis*, however, does not modify the necessary degree of the court's conviction but merely affects the assessment of evidence. As it is a matter of procedural rather than substantive law, tribunals are not required (but may of course opt) to apply *Anscheinsbeweise*, even where German law governs the substance of the dispute.[903]

3.168 Lastly, in a small number of other cases, German law seems to increase the threshold of the relevant standard of proof by stating that a specific requirement of a provision must be overtly (*offenbar*) fulfilled.[904]

2 Standard of Proof in Common Law

3.169 By contrast to the civil law standard of proof, the common law rule (which remains largely uniform across the jurisdictions) emphasizes the balance of probabilities.

i Balance of Probabilities

3.170 As a consequence of the duality of the traditional common law of evidence, there are two main standards of proof, namely the civil standard and the criminal standard. Both standards have been developed by case law. In criminal proceedings, the prosecution must prove the case beyond a reasonable doubt.[905] In civil cases, however, the well-known balance of probabilities applies. This means that the standard of proof is met where an allegation is more likely to be true than to be false, i.e., where the probability exceeds the threshold of 50%.[906] In *Miller v Minister of Pensions*, it was said:

> That degree is well settled. It must carry a reasonable degree of probability, but not so high as is required in a criminal case. If the evidence is such that the tribunal can say: 'we think it more probable than not', the burden is discharged, but if the probabilities are equal, it is not.[907]

3.171 Other definitions emphasize the inherent connection between the standard of proof and the burden of proof:

902. *See* below, Chapter 3, E.II.2.
903. *See* below, Chapter 3, E.II.2.
904. *See, e.g.*, sec. 319 (1), 562a, 660 (1) BGB, cf. Prütting, 'ZPO § 286' (n. 239) para. 43.
905. Keane and McKeown (n. 290) 85 et seq.
906. Rosemary Pattenden, 'The Risk of Non-Persuasion in Civil Trials: The Case Against a Floating Standard of Proof' (1988) Civil Justice Quarterly 220, 220.
907. *Miller v Minister of Pensions* [1947] 62 All ER 372 373, 374; *see also* Keane and McKeown (n. 290) 87; Schweizer (n. 868) 426.

> If a legal rule requires a fact to be proved (a 'fact in issue'), a judge or jury must decide whether or not it happened. There is no room for a finding that it might have happened. The law operates a binary system in which the only values are 0 and 1. The fact either happened or it did not. If the tribunal is left in doubt, the doubt is resolved by a rule that one party or the other carries the burden of proof. If the party who bears the burden of proof fails to discharge it, a value of 0 is returned and the fact is treated as not having happened. If he does discharge it, a value of 1 is returned and the fact is treated as having happened.[908]

3.172 In other words, the party bearing the burden of proof is required to fulfil the standard of proof by producing evidence which renders said party's submission to be more probable than not. It is, accordingly, the opposing party's task to produce evidence that is apt to reduce the probability below the required threshold.

ii *Modifications*

3.173 While the general civil standard is settled, certain exceptions exist where courts might apply a higher threshold in civil cases, especially where the matter in dispute either has criminal connotations or is related to criminal offences. Nevertheless, it is found that the trier of fact must maintain a certain flexibility. The underlying principle is that the more serious an allegation is, the less probable it is that it has occurred.[909] In *Re H & Ors (minors)*, it was famously held that:

> [w]hen assessing the probabilities the court will have in mind as a factor, to whatever extent is appropriate in the particular case, that the more serious the allegation the less likely it is that the event occurred and, hence, the stronger should be the evidence before the court concludes that the allegation is established on the balance of probability.

In illustration of this thesis, the ruling goes on to explain that, for example:

> [f]raud is usually less likely than negligence [and] (...) [d]eliberate physical injury is usually less likely than accidental physical injury.

Accordingly:

> [b]uilt into the preponderance of probability standard is a generous degree of flexibility in respect of the seriousness of the allegation.[910]

3.174 Similarly, it was found in Fiona Trust & Holding Corporation Ors v Privalov Ors that:

908. *In re B (Children) (FC)* [2008] UKHL 35 [2].
909. Keane and McKeown (n. 290) 109.
910. *H & Ors (minors), Re* [2000] UKHL 16 [73, 74].

> where a claimant seeks to prove a case of dishonesty, its inherent improbability means that, even on the civil burden of proof, the evidence needed to prove it must be all the stronger.[911]

3.175 A further review of the above statements and examples, however, raises doubts about whether these amount to a true modification of the standard of proof, i.e., whether they modify the threshold that must be met in order to consider an allegation true. In particular, the cited cases do not affect the abstract rule that the standard of proof is met where an allegation is more probable than not. Rather, the above examples refer to specific allegations and specific sets of facts. In other words, even in a case of fraud or corruption, the trier of fact must find the respective allegation to be more probable than not. The difference is that when considering the specific facts, the court may consider that 'the more serious the allegation, the less likely it is that the event occurred'. This suggests that these modifications may also apply as part of the assessment of evidence,[912] where the tribunal is not required to apply any strict rules of evidence, rather than as part of the standard of proof, where the tribunal is bound by the applicable substantive law.

3 *Challenges of Comparing Different Standards of Proof*

3.176 The current discussion in international arbitration and its comparative approach reveals that it is inherently difficult to consolidate the different standards of proof.

3.177 As will be detailed in this section, issues arise on two levels in particular. First, the question is whether the common law and civil law standards of proof, as outlined above, are actually different in their essence. Second, and connected with this first issue, it is doubtful whether the standard of proof as an abstractly formulated rule actually bears a significant influence on the outcome of the dispute.

3.178 The first issue is that it is intrinsically difficult to quantify 'probability', especially because the term is used in a subjective sense. Similar difficulties, of course, arise when seeking to specify or measure the trier of fact's 'conviction'. This suggests that the differences between the standards of proof are only terminological, rather than material.[913] Both the tests for the standard of proof are formulated ambivalently and, naturally, do not serve as accurate measuring devices. This is especially true for the common law test of balance of probabilities.

3.179 The term 'probability' has either an objective, i.e., a statistic or numeric meaning, or, alternatively, a subjective (or inductive) meaning, i.e., one that is based on personal assessment rather than reliable statistics.[914] According to the frequency

---

911. *Fiona Trust & Holding Corporation Ors v Privalov Ors* (n. 615) paras 1438, 1439 with reference to; *Jafari-Fini v Skillglass Ltd* [2007] EWCA Civ 261 [73].
912. *See* below, Chapter 3, E.I.
913. Smith and Nadeau-Séguin (n. 868) 141–145; Brinkmann (n. 360) 85 et seq.; Brinkmann (n. 366) 876 et seq.; *see* however Alfter (n. 868) 163, who rejects this proposition.
914. Brinkmann (n. 360) 23.

theory, the 'objective probability' is defined as the 'frequency of a specific outcome in a long, or infinite, series of trials'.[915] The application of this 'objective probability test' thus requires that the trier of facts has statistical evidence available based on (i) a relevant number of cases with, (ii) an identical underlying set of facts, and (iii) a confirmed evidentiary result. However, this is usually not the case. Civil disputes are commonly singular events, rather than repeatable experimental setups.[916] Accordingly, only under rare circumstances might a tribunal actually have the chance to apply the standard of probability test in an objective sense. It follows that, in most cases, it is the subjective probability which becomes decisive.

3.180 Unlike the 'objective probability', the terms 'subjective' or 'inductive probability' are based on the trier of facts' conviction.[917] A judge or arbitrator who must assess whether allegation 'A' is subjectively more probable than allegation 'B' can only rely on his personal assessment of the specific sets of facts. Consequently, 'probability' in a subjective sense resembles (or equals) civil law standards which are based on the inner conviction of the trier of facts, as pointed out above.[918] This suggests that the differences between the standards of proof across the jurisdictions are merely terminological. It thus may not make a difference whether a trier of fact decides based on its inner conviction or, alternatively, on a (subjective) preponderance of evidence.[919]

3.181 Beyond that, as a second issue, problems arise not only with the abstractness of the rules but also with their application. In particular, the question is what threshold must be met for a tribunal to consider itself sufficiently convinced, or respectively, for the allegation to be 'more likely than not'. The tribunal in *Croatia v MOL Hungarian* addressed this issue in the context of the distinction between the standard of the balance of probabilities and its enhancement in case of serious allegations ('something more'):

> The quantification of that 'something more', however, is elusive. To say that something more means 67% certainty, or to give any such number, is fatuous. Even the notion of preponderance cannot seriously be thought of as 51%; law cases are not scientific activities where absolute truth is thought of as a litre or a kilo, and the judge or arbitrator records the weight or volume of evidence with the effect that a total of 501 centilitres or grammes justifies the conclusion that something is 'true enough'.[920]

915. M Redmayne, 'Objective Probability and the Assessment of Evidence' (2003) 2 Law, Probability and Risk 275, 278.
916. *Ibid.*; Brinkmann (n. 360) 24.
917. Brinkmann (n. 360) 38.
918. *Ibid.*
919. Note that the proposition of synchronized or at least similar standards of proof has however also been objected to, especially due to lack of (relevant) proof for the hypothesis, *see* Alfter (n. 868) 163 et seq. However, since it is suggested that tribunals can and should apply a transnational standard of proof, this question does not call for a final evaluation, *see* below Chapter 3, D.II.
920. *Republic of Croatia v MOL Hungarian Oil and Gas Company Plc, PCA Case No. 2014-15* (n. 869) para. 119.

3.182 Defining an abstract rule on the standard of proof thus seems to be an attempt to objectify the highly subjective process of assessing evidence and decision-making. Current research on cognitive psychology suggests that most decisions, including evaluations and judgments, are not taken rationally based on objectively comprehensible criteria, but are based on 'intuitive heuristics that often produce nonnormative judgments'.[921] Intuition is, 'to a large extent, a highly unconscious procedure of information processing'.[922] In other words, the idea of the arbitrator who first reviews the applicable standard of proof and, with this standard in mind, makes rational decisions on individual issues seems to be an ideal rather than the reality. Rather, a trier of fact will usually first makes its decisions through an intuitive, subjective process and, in a second step, seek to justify this decision intersubjectively by applying presumably objective standards (i.e., the standard of proof) and testing its results against the rule.

3.183 Even though it remains difficult to prove that the different standards of proof are only terminological, there are strong arguments for the assumption that the different approaches do overlap or at least converge to a large degree. This blurs the practical significance of the distinction.

II Transnational Standard of Proof

3.184 Against the backdrop of the fading differences between international standards of proof, one can observe a trend towards a transnational standard of proof, namely, one of a balance of probabilities (*1*). As under the standards analysed above, modifications may apply in individual cases where it is deemed appropriate to either lower or heighten the threshold (*2*). In practice, tribunals have wide discretion when selecting and adapting the appropriate standard of proof, as it is a matter of applying the law, which is not subject to judicial review (*3*).

1 Balance of Probabilities

3.185 Despite the difficulties of reconciling the different standards of proof, one can observe a strong tendency towards a transnational standard of proof in international arbitration, driven especially by published awards and legal commentary. As pointed out, the relevant arbitration laws, rules and soft laws provide little guidance.[923] Nonetheless, a certain best practice towards a transnational standard of proof, independent of the underlying substantive law, has emerged.

3.186 As stated by, for example, *O'Malley*, the 'standard predominantly applied is quite often the balance of probabilities test'.[924] Specifically, this standard 'generally calls for a claim to be upheld if the tribunal is convinced by the evidence that the claim

921. Eldar Shafir and Robyn A LeBoeuf, 'Rationality' [2002] Annual Review of Psychology 491, 494.
922. Tichý (n. 868) 288.
923. *See* above, Chapter 3, D.I.
924. O'Malley (n. 407) para. 7.27.

is more likely than not true'.[925] This suggests that the standard of proof in international arbitration can be located somewhere between the common law rule of preponderance of probability and the civil law test of conviction.

3.187 In *Redfern/Hunter*, it is stated that:

> [t]he degree of proof that must be achieved in practice before an international arbitral tribunal is not capable of precise definition, but it may be safely assumed that it is close to the test of the 'balance of probability' (that is, 'more likely than not'). This standard is to be distinguished from the concept of 'beyond all reasonable doubt' required, for example, in countries such as the United States and England to prove guilt in a criminal trial before a jury.[926]

3.188 Similarly, *Born* observed that tribunals usually have recourse to a '"balance of probabilities" or "more likely than not" standard'.[927]

3.189 The approach is confirmed by various awards. In *Croatia v MOL Hungarian*, for example, the ICSID tribunal held that:

> [i]t is generally accepted that in civil cases the balance of probabilities is an appropriate standard of proof.[928]

3.190 The same was also found by a VIAC tribunal in *Aperture Software GmbH v Avocent Huntsville Corp*. Here, the tribunal decided by majority vote that the balance of probabilities standard of proof applied, independent of the principles applicable under Austrian procedural law:

> In view of Article 599(1) ZPO, the Tribunal is of the opinion that the rules on evidence developed by Austrian law for civil procedures handled by Austrian Courts have no bearing on this arbitration: the standard of evidence required in arbitration procedures located in Austria is the commonly accepted principle of balance of probabilities.[929]

3.191 The ALI/UNIDROIT Principles suggest a slightly different approach, which is meant to reflect a 'synthesis between the common law and civil law standard'.[930] According to Principle 22.1 of the ALI/UNIDROIT, '[f]acts are considered proven when the court is reasonably convinced of their truth'.[931]

925. *Ibid.*
926. Blackaby and others (n. 14) 378, 379, however expressly citing English case law.
927. Born (n. 338) 2488.
928. *Republic of Croatia v MOL Hungarian Oil and Gas Company Plc, PCA Case No. 2014-15* (n. 869) para. 115.
929. *VIAC Case No. SCH-5196, Final Award 17 October 2013* (n. 869) para. 119.
930. Brinkmann (n. 366) 889.
931. *See* Antonio Gidi, 'Transnational Rules of Civil Procedure – Study LXXVI – Doc 6 – Report on the Second Session, Rome, 2 to 6 July 2001' 38'According to a member, we should have only one standard of proof. We should not refer to local law, because it would be useless. This standard should not be the preponderance of evidence. This formula is a consequence of the adversarial system, without a judge who could initiate additional evidence on the court's own motion. We should adopt an intermediate standard, because this project changes the adversary

3.192 It follows that the ALI/UNIDROIT Principles lean towards the continental European tradition, i.e., the standard of conviction, while stating that this is 'functionally the same' as the 'preponderance of the evidence' standard.[932] The standard of proof under the Principles 'is neither the truth nor an objective mathematical probability nor the absolute conviction of the truth'.[933] The drafters of the Principles consider the term 'reasonably convinced', despite its vagueness, to be the 'best possible formula'[934] to leave flexibility and room for the development of a transnational standard of proof.[935] In other words, the prerequisite of '"reasonable" also indicates that the degree of conviction required is not the same for all cases'.[936] Thus far, however, there is no known case in which a tribunal has taken recourse to this standard of reasonable conviction.

3.193 When analysing the above examples on the balance of probabilities, one has to bear two issues in mind. First, the cited commentators predominately stem from common law jurisdictions, and thus analyse the issue against a particular background, presumably (largely) inspired by arbitrations with some connection to common law legal systems. The expressed views might, therefore, not necessarily be fully representative of arbitration outside of the common law (-dominated) legal sphere. Second, the development of a transnational standard of preponderance of probability is also driven by investment arbitration case law.[937] Usually, in investment arbitration, no specific domestic law applies, which is why no specific domestic standard of proof can be referred to. In the absence thereof, tribunals may be tempted to apply the standards of proof that they are familiar with.

3.194 Nevertheless, even though the standard of proof is, as pointed out above, frequently considered to derive from the *lex causae*,[938] the conducted survey confirms that the international arbitration community shows a trend towards applying a uniform standard of proof, independent of the applicable substantive law.

2 *Modifications*

3.195 In addition to the balance of probabilities test, there are certain modifications of the standard that tribunals frequently apply.

principle, in allowing the court to take evidence on its own motion. The proposed text is not enough to express that there is a connection of the possibility of the court to take evidence on its own motion, but we should say something about this.'

932. American Law Institute (ALI) and UNIDROIT (n. 203) para. P-21B.
933. Brinkmann (n. 366) 889.
934. Gidi (n. 931) 38.
935. *See* Brinkmann (n. 360) 890.
936. *See ibid.*
937. Sourgens, Duggal and Laird (n. 442) para. 5.09: 'The most common standard of proof in investor-state arbitration is this balance of probabilities or preponderance of evidence standard.'
938. Tichý (n. 868) 298 et seq.; Skontzos (n. 618) 577; Sachs and Niedermaier (n. 874) 133; Smith and Nadeau-Séguin (n. 868) 145.

3.196 To begin with, it is advocated that 'the more startling the proposition' is, the higher the threshold of evidence for the 'proposition to be fully established'.[939] Thus, in line with the traditional common law approach, especially in cases involving allegations of bribery, fraud or corruption, tribunals at times require evidence with a certain weight.[940] In *Karkey Karadeniz Elektrik Uretim v Pakistan*, for example, the Tribunal held that:

> the seriousness of the accusation of corruption in the present case, including the fact that it involves officials at the highest level of the Pakistani Government at the time, requires clear and convincing evidence. There is indeed a large consensus among international tribunals regarding the need for a high standard of proof of corruption.[941]

3.197 However, unlike the balance of probabilities standard, its modifications are less settled.[942] In *Croatia v MOL Hungarian*, for example, the tribunal found that:

> international tribunals and scholars have made diverging pronouncements with respect to the burden of proof to be applied to allegations of corruption.[943]
>
> In sum, no consensus has as yet emerged as to how to reconcile these conceptual approaches in theory.[944]

3.198 The ruling, based on an extensive survey of current prevalent practice, indicates that, while there is a certain tendency towards the application of a heightened standard in cases of criminal conduct, it may not amount to a general and undisputed principle.

3.199 Beyond that, in cases where it is likely that an event occurred, although access to evidence is limited, tribunals have also been known to lower the general standard of proof. This has applied particularly in expropriation cases involving victims of Nazi persecution, where tribunals had recourse to a 'relaxed standard of proof' (the so-called plausible standard).[945]

3.200 Similarly, it is also common practice to facilitate the quantification of damages by lowering the standard, thus allowing for certain estimations of the tribunal. As a tribunal found in an ICC proceeding, due to the difficulties of exactly quantifying the sum to be awarded:

> it appears equitable to fix them at about 50% and to reduce the damage claimed under this head by the plaintiff.[946]

939. Blackaby and others (n. 14) 379; similarly Waincymer (n. 343) para. 10.4.3.
940. Smith and Nadeau-Séguin (n. 868) 150.
941. *Karkey Karadeniz Elektrik Uretim A.S. v Islamic Republic of Pakistan, ICSID ARB/13/1* (n. 869) para. 492.
942. Smith and Nadeau-Séguin (n. 868) 150, 151.
943. *Republic of Croatia v MOL Hungarian Oil and Gas Company Plc, PCA Case No. 2014-15* (n. 869) para. 116.
944. *Ibid.*, 118.
945. Waincymer (n. 343) 770, 771.
946. Unpublished, cited after Smith and Nadeau-Séguin (n. 868) 151.

Nonetheless, while approximations are inevitable when assessing damages,[947] the tribunal must always base its estimation on tangible fact and consider all relevant evidence presented by the parties.[948] It must further present its reasoned considerations for the findings within the final award.[949]

3.201 The above examples show that, while it may be challenging to formulate an abstract principle regarding modifications to the standard of proof, international tribunals embrace their powers to define and adapt an appropriate standard of proof, largely independent of the underlying substantive law.

3 *Practical Considerations*

3.202 The above examples confirm that there is a strong tendency towards a transnational standard of proof independent of the substantive law. Overall, arbitral tribunals enjoy the freedom to apply the above standards where they consider them appropriate. As has been pointed out, the standard of proof, as well as modifications thereof, is an issue in the 'grey zone' between substantive and procedural law. Since it is the tribunal's immanent task to apply the law and thus define the material scope thereof, the decision of whether or not the standard of proof forms part of the applicable substantive law is left to the tribunal. Consequently, while the tribunal must respect the parties' substantive choice of law clause, it is within the tribunal's power and responsibility to decide whether this also covers the standard of proof. Within a subsequent enforcement or annulment proceeding, state courts are not entitled to undertake a *révision au fond* and are, therefore, not in a position to review the tribunal's qualification of the issue.

3.203 Moreover, the principle of free assessment of evidence lies at the core of the tribunal's power to control evidence and grants it the responsibility to determine the weight or value of the evidence as it deems appropriate. That is, where the tribunal finds that a specific event is inherently less likely to occur, it is free to consider this specific likelihood when assessing evidence, independent of the (presumably) applicable standard of proof.

3.204 This was confirmed, for example, by the Higher Regional Court of Frankfurt, with a similar reasoning which emphasized the tribunal's control over evidence procedures. After a party challenged an award, relying (*inter alia*) on a presumably 'wrong' application of the standard of proof, the court rejected the challenge, stating:

> Without infringing the prohibition of a révision au fond in the proceedings for a declaration of enforceability, it cannot be examined whether the arbitral tribunal was right to assume, on the basis of the available evidence, (...), that a determination of probability corresponding to reduced requirements for the standard of

947. *Himpurna California Energy Ltd v PT (Persero) Perusahaan Listruik Negara, Ad-Hoc Award of 4 May 1999* [2000] XXV Ybk Comm Arb 13 [376].
948. *See* below, Chapter 3, E.I.1.
949. *See* below, Chapter 3, E.I.4.

> proof could be made. The assessment of evidence by the arbitral tribunal in proceedings for a declaration of enforceability cannot, in principle, be replaced by the state court's own assessment of evidence.[950]

3.205 On a practical note, the tribunal may, for reasons of legal certainty, consider including a specific provision on the standard of proof in the first procedural order.

III Conclusion

3.206 The standard of proof remains one of the most disputed topics in international arbitration. This is particularly true because many commentators consider it to be subject to the applicable substantive law. The substantive laws, however, reveal a notable divide between common law and civil law countries: while common law courts usually apply a balance of probability test, civil law courts mostly decide based on their inner conviction. The question remains, however, whether these differences actually influence the outcome, or whether they are merely terminological.

3.207 Nevertheless, even though it is frequently argued that the standard of proof is a matter of substantive law and thus governed by the *lex causae*,[951] there is also a strong trend to apply a transnational standard of proof, independent of the *lex causae*, namely the standard of the balance of probabilities. Doing so lies within the tribunal's discretion. In any case, for the sake of legal certainty, tribunals are encouraged to clarify the applicable standard of proof at the outset of the proceeding as part of the first procedural order.

E ASSESSMENT AND FACILITATIONS OF EVIDENCE

3.208 In both common law and civil law traditions, domestic procedural codes impose (varyingly) strict rules on the assessment of evidence. The common law of evidence has a lengthy history and was designed to accommodate fact-finding procedures involving jurors or lay justices.[952] That is, contrary to what one might suspect, the common law of evidence does not primarily aim at facilitating the taking of evidence. Rather, one of its main purposes is to exclude means of evidence which laypersons may over- or underestimate.[953] In criminal proceedings, for example, character evidence (such as prior convictions) is inadmissible, since a juror might attribute more probative value to it than a professional judge.[954]

950. *OLG Frankfurt a. M., Order of 2 February 2017* (n. 255) para. 51.
951. Tichý (n. 868) 298 et seq.; Skontzos (n. 618) 577; Sachs and Niedermaier (n. 874) 133; Smith and Nadeau-Séguin (n. 868) 145.
952. Keane and McKeown (n. 290) 3.
953. *Ibid.*, 3 et seq.; *see also* above Chapter 3, C.III.
954. *Ibid.*, 3.

3.209 Other jurisdictions, such as Germany, expressly promote the principle of free assessment of evidence,[955] while still (somewhat paradoxically) obliging the courts to adhere to a considerable number of different evidentiary rules. For example, in German civil procedure, the use of digital documents is highly restricted (and in practice nearly impossible),[956] and the parties' expert reports bear no evidentiary quality.[957]

3.210 As will be shown below, there is no room for these overly formalistic approaches in international arbitration. In line with the tribunal's power to determine admissibility,[958] the principle of free assessment of evidence grants the tribunal wide discretion to analyse the proof as it deems appropriate (*I*). When assessing evidence, tribunals frequently have recourse to certain facilitations, such as circumstantial evidence, *prima facie evidence* and adverse inferences (*II*).

I The Principle of Free Assessment of Evidence

3.211 In international arbitration, it is the tribunal's immanent task to assess and weigh the evidence,[959] independent of whether any strict rules of evidence are applied.

3.212 Many arbitration laws and rules expressly stipulate the tribunal's power of free assessment of evidence, which amounts to a general and transnational principle. The Model Law, for example, states in Article 19 (2) Second Sentence that the 'power conferred upon the arbitral tribunal includes the power to determine the admissibility, relevance, materiality and weight of any evidence'. In sometimes varying language, the same is confirmed by other national arbitration laws, such as section 1042(4) Second Sentence of the ZPO[960] and Article 25 (2) Second Sentence of the Spanish Arbitration Act[961]. Similar provisions can be found in different arbitration rules, such as Article 27.4 of the UNCITRAL Rules,[962] Article 31.1 SCC Rules[963], Article 22.7 ICDR Rules,[964]

955. Section 286 (1) ZPO: '(1) The court is to decide, at its discretion and conviction, and taking account of the entire content of the hearings and the results obtained by evidence being taken, if any, whether an allegation as to fact is to be deemed true or untrue. The judgment is to set out the reasons informing the conviction of the judges.'
956. *See* above, Chapter 3, B.III.
957. *See* above, Chapter 3, B.II.
958. *See* above, Chapter 3, C.
959. O'Malley (n. 407) 7.12.
960. Section 1042(4) Second Sentence ZPO: 'The arbitral tribunal is authorised to decide on the admissibility of the taking of evidence, to so take evidence, and to assess the results at its sole discretion.'
961. Article 25 (2) Second Sentence of the Spanish Arbitration Act: 'Esta potestad de los árbitros comprende la de decidir sobre admisibilidad, pertinencia y utilidad de las pruebas, sobre su práctica, incluso de oficio, y sobre su valoración.'
962. Article 27.4 UNCITRAL Rules: 'The arbitral tribunal shall determine the admissibility, relevance, materiality and weight of the evidence offered.'
963. Article 31.1 SCC Rules: 'The admissibility, relevance, materiality and weight of evidence shall be for the Arbitral Tribunal to determine.'
964. Article 22.7 ICDR Rules: 'The tribunal shall determine the admissibility, relevance, materiality, and weight of the evidence.'

Article 22.2 HKIAC Rules,[965] Article 27.4 PCA Rules.[966] Article 22.1 (vi) of the LCIA Rules (with a wording resembling Article 34 (1), (2) (f) English Arbitration Act)[967] states that the tribunal may

> (...) decide whether or not to apply any strict rules of evidence (or any other rules) as to the admissibility, relevance or weight of any material tendered by a party on any issue of fact or expert opinion (...).

3.213 Other arbitration laws[968] or rules[969] do not contain any specific rules on the assessment of evidence, thus, in the absence of stipulations to the contrary, leaving the assessment of evidence to the general discretion of the tribunal.

3.214 The principle of free assessment is further confirmed by Article 9.1 of the IBA Rules.[970] The Prague Rules, however, do not expressly address the issue. Yet, the tribunal's powers to freely assess evidence are implied by Article 2 (4) (e) (iv), according to which the tribunal, *inter alia,* shall give its preliminary views on the 'weight (...) of evidence submitted by the parties'. ALI/UNIDROIT Principle 16.6 and Rule 28.2 put this into more precise terms, stating that the trier of fact 'should make free evaluation of the evidence and attach no unjustified significance to evidence according to its type or source'.

3.215 That being said, the tribunal's power of free assessment amounts to a transnational principle which states that the tribunal may examine and draw inferences from the evidence as it deems appropriate. When assessing the evidence submitted, the tribunal may also consider the course and development of the proceeding, the conduct of the parties, as well as all other impressions it may draw inferences from.[971] In particular, the tribunal may freely weigh the evidence as it deems appropriate (*1*), without being bound by any rules on the value of different means of evidence (*2*) or other domestic laws of evidence (*3*). To compensate for the tribunal's considerable power, it is required to give reasons for its findings on the facts in the award (*4*).

965. Article 22.2 HKIAC Rules: 'The arbitral tribunal shall determine the admissibility, relevance, materiality and weight of the evidence, including whether to apply strict rules of evidence.'
966. Article 27.4 PCA Rules: 'The arbitral tribunal shall determine the admissibility, relevance, materiality and weight of the evidence offered.'
967. Article 34 (1), (2) (f) English Arbitration Act: 'It shall be for the tribunal to decide all procedural and evidential matters, subject to the right of the parties to agree any matter. Procedural and evidential matters include (...) whether to apply strict rules of evidence (or any other rules) as to the admissibility, relevance or weight of any material (oral, written or other) sought to be tendered on any matters of fact or opinion, and the time, manner and form in which such material should be exchanged and presented (...).'
968. *See, inter alia,* the arbitration acts of the US and Brazil.
969. *See, inter alia,* the ICC Rules, Vienna Rules and SCAI Rules.
970. Article 9.1 IBA Rules: 'The Arbitral Tribunal shall determine the admissibility, relevance, materiality and weight of evidence.' *See* for exceptions Art. 9.1 and 9.2 IBA Rules.
971. *See* below on adverse inferences, Chapter 3, E.II.3.

1 Weight of Evidence

3.216 The principle of the free assessment of evidence grants the tribunal wide freedom, but of course, also stipulates the duty to examine and weigh relevant evidence, which must be reflected in the award accordingly.[972]

3.217 To weigh the evidence means to assess whether it has a 'persuasive effect on the arbitrator's mind',[973] i.e., to determine whether the content of the evidence renders a factual assertion to be more or less likely. Accordingly, the term 'weight of evidence' defines the cogency or the probative worth of evidence in relation to the facts in issue.[974] In other words: assessing evidence means testing it against the applicable standard of proof in order to verify whether the threshold is met. The tribunal is free in assessing evidence and its findings may not be reviewed during annulment and enforcement procedures.[975] While there are no hard and fast rules or tests for the operative procedure, logically the assessment requires three steps, which determine whether the evidence in question is (i) relevant, (ii) credible and (iii) sufficient.[976]

3.218 As detailed above, evidence is relevant if it renders a factual allegation to be more likely.[977] The principle of free assessment of evidence states that it is the tribunal's task to determine relevance. If a witness, for example, testifies that he or she has no independent knowledge of the issue in dispute, the tribunal is not able to draw any conclusions from the testimony and shall therefore discard it as irrelevant.[978]

3.219 Subsequently, and only if the evidence proves to be relevant, the tribunal must examine whether it is credible, i.e., reliable.[979] Accordingly, it shall, for instance, determine whether a witness is to be believed, an expert is qualified and has correctly examined the issue in question, or whether a document is authentic. The tribunal is free to make its observations and draw conclusions under due consideration of all relevant circumstances. Nonetheless, it can be observed that tribunals frequently have recourse to certain empirical values and principles. For instance, documents are

972. *See* on the tribunal's duty to give reasons below Chapter 3, E.I.3.
973. Pilkov (n. 422) 152, 153 et seq.; *see* for the weight of evidence under English law Keane and McKeown (n. 290) 33 et seq.; *see* for German law Prütting, *Gegenwartsprobleme Der Beweislast* (n. 603) 58; Greger (n. 870) 8.
974. *See* for the terminology in England and Wales: Keane and McKeown (n. 290) 33.
975. *OLG Frankfurt a. M., Order of 2 February 2017* (n. 255) para. 51: 'Without infringing the prohibition of a révision au fond in the proceedings for a declaration of enforceability, it cannot be examined whether the arbitral tribunal was right to assume, on the basis of the available evidence, (…), that a determination of probability corresponding to the reduced requirements for the standard of proof could be made. The assessment of evidence by the arbitral tribunal in proceedings for a declaration of enforceability cannot, in principle, be replaced by the state court's own assessment of evidence because of the prohibition of a revision of the fund.' (Translation by the author).
976. Pilkov (n. 422) 147–154.
977. *See* above, Chapter 2, C.III.1.a.iii. and iv; Chapter 3, C.II.
978. If such testimony, however, contradicts the content of the previously submitted written witness statement, the tribunal may of course draw inferences from the inconsistency of the party's submissions.
979. Pilkov (n. 422) 152, 153.

presumed to be authentic unless the opposite is proven.[980] Moreover, unlike in some domestic jurisdictions, there is no bias against party witnesses or witnesses closely related to one of the parties.[981]

3.220 Lastly, if the evidence is relevant and appears reliable, it is the tribunal's task to analyse whether it is sufficient to meet the standard of proof,[982] i.e., whether it renders the allegation in dispute to be more probable or not, or, respectively, reasonably convincing.[983] Here, too, the tribunal is not bound by any fixed rules. As will be detailed in the following section, when testing the sufficiency, the tribunal may, for example, be required to decide whether an utterly uncorroborated witness statement could be the basis for a decision or a whether a subsequently (rather than contemporaneously) drafted document is likely to prove the issue in question.

2 No Hierarchy of Means of Evidence

3.221 There are no hard and fast rules as to the hierarchy of different kinds of evidence. That is, all evidence is generally considered equally valuable, independent of whether it is witness evidence, documentary evidence or expert evidence. This differs from the common practice in domestic litigation, where, in certain civil law countries, contemporaneous documents are perhaps considered to be the most valuable, whereas, in common law litigation, there is a certain tendency to prefer oral testimony that can be tested and cross-examined during a hearing.[984]

3.222 Nonetheless, there are also certain observable tendencies in the international arbitration practice. While not amounting to a general principle, some tribunals have considered contemporaneous writings 'as the more reliable form of evidence'.[985]

3.223 Moreover, there is a tendency to reject witness testimonies if they are utterly and inexplicably uncorroborated by other means of evidence. As was held in the Dissenting and Concurring Opinion of Assadollah Noori in *TME International, Inc v The Government of the Islamic Republic of Iran*:

> International fora will consider (...) oral evidence only in so far as it finds corroboration in the documentary evidence dating from the time concerned.[986]

980. *See* above, Chapter 3, B.III.
981. O'Malley (n. 407) para. 7.13 (x).
982. Pilkov (n. 422) 153.
983. *See* above, Chapter 3, D.
984. Khodykin, Mulcahy and Fletcher (n. 803) para. 7.142; Groz (n. 803).
985. As stated in the first edition of O'Malley (n. 804) para. 7.11.
986. *TME International, Inc v The Government of the Islamic Republic of Iran, National Iranian Oil Company and others, IUSCT Case No 357 (473-357-1)* Dissenting and Concurring Opinion of Assadollah Noori of 23 April 1990 [27] with reference to the following authorities in Fn. 22: '*See*: The Kronprins Gustaf Adolf and the Pacific Case (1932), U.S. Department of State, Arbitration between United States and Sweden under Special Agreement of December 17, 1930, Arbitration Decisions and Records of Proceedings: Arbitration Series No. 5, Part 6 (Washington, D.C., 1932). In the Murphy Case, the U.S.-Chilean Mixed Commission (1892) regarded affidavits as constituting not evidence per se, but rather as collateral and circumstantial elements (secondary evidence) which could be relied upon to support findings based upon

3.224 The ICSID tribunal in *Vestey Group Ltd. v Bolivarian Republic of Venezuela* came to a similar conclusion. In the final award, the tribunal rejected the witness statement by the former minister Juan Carlos Loyo, who had testified to have made vital representations to the claimant's proxies via telephone. The tribunal, however, found that this allegation 'without any corroboration' appeared 'insufficient'.[987] In *Continental Transfert Technique Ltd. v Federal Government of Nigeria*, the ad hoc tribunal denied the probative value of a key witness statement based on 'the inconsistencies in [the witness statement] and the lack of corroboration'.[988] Similar approaches have been adopted by the Iran US Claim Tribunal (IUSCT)[989] and also in the ambit of commercial arbitration.[990]

3.225 Nevertheless, and importantly, the principle of free assessment of evidence leaves the decision in any particular procedural situation to the tribunal. If a tribunal, after the examination of the witness, comes to the conclusion that the testimony was sound and credible, it may very well rely solely thereon, despite the lack of corroboration.

3.226 Accordingly, it was found that even where documentary evidence clearly contradicts a witnesses' testimony, the tribunal is not required to automatically disregard the testimony. In *Plama Consortium v Bulgaria*, the tribunal noted that while the witness's evidence was 'materially inconsistent with parts of that documentation', the fact remained that he had:

> testified under cross-examination before the Tribunal at the September Hearing; his own testimony remained unequivocal on the relevant issues; and on the existing materials, the Tribunal would not wish to reject his evidence as false at this stage of the proceedings.[991]

---

other, solid evidence. In that same case, the Commission ruled: '[W]e must (...) take them [affidavits] into consideration not as evidence, but only as elements which in certain cases may contribute to a limited extent, collateral or secondary, to confirm or strengthen a conviction appearing to be based on proof of a more conclusive character.' Minutes of Proceedings 123, 127 (1894). *See also* 3 Moore, Arbitration 2262. The U.S.-German Mixed Claims Commission (1922) dismissed the claims in both the Hire Case and the Gillenwater Case, since they were based on uncorroborated affidavits or because other witnesses gave testimony against the claims. (Administrative Decisions and Opinions [1926] pp. 648, 798–801). In the Corfu Channel Case, the International Court of Justice ruled that 'personal knowledge [is] not sufficient to prove' a claim (ICJ Reports, 16–17, 68–69).'

987. *Vestey Group Ltd. v Bolivarian Republic of Venezuela, ICSID ARB/06/4* (n. 672) paras 314, 315.
988. *Continental Transfert Technique Ltd v Federal Government of Nigeria, Ad Hoc Final Award of 14 August 2008* Arbitrator Intelligence Materials 125.
989. *See Robert R Schott v Islamic Republic of Iran, Ministry of Mines and Industries of Iran and others, IUSCT Case No 268 (474-268-1)* Award of 14 March 1990 [41, 57]; *Dadras International v The Islamic Republic of Iran, Kan Consulting Engineers and others, IUSCT Case No 214 (578-214-3)* Award of 25 February 1997 [33–39].
990. Cf., *inter alia, Scantop Enterprises Co v Winplus Co, ICDR Case No 50 155 T 00530 11, Interim Award of 4 April 2014* Arbitrator Intelligence Materials 16, 17: 'The tribunal rejected financial information provided by the Claimant's accountant. It found that the evidence was completely unacceptable as evidence due to its lack of independent corroboration.'
991. *Plama Consortium Limited v Republic of Bulgaria, ICSID ARB/03/24* Decision on Jurisdiction of 8 February 2005 [178].

3.227 This ruling indicatively shows the tribunal's broad freedom and discretion to decide on a case-by-case basis under due consideration of all circumstances, unfettered by any strict evidentiary principles or domestic rules.

3 *No Recourse to Domestic Rules of Evidence*

3.228 Importantly, as has, *inter alia,* been addressed in the above section on the admission of evidence,[992] domestic laws of evidence do not apply in international arbitration. As has been pointed out above, national jurisdictions provide many different rules that courts must adhere to when determining the reliability, credibility and sufficiency of evidence. For example, since the sixteenth century,[993] there has historically been an adverse attitude towards hearsay evidence in common law, especially as it lacks directness of perception and cannot readily be tested by cross-examination.[994] An international arbitral tribunal is not bound by any rule to this effect and could even decide a case based exclusively on hearsay, if it is sufficiently convincing. Similarly, a tribunal may also accept electronic documents into evidence, even where these do not reflect a 'qualified electronic signature' as required under German law.[995]

3.229 By contrast, there are some formal substantive requirements that directly affect the material validity of declarations. In particular, the written form requirement may be part of the substantive law and, to that extent, must be adhered to.[996] If a contract lacks the proper form, this is a matter of the *lex causae,* rather than a question of the assessment of evidence.

4 *Duty to Give Reasons*

3.230 Lastly, as a complement to the tribunal's broad powers to weigh evidence, it is subject to the duty to give reasons for its findings. Nearly forty years ago, in 1985, *Carbonneau* noted that it was the:

> prevalent practice (…) to render international arbitral awards without explaining the reasons by which the decision was reached.[997]

992. *See* above, Chapter 3, C.
993. Before then, hearsay was considered admissible and was only occasionally excluded. For an overview, *see* John H Wigmore, 'The History of the Hearsay Rule' (1904) 17 Harvard Law Review 437.
994. Keane and McKeown (n. 290) 350; Note that in civil proceedings, the hearsay rule has been virtually abolished, *see, inter alia, Post Office Counters Ltd v Mahida* (n. 854) 24.
995. *See* above, Chapter 3, B.III.
996. Cf. the considerations referring to the principle of free assessment under the ALI/UNIDROIT Principles, American Law Institute (ALI) and UNIDROIT (n. 203) para. P-16G.
997. Thomas E Carbonneau, 'Rendering Arbitral Awards with Reasons: The Elaboration of Common Law of International Transactions' (1985) 23 Columbia Journal of Transnational Law 579, 581.

3.231 Nowadays, the practice of rendering unreasoned awards, which is rooted in the English common law tradition,[998] has been virtually abolished in international proceedings.

3.232 A successful party is usually content with the operative part of the award, based on which it can enforce or protect its rights. The defeated party, however, has an intrinsic interest in the reasons of the award in order to assure itself that the tribunal fully heard and appreciated its submissions and took all relevant aspects into account. The text of the arbitral award furthers serves as the main basis for any enforcement or annulment proceedings and will be examined (by the national courts in particular) for public policy violations. Accordingly, giving reasons 'is a salutary discipline to all whose judgments may adversely affect their fellow citizens'.[999]

3.233 A reasoned award not only allows for external verification, but drafting it also offers a measure of self-review, as it 'concentrates the mind'[1000] of the arbitrator. It is, in fact, frequently the very act of formulating a decision that obliges the arbitrator to reflect on whether the ruling is correct and justifiable and whether the reasons are sound.[1001] That is, reasoned awards enhance the quality as well as 'the legitimacy of the arbitral process in the eyes of the arbitrators, the parties and the public, including national courts'.[1002]

3.234 Therefore, in modern arbitration, while a tribunal is free in the assessment of evidence, as a general and transnational principle, it must give reasons for its decision. This is confirmed by the Model Law, as well as (*inter alia*) the arbitration laws of Germany,[1003] England,[1004] Brazil,[1005] Switzerland,[1006] Austria[1007] and Italy.[1008] Provisions to this effect can also be found in many arbitration rules, such as the UNCITRAL

998. Carbonneau (n. 997): '[T]he writ procedure provided for having an arbitral award reviewed on the merits by a court for an error of law. To avoid such review, it became commonplace for English arbitral tribunals to render awards without providing the underlying reasons.'
999. Coleman v Dunlop Ltd, 26 November 1997, unreported, cited after HL Ho, 'The Judicial Duty to Give Reasons' (2000) 20 Legal Studies 42, 48.
1000. *Tramountana Armadora SA v Atlantic Shipping Company SA (The Vorros)* [1978] 2 All ER 870 [872].
1001. *See* Mathilde Cohen, 'When Judges Have Reasons Not to Give Reasons: A Comparative Law Approach' (2015) 72 Washington and Lee Law Review 483, 504–512.
1002. SI Strong, 'Reasoned Awards in International Commercial Arbitration' (*Kluwer Arbitration Blog*, 19 February 2016).
1003. Section 1054 (2) ZPO: 'The reasons for the arbitration award are to be provided unless the parties to the dispute have agreed that no reasons need be provided, or unless the parties have agreed on the wording of the arbitration award in the sense as defined by section.'
1004. Article 52 (4) English Arbitration Act: 'The award shall contain the reasons for the award unless it is an agreed award or the parties have agreed to dispense with reasons.'
1005. Article 26 Brazilian Arbitration Act: 'The arbitral award must contain: I – A report including the names of the parties and a summary of the dispute; II – The grounds of the decision with due analysis of factual and legal issues (…).'
1006. Article 189 (2) Second Sentence PILA: 'The award shall be made in writing, with reasons, dated and signed.'
1007. Section 606 (2) Austrian Code of Civil Procedure: 'Unless the parties have agreed otherwise, the award shall state the reasons upon which it is based.'
1008. Section 823 (5) Italian Code of Civil Procedure: 'The award must contain (...) a brief statement of the reasons.'

Rules,[1009] ICC Rules,[1010] DIS Rules,[1011] LCIA Rules (2020),[1012] SCC Rules,[1013] Vienna Rules,[1014] ICDR Rules,[1015] HKIAC Rules,[1016] SCAI Rules,[1017] PCA Rules[1018] and ICSID Rules.[1019] Moreover, according to ALI/UNIDROIT Principle 23.2, the award should 'be accompanied by a reasoned explanation of the essential factual, legal, and evidentiary basis of the decision'.

3.235 As an exception to this transnational principle, unreasoned awards are still customary in domestic arbitration in the United States. According to R-46 of the AAA Rules:

> [t]he arbitrator need not render a reasoned award unless the parties request such an award in writing prior to appointment of the arbitrator or unless the arbitrator determines that a reasoned award is appropriate.

3.236 This rule may explain why the AAA at times seems to struggle with the prejudice that AAA tribunals have the tendency to 'split the baby'.[1020]

3.237 The question remains what level of detail is required? The approach across the jurisdictions does vary to a certain degree. In Australia, for example, in *Bremer Handelsgesellschaft mbH v Westzucker GmbH (No 2)*, it was held that:

1009. Article 34.3 UNCITRAL Rules: 'The arbitral tribunal shall state the reasons upon which the award is based, unless the parties have agreed that no reasons are to be given.'
1010. Article 32.2 ICC Rules: 'The award shall state the reasons upon which it is based.'
1011. Article 39.1 (ii) DIS Rules: 'Each arbitral award shall be made in writing and shall state:

> the arbitral tribunal's decision and the reasons upon which it is based, unless the parties have agreed that reasons need not be given or the award is by consent pursuant to Article 41 (...).'

1012. Article 26.2 First Sentence LCIA Rules: 'The Arbitral Tribunal shall make any award in writing and, unless all parties agree in writing otherwise, shall state the reasons upon which such award is based.'
1013. Article 42.1 SCC Rules: 'The Arbitral Tribunal shall make its award in writing, and, unless otherwise agreed by the parties, shall state the reasons upon which the award is based.'
1014. Article 36.1 Vienna Rules: 'Awards shall be in writing. Awards shall state the reasons on which they are based unless all parties have agreed in writing or in the oral hearing that the award may exclude the reasons.'
1015. Article 33.1 Fifth Sentence ICDR Rules: 'The tribunal shall state the reasons upon which an award is based, unless the parties have agreed that no reasons need be given.'
1016. Article 35.4 HKIAC Rules: 'An award shall state the reasons upon which it is based unless the parties have agreed that no reasons are to be given.'
1017. Article 32.3 SCAI Rules: 'The arbitral tribunal shall state the reasons upon which the award is based, unless the parties have agreed that no reasons are to be given.'
1018. Article 34.3 PCA Rules: 'The arbitral tribunal shall state the reasons upon which the award is based, unless the parties have agreed that no reasons are to be given.'
1019. Article 47 ICSID Rules: '(1) The award shall be in writing and shall contain: (...) (g) a statement of the facts as found by the Tribunal; (h) the submissions of the parties; (i) the decision of the Tribunal on every question submitted to it, together with the reasons upon which the decision is based (...).'
1020. Ryan Boyle and Susan D Lewin, 'ADR Does Not Mean Splitting the Baby' [2019] Corporate Counsel Business Journal.

> [a]ll that is necessary is that the arbitrators should set out what, on their view of the evidence, did or did not happen and should explain succinctly why, in the light of what happened, they have reached their decision and what that decision is.[1021]

3.238 In Germany, where the procedural law provides strict thresholds for reasoning domestic sentences,[1022] the requirements applicable to awards are likewise stricter. Yet, while the tribunal must fully and completely consider the parties' submissions, it is not required to address every argument, especially those it does not deem relevant. As the Federal Court of Justice held:

> An infringement of Article 103 (1) of the Basic Law [i.e. the right to be heard] requires that special circumstances in the individual case make it clear that the factual submissions of a party were either not taken into account at all or were not considered in the decision. If the [tribunal] does not address in its reasons for the decision the essential core of a party's factual submission on an issue that is of central importance to the proceedings, this indicates that the submission was not taken into account, unless, in the court's legal opinion, it was irrelevant or obviously unsubstantiated. In contrast, the fundamental procedural right to a fair hearing does not oblige the [tribunal] to deal with a party's submissions in the way the party itself considers correct.[1023]

3.239 If it becomes apparent that a tribunal has not duly and fully taken into account a party's pleading and evidence, this amounts to a violation of the right to be heard, thus rendering the award unenforceable.[1024] Similar decisions have been made by domestic courts in other jurisdictions. In *Billiton*, the Victorian court of appeal set aside an award due to insufficient reasoning.[1025]

3.240 Due to the (slightly) diverging approaches on the required level of reasoning, it remains challenging to formulate a universal standard. In light of the vital significance of reasoned decisions to the parties' right to be heard, it is submitted that awards must always reflect (i) the parties, (ii) the procedural history, (iii) relevant submissions of facts and evidence, (iv) prayers for relief as well as (v) all decisions on material issues in dispute. Further, the tribunal must also address all (vi) relevant and material evidence which the parties have submitted, (vii) reasons for not admitting evidence (at least in dubious cases), and lastly, (viii) the assessment of evidence.

3.241 In any case, unreasoned awards are only acceptable if expressly permitted by the arbitration rules or where the parties have given their consent. Otherwise, careful reasoning is essential, both in the interest of the losing party and quality assurance.

1021. *Bremer Handelsgesellschaft mbH v Westzucker GmbH (No 2)* [1981] 2 Lloyd's Rep 130 [132, 133].
1022. Cf. sec. 313 ZPO.
1023. *BGH, Order of 21 April 2016* [2016] SchiedsVZ 339 [22, 23], translation by the author. Note, however that the award is not required to reflect every single argument brought forward.
1024. *Ibid.*
1025. *Oil Basins Ltd v BHP Billiton Ltd* (2007) 18 VR 346, cited after Peter Gillies and Niloufer Selvadurai, 'Reasoned Awards: How Extensive Must the Reasoning Be?' (2008) 74 Arbitration 125, 128 et seq.

II Facilitations of Evidence

3.242 In light of the principle of free assessment of evidence, and subject to the parties' right to be heard and right to a fair trial, the tribunal may resort to the facilitations of evidence it deems appropriate. It remains a discretionary decision; no party has the right to demand their application. Although facilitations of evidence may appear in different variations, the most common types shall be briefly outlined below, in particular, circumstantial evidence (*1*), *prima facie evidence* (*2*) and drawing adverse inferences (*3*).

1 Circumstantial Evidence

3.243 The traditional English law of evidence distinguishes between direct and indirect, i.e., circumstantial, evidence. When giving direct evidence, a party may produce the very document or physical thing in dispute or adduce the testimony of a witness who has directly perceived the fact with his or her own senses.[1026] In order to be classified as direct, the evidence must therefore be directly connected to the fact that must be proved. A witness, for example, who testifies in relation to a car accident, must have perceived the very moment of the collision. In the case of a disputed contract, the contractual document itself may serve as direct evidence that the parties concluded the contract in dispute. The term 'circumstantial evidence', i.e., indirect evidence, describes 'evidence of relevant (...) facts from which the existence or non-existence of a fact in issue may be inferred'. Circumstantial evidence may, for example, relate to the negotiations leading to the conclusion of the contract or the parties' subsequent conduct.

3.244 In international arbitration, the tribunal's broad powers to assess evidence allow 'reasonable inferences' to be drawn,[1027] independent of whether it is taking direct or indirect evidence.[1028] In fact, tribunals frequently have no choice but to resort to circumstantial evidence.

3.245 As noted, for example, in *Tokios v Ukraine*, the tribunal felt compelled to:

> form an idea, necessarily based on secondary and circumstantial evidence since direct evidence [was] out of reach.[1029]

1026. Keane and McKeown (n. 290) 11, 14; for Germany *see* Prütting, 'ZPO § 284' (n. 880) paras 24, 25.
1027. Sourgens, Duggal and Laird (n. 442) para. 8.08.
1028. O'Malley (n. 407) para. 7.13 (iii): 'A tribunal may, within its discretion, give dispositive weight to circumstantial evidence.'; *see also* American Law Institute (ALI) and UNIDROIT (n. 203) para. R-25C: 'In some legal systems there are rules limiting in various ways the use of circumstantial evidence. However, these rules seem unjustified and are very difficult to apply in practice. More generally, there is no valid reason to restrict the use of circumstantial evidence when it is useful to establish a fact in issue. Therefore, generally, the court may consider any circumstantial evidence provided it is relevant to the decision on the facts of the case.'
1029. *Tokios Tokelés v Ukraine, ICSID ARB/02/18* (n. 646) para. 14; confirmed by *Alpha Projektholding GmbH v Ukraine, ICSID ARB/07/16* (n. 647) 373.

3.246 Tribunals have the authority to base their awards on the evidence they deem appropriate, independent of whether it can be classified as direct or circumstantial evidence. Rather, since in many cases direct evidence is not readily available, parties may and must in their own interest submit indirect evidence to prove their case.

2 Prima Facie Evidence

3.247 In international arbitration, parties frequently seek to rely on *prima facie evidence* in different procedural contexts. In Latin, prima facie means 'on/at first appearance'.[1030] Accordingly, *prima facie evidence* describes a type of evidence that allows certain preliminary conclusions to be drawn. Nevertheless, the term is ambiguous to say the least, as both case law and commentators seem to apply inconsistent definitions.[1031]

i *Terminology*

3.248 Especially in the common law tradition, *prima facie evidence* has a 'lighter',[1032] and a 'heavier'[1033] meaning. It can either mean 'evidence adduced by a party so weighty that it could reasonably justify a finding in its favour', or 'evidence adduced by a party which is, in the absence of contradictory evidence, so weighty that it does justify a finding in its favour'.[1034] In the first case, in which it is sometimes also referred to as 'conclusive evidence',[1035] *prima facie evidence* is treated as a factual presumption,[1036] at times amounting to a shift of the burden of proof.[1037]

3.249 In domestic US litigation proceedings, the second case is frequently used as a test to determine whether the case is strong enough to go to the jury or is liable to be struck out.[1038] It is, however, questionable whether it is appropriate to apply this test in arbitration proceedings, where the procedural structure is fundamentally different from litigation procedures with lay jurors, and where tribunals usually do not strike out cases on a preliminary basis.[1039] In particular, parties in international arbitration usually have the right to make their case and present evidence up until the cut-off

1030. Georg Nils Herlitz, 'The Meaning of the Term "Prima Facie"' (1994) 55 Louisiana Law Review 391, 392.
1031. Barceló III (n. 631) 25 et seq.; Ho Cheol Kim, 'Burden of Proof and the Prima Facie Case: The Evolving History and Its Applications in the WTO Jurisprudence' (2007) 6 Richmond Journal of Global Law & Business 245, 246 et seq.
1032. Herlitz (n. 1030) 395.
1033. *Ibid.*, 397, 398.
1034. Keane and McKeown (n. 290) 33.
1035. *Ibid.*
1036. *See also* Herlitz (n. 1030) 397, 398.
1037. Barceló III (n. 631) 26.
1038. Roscoe Steffen, 'The Prima Facie Case in Non-Jury Trials' (1959) 27 The University of Chicago Law Review 94, 95 et seq.
1039. *See*, however, for instance, Art. 41.5 ICSID Rules according to which a tribunal can decide on a preliminary basis that a claim is manifestly without merit.

date.[1040] Consequently, pleadings in international arbitration are generally not struck out if they lack *prima facie evidence*, in the first meaning of the term. Moreover, it must be emphasized that '*prima facie evidence*' differs from the term 'prima facie case'. While the former refers to a piece of evidence to establish a single fact, the latter applies where one side produces 'some evidence of each of several elements of a conclusion of law'.[1041]

3.250 Moreover, a quite elaborate, albeit at times inconsistent, case law in WTO disputes on *prima facie evidence* has been established, mainly operating with shifts of the burden of proof.[1042]

ii *Evidence of First Appearance*

3.251 Adding to the confusion, German procedural law[1043] operates with a related, albeit distinguishable, instrument which is referred to as 'evidence of first appearance' (*Anscheinsbeweis*).[1044] Despite the somewhat misleading name, evidence of first appearance is not a real means of evidence, but suggests the consideration of empirical principles (*Erfahrungssätze*) when assessing evidence.[1045] The exact delimitation of factual presumptions is often difficult, maybe even impossible. German courts have developed different case groups to this effect, especially, for example, in tort law,[1046] construction law[1047] and in certain areas of capital markets law.[1048] In these areas, recurring patterns of facts (such as a typical car accident) allow conclusions to be drawn (e.g., regarding the causality between a violation of duties and damage), even though not all issues are fully established and provable. *Anscheinsbeweis* is thus, in fact, a standardized form of circumstantial evidence, meaning that where the factual pattern 'XY' is established, the conclusion 'Z' can be drawn, even if there is no evidence for 'Z'. However, it does not amount to an irrebuttable presumption. Rather, the opposing party is required to bring sufficient evidence, not to (necessarily) convince the trier of facts of the contrary, but merely to shake the prior conviction of 'Z'.[1049] This means that an evidence of first appearance is rebutted if the other party establishes 'facts from which the serious possibility of a deviating course of events arises'.[1050]

1040. *See* above, Chapter 2, A.IV.
1041. Herlitz (n. 1030) 406.
1042. Barceló III (n. 631) para. III; *see also* Kim (n. 1031).
1043. Spellenberg, 'Rom I-VO Art. 18' in Franz Jürgen Säcker and others (eds), *Münchener Kommentar zum BGB* (8th edn, C.H. Beck 2021) para. 26.
1044. Prütting, 'ZPO § 286' (n. 239) paras 50 et seq.; while Anscheinsbeweise are commonly accepted to form part of the customary law, they lack a written legal basis, cf., *inter alia*, Nadine Reimer, 'Anscheinsbeweis Und Parteivernehmung Im Verkehrszivilprozess' [2018] NZV 258, 259.
1045. Prütting, 'ZPO § 286' (n. 239) para. 50.
1046. Bacher (n. 603) para. 95.3; Prütting, 'ZPO § 286' (n. 239) para. 77.
1047. Bacher (n. 603) para. 95.8.
1048. *Ibid.*, 96.3.
1049. *BGH, Judgment of 7 February 2013* [2013] NJW 1092 [28].
1050. *Ibid.*, translation by the author.

3.252 This was confirmed in a landmark decision in 2018, where the Federal Court of Justice redefined the scope of the application of *Anscheinsbeweise* in antitrust litigation.[1051] The question at issue was whether (proven) illicit agreements between competing players in the market 'typically' lead to increased prices for their customers. The background of this question is that it is commonly difficult to positively establish the causality between such an illicit agreement and price increases, while the aggrieved party bears the burden of proof for establishing this link. The court found that there was no sufficiently high probability that the agreements would actually be successfully implemented, i.e., that the typical course of events will bring about the intended price increase.[1052]

3.253 From the above, two main conclusions follow, namely first that the German approach towards '*Anscheinsbeweise*' should not be confused with *prima facie evidence* frequently cited in other jurisdictions as well as in international arbitration. Second, due to their procedural nature, tribunals are free to decide whether case law in a particular case on *Anscheinsbeweise* will apply or not. They are not part of the substantive rules and thus are not covered by a choice of law clause in favour of German law.

iii *Prima Facie Evidence in the Arbitral Practice*

3.254 Just as across jurisdictions, there are different definitions of *prima facie evidence* in international arbitration. Some institutional rules refer to a prima facie standard in organizational and preliminary matters, specifically to be applied to the validity and scope of the arbitration agreement.[1053]

3.255 In the ambit of investor-state arbitration, a prima facie standard of evidence may further apply during the jurisdiction phase, where 'the claimants allege the facts at the jurisdictional phase and the tribunal will examine these facts to see, if proven subsequent, would fall within the scope of the applicable treaty'.[1054]

3.256 Beyond that, in international arbitration, *prima facie evidence* is frequently referred to as 'evidence, which, unexplained or uncontradicted, is sufficient to maintain the proposition affirmed'; or, more broadly, 'a case sufficient to call for an answer'.[1055] This was aptly summarized by *Aghahosseini* in the dissenting vote in *Dadras International*:

1051. *BGH, Judgment of 11 December 2018* [2019] NJW 661; recently confirmed by *BGH, Judgment of 23 September 2020* [2021] NJW 848 [38].
1052. *BGH, Judgment of 11 December 2018* (n. 1051) paras 50 et seq., 57.
1053. Notably, the same institutional rules refer to a *prima facie* standard in organizational and preliminary matters, *see, e.g.*, Art. 6.4 ICC Rules: 'In all cases referred to the Court under Article 6(3), the Court shall decide whether and to what extent the arbitration shall proceed. The arbitration shall proceed if and to the extent that the Court is prima facie satisfied that an arbitration agreement under the Rules may exist.' Further references can be found in Art. 6.4 (i)-(iii) ICC Rules; Art. 19.5, 27.1 (a) HKIAC Rules, Art. 9.3 Third Sentence DIS Rules.
1054. Sourgens, Duggal and Laird (n. 442) para. 5.06.
1055. *See* O'Malley (n. 407) para. 7.32 with further references.

> In other words, where a prima facie case, in the sense of discharged 'conclusive' evidence, is made out, the opponent must offer evidence pointing to some reasons 'for doubting'. If he does so, then, and this is most important, the evidence before the tribunal, whether adduced by the proponent in support of his contention or by the opponent in support of his denial, must be considered together in order to determine whether or not the proponent's burden of proof is met:
>
> The question whether a fact in issue has been proved can only be answered after both parties have called their evidence.[1056]

Accordingly, in this interpretation, *prima facie evidence* does not shift the burden of proof but must be considered during the assessment of evidence.

3.257 It follows that the term '*prima facie evidence*' is multifaceted and rather difficult to pin down. In the most common use in international arbitration, it refers to conclusive evidence which the opposing party must rebut in order to avoid an adverse decision. However, due to its diverging meanings, the terminology must be handled with due care in order to prevent confusion throughout the proceedings.

3 Adverse Inferences

3.258 Lastly, a tribunal may always resort to adverse inferences. Lacking coercive powers, adverse inferences are one of the most powerful tools tribunals are equipped with. When drawing adverse inferences, the tribunal may consider the parties' conduct, including all acts and omissions, when assessing evidence. In particular, adverse inferences are applied where a party, without proper justification, fails to comply with an order of the tribunal which relates to an evidentiary matter, e.g., an order to produce documents or other means of evidence.[1057] In this case, the tribunal may consider the party's failure to comply when deciding on the facts. Similar approaches are also prevalent in certain domestic jurisdictions.[1058]

3.259 Some commentators advocate that the instrument of adverse inferences is a matter of interpretation of the contract and is thus governed by the applicable substantive law.[1059] The more accurate view, however, is that the authority to draw inferences both from the evidence and from the parties' conduct lies at the very core of the tribunal's power of free assessment of evidence. It is, therefore, a matter of procedural nature, subject to wide arbitral discretion.[1060] This also means that while adverse inferences pertain to the canon of transnational law,[1061] the principle of free assessment prohibits the prescription of any hard and fast rules. Subject to the right to free trial and the right to be heard, the tribunal is thus free to draw inferences as it

1056. *Dadras International, Per-Am Construction Corporation v The Islamic Republic of Iran, Tehran Redevelopment Company, IUSCT Case Nos 213 and 215 (567-213/215-3)* Dissenting Opinion of Mohsen Aghahosseini of 7 November 1995 [131].
1057. Sachs and Niedermaier (n. 874) 130 et seq.
1058. *See* for German law (critically), Laumen (n. 656) 3744 et seq.; *see* for English law Keane and McKeown (n. 290) 453 et seq.
1059. *See* Nairn, Nelson and Henin (n. 169) 160, 161 for further references.
1060. Sachs and Niedermaier (n. 874) 146.
1061. Nairn, Nelson and Henin (n. 169) 163 et seqq.

deems appropriate. This is true for both adverse and beneficial inferences; the very idea that specific requirements must be met contradicts the principle of free assessment.

3.260 This may explain why arbitration laws and rules are mostly silent on the issue, thus leaving the matter to the general discretion of the tribunal. There are, however, some exceptions. For instance, Article 41 (7) (b) of the English Arbitration Act states that:

> [i]f a party fails to comply with any (...) kind of peremptory order, then, (...), the tribunal may (...) draw such adverse inferences from the act of non-compliance as the circumstances justify.

3.261 Explicit provisions to this effect can also be found under the SCC Rules[1062], the ICDR Rules,[1063] the ALI/UNIDROIT Principles and Rules[1064] as well as the Prague Rules.[1065] The provision under the IBA Rules is slightly narrower, stating that:

> if a Party fails without satisfactory explanation to produce any Document (...), the Arbitral Tribunal may infer that such document would be adverse to the interests of that Party.[1066]

3.262 Accordingly, the provision is expressly limited to the drawing of inferences based on document production requests and orders, rather than extending to other forms of evidence.

3.263 Quite famously, in 2006, *Sharpe* developed the following five main requirements, which since then have been frequently referred to, both in commercial[1067] and investment arbitration:[1068]

> (1) the party seeking the adverse inference must produce all available evidence corroborating the inference sought;
> (2) the requested evidence must be accessible to the inference opponent;

1062. Article 35.3 SCC Rules: 'If a party, without good cause, fails to comply with any provision of, or requirement under, these Rules or any procedural order given by the Arbitral Tribunal, the Arbitral Tribunal may draw such inferences as it considers appropriate.'
1063. Article 24.9 ICDR Rules: 'In the event a party fails to comply with an order for information exchange, the tribunal may draw adverse inferences and may take such failure into account in allocating costs.'
1064. *See* ALI/UNIDROIT Rule 28.3.3 'The court, on its own motion or motion of a party, may: Impose sanctions on a person for unjustified failure to attend to give evidence, to answer proper questions, or to produce a document or other item of evidence, or who otherwise obstructs the proceeding.'
1065. Article 10 Prague Rules: 'If a party does not comply with the arbitral tribunal's order(s) or instruction(s), without justifiable grounds, the arbitral tribunal may draw, where it considers appropriate, an adverse inference with regard to such party's respective case or issue.'
1066. Article 9.6 IBA Rules: 'If a Party fails without satisfactory explanation to produce any Document requested in a Request to Produce to which it has not objected in due time or fails to produce any Document ordered to be produced by the Arbitral Tribunal, the Arbitral Tribunal may infer that such document would be adverse to the interests of that Party.'
1067. Nairn, Nelson and Henin (n. 169) 168 with further references.
1068. Cf. Michael Polkinghorne and Charles B Rosenberg, 'The Adverse Inference in ICSID Practice' (2015) 30 ICSID Review 741, 746.

(3) the inference sought must be reasonable, consistent with facts in the record and logically related to the likely nature of the evidence withheld;
(4) the party seeking the adverse inference must produce *prima facie* evidence; and
(5) the inference opponent must know, or have reason to know, of its obligation to produce evidence rebutting the adverse inference sought.[1069]

3.264 It must be emphasized that these prerequisites serve as mere guidelines and orientation and do not amount to a hard and fast rule, which would compromise the arbitral discretion. If, however, these points are cumulatively fulfilled, the tribunal can confidently proceed to draw inferences without running the risk of violating any presumed right to be heard.

3.265 In *Metal-Tech v Uzbekistan*, it was established that the claimant had paid $4 million to 'consultants' to perform 'lobbyist activity'.[1070] The tribunal then ordered the claimant to produce further evidence (documents and witness testimony) to show the legitimate purpose of this payment.[1071] As the claimant failed to do so, the tribunal held:

> While the Tribunal does not believe that the Claimant sought to conceal evidence, the inference that inexorably emerges from this dearth of evidence is that the Claimant can provide no evidence of services, because no services, or at least no legitimate services at the time of the establishment of the Claimant's investment, were in fact performed. The Tribunal will bear this inference in mind when further assessing the facts.[1072]

3.266 Generally, however, tribunals are rather reluctant to resort to inferences. As stated, for example, by the Tribunal in an SCC proceeding:

> Whilst we agree we have the jurisdiction to draw adverse inferences, this jurisdiction is one which is to be exercised with discretion and only where required to reach a determination of an issue in dispute.[1073]

3.267 Importantly, unlike (*inter alia*) suggested by the commentary to the ALI/UNIDROIT Principles,[1074] adverse inferences do not amount to a shift of the burden of proof.[1075] Especially where the party, according to the general rules, has no means of proving an assertion, shifting the burden of proof would put this party in an unduly favourable position. For example, a buyer may claim that, after concluding the main contract, the parties had agreed to a reduction of the purchase price through an

1069. Sharpe (n. 169) 551.
1070. *Metal-Tech Ltd. v Republic of Uzbekistan, ICSID ARB/10/3* (n. 557) para. 247.
1071. *Ibid.*, 248.
1072. *Ibid.*, 265; *see* for a further overview of adverse inferences in the ICSID Practice, Polkinghorne and Rosenberg (n. 1068) 744 et seq.
1073. *SCC Case No 2018/072, Final Award of 29 October 2019* [2020] XLV Ybk Comm Arb 1 [161].
1074. American Law Institute (ALI) and UNIDROIT (n. 203) 42 Drawing such inferences can be considered a sanction, *see* Principle 17.3, or a shifting of the burden of proof, *see* Principle 21.1.
1075. Sharpe (n. 169) 552.

oral amendment, naming a seller's representative as witness. If the seller, against the tribunal's orders, fails to make said witness available, shifting the burden of proof would mean that the tribunal would consider the buyer's allegation to be true unless positively proven false. Without any taking of evidence, and despite it being disputed, the tribunal would thus consider that the parties had reached such an oral agreement. Yet, especially if the buyer itself fails to submit any other evidence, it would get more than it bargained for. In such case, it is thus more appropriate to consider the seller's conduct as one of a number of factors when assessing the evidence rather than fully shifting the burden of proof.

III Conclusion

3.268 The assessment of evidence lies at the core of the tribunal's mandate and authority. According to the widely accepted transnational principle of free assessment of evidence, the tribunal is not restricted by any formal rules but may evaluate the evidence as it deems appropriate. When weighing the evidence, the tribunal usually examines whether it is relevant, credible and sufficient to meet the standard of proof. Although there is no formal hierarchy of the different means of evidence, contemporaneous documents are frequently considered to be highly reliable, whereas inexplicably uncorroborated witness statements may raise questions. In any case, the tribunal's power to assess the evidence is unfettered and not restricted by any domestic laws of evidence, which do not apply in international arbitration. The tribunal's broad powers are complemented by its duty to give reasons for its decision.

F SUMMARY

3.269 This second part of the survey of fact-finding rules corroborates the above conclusions concerning the development of a transnational *Lex Evidentiae* in international arbitration. In line with the ongoing synchronization of the rules on the gathering of facts, one can likewise observe a synchronization of the rules on the determination of facts, i.e., the taking of evidence. The trend towards a uniform law of evidence in international arbitration – the *Lex Evidentiae* – is driven by both (i) uncodified best practices, such as the development of a transnational rule on the burden and standard of proof, and (ii) codified best practices, such as the provisions of the IBA Rules on witness and documentary evidence.

3.270 Notably, especially with regard to the admission and assessment of evidence, the arbitration laws and rules are also becoming largely homogeneous, reflecting identical or similar provisions, thus further contributing to transnationalization. Nevertheless, here, the detailed questions concerning the application of the law are also determined in more detail by soft law, legal commentary and awards.

CHAPTER 4

Results of the Study

4.1 This final part of the study sums up its main findings (*A*) and provides a final, concise overview of the transnational rules of fact-finding in international arbitration (i.e., the *Lex Evidentiae*) as identified by the present analysis (*B*).

A SUMMARY OF FINDINGS

4.2 As this study shows, the relation between facts and law remains complicated. Just as reflected by the initially cited dialogue between *Camilla* and *Gantenbein*, in international arbitration the truth is frequently relative; the established facts are but a mere compromise that serves to reconcile the requirements of justice, efficiency and proportionality. Despite these overwhelming difficulties, the international arbitration community has developed a robust and reliable programme capable of establishing the facts to a satisfactory degree even in highly complex cases.

4.3 In Chapter 1, this study examines the theoretical underpinning of the law of evidence in international arbitration (*Lex Evidentiae*). The first key take-away of this is that the current practice and law of evidence in international arbitration does not seem to fit into traditional positivist theories which still heavily rely on the law-making of national – or, at times international – legislators. Rather, the *Lex Evidentiae*, as conceptualized in this study, mainly derives from and is shaped by practice – the stakeholder's experience and the replication thereof. The thus established practices become legally binding transnational law where they are backed by the means to ensure their compliance. In the case of international arbitration, compliance is safeguarded via inner-procedural mechanisms, such as the drawing of adverse inferences or cost decisions, or via external mechanisms, such as the enforcement of awards. The recourse to domestic courts is, however, not usually necessary, since, in 80%–90% of cases, parties voluntarily comply with the decisions of the tribunal.

4.4 The following sections apply the theoretical underpinning to analyse the current arbitral practice in fact-finding. Based on the above definition, the analysis is two-pronged, first addressing the rules of fact-gathering and, second, the rules of fact-determination, i.e., the taking of evidence.

4.5 Accordingly, Chapter 2 examines the gathering of facts. The gathering of facts is the first crucial phase in arbitral proceedings, during which the parties define the scope of the dispute and present their respective version and understanding of the facts. It thus begins with the parties' submissions in the form of fact pleadings (Chapter 2, A). This study confirms that, although thus far, little attention seems to have been paid to the topic in international arbitration, the issue is of utmost importance. In many cases, it is not the taking of evidence which decides the dispute, but the parties' very pleadings. If these are poorly drafted or insufficient, the tribunal may not even proceed to take evidence on crucial issues. Nonetheless, based on a survey of the arbitration laws, rules, commentary and, where available, case law, certain general and transnational principles can be distilled, namely that (i) the parties must, in their own interest, plead the facts they rely upon, (ii) the burden of pleading follows the burden of proof but may be modified by the tribunal, (iii) the parties must provide a certain level of detail and may not simply or generally deny the opposing party's allegations without further explanation and, finally, (iv) that domestic pleading requirements do not apply.

4.6 The next section (Chapter 2, B) addresses the information and disclosure duties of the parties. As a preliminary issue, the meaning of the term 'truth' in a procedural context is examined, outlining the difficulties of establishing the truth in an objective sense within a procedural framework, be it arbitration or litigation. These difficulties are caused by concerns of efficiency, the limited tools of actual truth-seeking, known shortcomings of the memory of parties and witnesses as well as recurring issues of dishonesty. Nonetheless, parties to international arbitrations are generally expected to submit the facts fully and truthfully, without being entitled to withhold adverse information (as is the case in certain domestic jurisdictions). The mandatory exchange of information in international arbitration is usually performed through document production, generally based on the prerequisites of the IBA Rules. As this study confirms, the latter have become a truly transnational set of rules. Other means of discovery and disclosure proceedings, such as depositions and interrogatories, are rather unusual, albeit possible subject to the tribunal's discretion.

4.7 The then following section (Chapter 2, C) examines the powers of the tribunal to engage in the gathering of facts. The first section summarizes adversarial and inquisitorial approaches to fact-finding. After pointing out frequent misunderstandings, the subsequent analysis of the current arbitration laws, rules and soft laws show that there is a palpable trend to strengthen the tribunal's mandate to proactively engage in fact-finding procedures. Under most of these sets of rules, the tribunal has at least limited powers to actively order the parties to produce documents and other means of evidence. Some sets of rules go so far as to expressly grant the tribunal the power to 'undertake investigation and collect evidence' (Article 43 CIETAC Rules); to 'establish the facts of the case by all appropriate means' (Article 25.1 ICC Rules), or to 'on its own initiative[,] collect evidence, question parties or witnesses, request the parties to submit evidence, and call experts' (Article 29.1 Vienna Rules). In practice, however, tribunals are still rather reluctant to fully employ their powers, leaving the main responsibility of fact-finding to the parties. The predominant approach in international arbitration can therefore be described as semi-inquisitorial. Only under exceptional circumstances, such as in cases of corruption, fraud or similar allegations, is the tribunal's mandate to independently investigate undisputed. Nonetheless, recent amendments to the above sets of rules suggest that the international arbitration community can expect a further strengthening of the position of the tribunal. Different techniques of proactive fact-finding are already in more common use, such as the recourse to public knowledge, specific disclosure orders as well as defining the issues in dispute.

4.8 Chapter 3 deals with the rules pertaining to the determination of facts (the taking of evidence). The first section (Chapter 3, A) addresses the introduction of evidence into the dispute. Most laws and sets of rules do not provide any specifics but rather stipulate that parties shall submit the evidence they seek to rely upon. The question of who bears the risk of evidence, and ultimately the risk of a *non liquet*, is answered by the burden of proof and its distribution. The general allocation following *actori incumbit* amounts, nowadays, to a transnational principle. Accordingly, the burden of proof lies upon a party which substantially asserts the affirmative of an issue (i.e., claims and affirmative defences). In case of doubt, the tribunal shall consult the applicable substantive law to determine whether a party is pleading an affirmative or a mere denial and to determine whether legal presumptions may apply. In addition, under due consideration of the principle of procedural fairness, the tribunal is, in theory, also empowered to reverse the burden of proof in individual cases. In any case, under exceptional circumstances, the tribunal may take evidence ex officio as part of its investigatory powers.

4.9 The second section (Chapter 3, B) describes the different means of evidence, i.e., fact witnesses, experts, documents and real evidence. Parties usually introduce their witnesses by means of written witness statements, which serve as the basis for the testimonies to be examined during the hearing. The examination can be conducted either in a party-led way (i.e., through direct, cross and re-direct examination as set out under Article 8.4 of the IBA Rules) or in a tribunal-led manner, as suggested by, *inter alia*, 5.9 of the Prague Rules. Moreover, there is a growing tendency to jointly examine witnesses by means of witness conferencing ('hot-tubbing').

4.10 Experts can be appointed either by the parties or, upon consultation with the parties, by the tribunal. As a compromise, the Sachs Protocol suggests that parties exchange a list of potential experts, which each party may comment on. Based on the suggestions, the tribunal may then select and instruct two experts to analyse the issues in question as an expert team. Similar to witness evidence, expert evidence is usually introduced in writing through expert reports, based on which the experts are examined during the hearing.

4.11 Lastly, parties may rely on real evidence (also referred to as physical evidence), i.e., objects to be produced before the tribunal or site visits. Site visits are rather rare but can be particularly helpful in technical disputes and investment arbitrations.

4.12 As analysed in the following section (Chapter 3, C), as a transnational and undisputed rule, the tribunal may and must decide on the admissibility of evidence. Assessing the relevance is the tribunals' own and immanent task and, in doing so, it is not bound by any domestic rules. Tribunals usually have recourse to the test of relevance and admissibility. Evidence is relevant if it renders a contention to be more likely and is material if it may bear on the outcome of the dispute. In light of the parties' right to be heard and present evidence, the threshold for rejecting evidence is high. The same standard of relevance and materiality applies when deciding on requests to produce evidence under the IBA Rules. Nonetheless, when judging the admissibility, the tribunal's perspective is different. At the beginning of the proceeding, when dealing with document production, the tribunal does not yet have sufficient information to decide whether evidence will become relevant and material, thus a more lenient approach is recommended. When taking evidence, however, the dispute is already fairly developed, thus allowing for a more informed decision. Moreover, the tribunal may be required to consider exclusionary rules when deciding on the admissibility of evidence and will, in particular, exclude evidence on the grounds of privilege, (commercial) confidentiality and potential issues of illegally obtained evidence.

4.13 When taking evidence, the tribunal must assess the evidence against the applicable standard of proof (Chapter 3, D). The standard of proof describes the threshold that must be met for a factual assertion to be considered true. As the standard of proof is predominantly found to be an issue in substantive law, the first subsection (Chapter 3, D.I) examines the application across different jurisdictions. In doing so, the prevalent approaches in England and Wales and the United States are contrasted with the standard of proof in Germany. The main difference is that, in the common law tradition, a balance of probabilities applies, whereas in Germany, in line with the civil law tradition, the standard of proof is met if the trier of fact is sufficiently convinced. Owing to its very nature, however, there are inherent difficulties in comparing different standards of proof. The evaluation of evidence is a mainly subjective process, which the standard of proof seeks to put into objective terms. It is thus questionable whether a trier of fact who decides according to a balance of probability would decide differently when applying the standard of conviction. This is especially true since applying a subjective standard of probability, as opposed to an objective and numeric standard of probability, ultimately requires a subjective evaluation and is thus, in essence, a matter of conviction.

4.14 As the next section (Chapter 3, D.II) analyses, however, there is a strong tendency in international arbitration to apply a uniform standard of proof, independent of the applicable substantive law. Different commentators and awards in that context suggest the general application of a balance of probabilities standard, which may, in individual cases (e.g., allegations of fraud or corruption), be subject to certain modifications.

4.15 As a further transnational rule, the tribunal is free to assess the evidence as it deems appropriate (principle of free assessment of evidence, Chapter 3, E.I). This is confirmed by all the analysed laws and sets of rules. The principle of free assessment of evidence means that, when weighing evidence, the tribunal is not bound to adhere to domestic rules of evidence, such as the prohibition of hearsay or the four-corners rule. In order to balance the tribunal's great powers, however, it is required to give reasons for its decisions.

4.16 The power to freely assess evidence also means that the tribunal may resort to facilitations of evidence (Chapter 3, E.II). It may, *inter alia*, consider circumstantial evidence or draw inferences (including adverse inferences) if it deems it appropriate to do so. As for *prima facie evidence*, the terminology is highly ambiguous in an international context. It is, however, frequently used to describe 'evidence, which, unexplained or uncontradicted, is sufficient to maintain the proposition affirmed' and frequently applied in an international context.

4.17 In sum, the present survey confirms that there is a consolidated, transnational law of fact-finding in international arbitration, with rules relating to all important steps of fact-gathering and the taking of evidence. Rather than being the product of national or international formalized legislative procedures, the law has been developed and stabilized by its practical application. This process is strongly driven by private codification bodies, such as the IBA, but also by the arbitral institutions and their regular, comprehensive reforms of the arbitration rules under due consideration of current developments. Moreover, legal commentary as well as published awards, both in investment and commercial arbitration proceedings, further contribute to the consolidation of the fact-finding rules.

4.18 It remains, however, important to emphasize that, due to its transnational character, said body of rules is fluid and highly adaptable. Rather than being carved in stone, it has developed over the past decades and can and will develop further over the years.

B THE *LEX EVIDENTIAE*: SUMMARY OF RULES

I Gathering of Facts

Pleading of Facts

(a) Each party shall plead the facts it seeks to rely upon. The parties shall, so far as practicable, set forth detail as to time, place, participants and events.
(b) The parties are expected to make their submissions completely and truthfully.
(c) The burden of pleading follows the burden of proof.

(d) A party shall address all of its opponents' relevant statements either by admitting or denying with explanation. A party that justifiably has no independent information may declare its lack of knowledge.
(e) Subject to the tribunal's powers to clarify the facts, it may consider the failure to address relevant allegations as an admission.
(f) The tribunal shall set a cut-off date subsequent to which further pleadings and evidence must be rejected, unless the delay is reasonably justified.

Exchange of Information

(a) Subject to the below, no party may withhold relevant information from the tribunal and the other parties.
(b) The tribunal may, at its own discretion or at the request of a party, order the parties to produce documents or other information in a manner it deems appropriate.
(c) The tribunal shall grant a request to produce documents only if:
    (i) it contains a description of each requested document sufficient to identify it or a description in sufficient detail (including subject matter) of a narrow and specific requested category of documents that are reasonably believed to exist;
    (ii) the requesting party demonstrates that the documents are relevant to the case and material to its outcome;
    (iii) the documents are neither privileged nor sufficiently confidential; and
    (iv) the request is proportionate to the meaning and relevance of the information sought.

Proactive Case Management

(a) The tribunal may define issues which it considers to be relevant.
(b) At its own motion or at the request of the party, the tribunal may order the parties:
    (i) to supplement, specify or clarify its pleadings regarding specific issues; and
    (ii) to produce specific relevant documents or other means of evidence which may become relevant.
(c) Subject to prior consultation with the parties, the tribunal may have recourse to public knowledge.
(d) Where necessary and appropriate and under due consideration of the principle of procedural fairness, the tribunal may undertake independent measures to clarify the facts. The tribunal must disclose all activities and results to the parties and grant them the right to comment.

Taking of Evidence

Submission of Evidence

(a) Parties shall submit the evidence they seek to rely upon.
(b) The burden of proof lies upon a party which substantially asserts the affirmative of an issue (*actori incumbit*).
(c) The tribunal may apply legal presumptions as part of the applicable law.
(d) Where appropriate, the tribunal may:
    (i) shift the burden of proof; and/or
    (ii) take evidence at its own motion.

Means of Evidence

(a) Witness Evidence
    (i) Witnesses must testify truthfully.
    (ii) Each party shall produce written statements of the witnesses it seeks to rely on.
    (iii) It lies within the tribunal's discretion whether to control the examination of the witnesses or leave it to the parties:
        (1) Party-led examination
            (a) During the oral hearing, the written witness statement may replace the direct examination.
            (b) Parties have the right to cross-examine the producing party's witness. The producing party may address issues raised during the cross-examination during the re-direct examination.
            (c) Subsequent to the parties, the tribunal may question the witnesses.
        (2) Tribunal-led examination
            (a) If the tribunal decides to control the examination of the witness, it shall first question the witness regarding all issues it deems relevant. It is not bound by the parties' submissions.
            (a) Subsequent to the tribunal, the parties have the right to question the witnesses in an order the Tribunal deems appropriate.
    (iv) If two or more opposing witnesses disagree, they may be examined at the same time (witness conferencing).
(b) Documents
    (i) Parties shall annex copies of the documents which they seek to rely upon to their submissions. Notarizations or other forms of authentication are not required.
    (ii) If necessary, the tribunal shall take evidence as to the authenticity of the document in a manner it deems appropriate.
(c) Experts
    (i) The parties as well as the tribunal, upon consultation with the parties, may instruct experts to give evidence.

(ii) In the interest of cost and time, the tribunal shall discuss with the parties the use and limitation of experts during an early case management conference.
(iii) The rules on witness examination apply *mutatis mutandis*.

(d) Other Means of Evidence

Evidence may be taken in the form of any other means of evidence from which inferences can be drawn, including real evidence and site visits.

Admission of Evidence

(a) The power conferred upon the arbitral tribunal includes the power to determine the admissibility of evidence.
(b) Evidence is generally admissible if it renders a contention to be either more or less likely (relevance) and might bear upon the final decision (materiality).
(c) Evidence may be disregarded on the grounds of privilege, confidentiality, illegality, or similar reasons.

Standard of Proof

(a) The general standard of proof is met if a contention is more likely than not.
(b) The Tribunal may have recourse to a specific standard of proof under a law or set of rules with a sufficiently close connection to the dispute.
(c) If the circumstances require it, and subject to the duty to state reasons (§5.c), the tribunal may lower or heighten the standard of proof.

Assessment of Evidence

(a) The tribunal is free to assess the evidence in a way it deems appropriate. It is free to consider circumstantial evidence to reach its conclusion.
(b) The tribunal may draw reasonable inferences, including adverse inferences, from the evidence as well as from the conduct of the parties and their counsel.
(c) In its decision, the tribunal shall state the reasons by which the decision was reached.

Bibliography

1999 IBA Working Party and 2010 Rules of Evidence Review Subcommittee, *Commentary on the Revised Text of the 2010 IBA Rules on the Taking of Evidence in International Arbitration* (2010)

1999 IBA Working Party, 2010 Rules of Evidence Review Subcommittee and 2020 IBA Rules of Evidence Review Task Force, *Commentary on the Revised Text of the 2020 IBA Rules on the Taking of Evidence in International Arbitration* (2021)

Abbud A, Levy D and Alves RF, *Brazilian Arbitration Act: A Case Law Guide* (Kluwer Law International 2019)

Aimoré Carreteiro M, 'Burden and Standard of Proof in International Arbitration: Proposed Guidelines for Promoting Predictability' (2016) XIII Revista Brasileira de Arbitragem 82

Al-Baharna DHM, 'International Commercial Arbitration in a Changing World' (1994) 9 Arab Law Quarterly 144

Alfter P, *Das Beweismaß in der internationalen Handelsschiedsgerichtsbarkeit* (Springer 2019)

American Law Institute (ALI) and UNIDROIT, *ALI/UNIDROIT Principles of Transnational Civil Procedure* (Cambridge University Press 2006)

Anderson T, Schum DA and Twining WL, *Analysis of Evidence* (Cambridge University Press 2005)

Andrews N, 'The Adversaral Principle: Fairness and Efficiency' in AAS Zuckerman and Ross Cranston (eds), *Reform of Civil Procedure: Essays on 'Access to Justice'* (Clarendon Press; Oxford University Press 1995)

'Arbitration Centres | United Nations Commission on International Trade Law' < https://uncitral.un.org/en/texts/arbitration/contractualtexts/arbitration/centres >

Arroyo M, *Arbitration in Switzerland: The Practitioner's Guide* (2nd edn, Kluwer Law International 2018)

Ashford P, *The IBA Rules on the Taking of Evidence in International Arbitration: A Guide* (Cambridge University Press 2012)

Bacher, 'ZPO § 284' in Vorwerk and Wolf (eds), *Beck'sche Online-Kommentar ZPO* (39th edn, C.H. Beck 2020)

Baizeau D and Hayes T, 'The Arbitral Tribunal's Duty and Power to Address Corruption Sua Sponte' (2017) 19 ICCA Congress Series 225

Bar Council - Ethics Committee of The General Council of the Bar, *Witness Preparation* (21)

Bar Standards Board, *The BSB Handbook* (Version 46, 2020)

Barceló III, JJ, 'Burden of Proof, Prima Facie Case and Presumption in WTO Dispute Settlement' (2009) 42 Cornell International Law Journal 23

Benedicter G, *Die Sachverhaltsermittlung Im Zivilprozess* (Hochschulschrift 2005)

Benzing M, *Das Beweisrecht vor internationalen Gerichten und Schiedsgerichten in zwischenstaatlichen Streitigkeiten* (Springer 2010)

Berger KP, 'Evidentiary Privileges: Best Practice Standards versus/and Arbitral Discretion' (2006) 22 Arbitration International 501

Berger KP, *The Creeping Codification of the New Lex Mercatoria* (2nd edn, Kluwer Law International 2010)

Berger KP, 'Common Law vs. Civil Law in International Arbitration: The Beginning or the End?' (2020) 36 Journal of International Arbitration, 295

Berger KP and Jensen JO, 'The Arbitrator's Mandate to Facilitate Settlement' (2017) 40 Fordham International Law Journal 887

Berger TA, 'The Ethical Limits of Discrediting the Truthful Witness: How Modern Ethics Rules Fail to Prevent Truthful Witnesses from Being Discredited Through Unethical Means' (2015) 99 Marquette Law Review 285

Berman PS, *Global Legal Pluralism: A Jurisprudence of Law Beyond Borders* (Cambridge University Press 2012)

Bermann GA, 'The Self-Styled "Autonomy" of International Arbitration' (2020) 36 Arbitration International 221

Besson S and Tasioulas J, *The Philosophy of International Law* (Samantha Besson and John Tasioulas eds, Oxford University Press 2010)

Blackaby N and others, *Redfern and Hunter on International Arbitration* (6th edn, Oxford University Press 2015)

Błaszczak Ł and Kolber J, 'Annulment and Enforcement of Arbitral Awards in Poland' (2012) 30 ASA Bulletin 564

Blavi F and Vial G, 'Burden of Proof in International Commercial Arbitration: Are We Allowed to Adjust the Scales' (2016) 39 Hastings International and Comparative Law Review 41

Böckstiegel K-H, Kröll S and Nacimiento P (eds), *Arbitration in Germany: The Model Law in Practice* (2nd edn, Kluwer Law International 2015)

Born G, 'A Code of Conduct for Counsel in International Arbitration' (*Kluwer Arbitration Blog*, 16 November 2010)

Born G, *International Commercial Arbitration* (3rd edn, Kluwer Law International 2021)

Bösch M and Rohn P, 'Switzerland' in Amy Cohen Kläsener (ed.), *The Guide to M&A Arbitration* (Global Arbitration Review 2018)

Boyle R and Lewin SD, 'ADR Does Not Mean Splitting the Baby' [2019] Corporate Counsel Business Journal

Brand P-A, 'Grenzen Zivilprozessualer Wahrheit Und Gerechtigkeit' [2017] NJW 3558

Brinkmann M, 'The Synthesis of Common and Civil Law Standard of Proof Formulae in the Ali / Unidroit Principles of Transnational Civil Procedure' (2004) 9 Uniform Law Review 875

Brinkmann M, *Das Beweismaß Im Zivilprozess aus rechtsvergleichender Sicht* (Heymanns 2005)

Broglia Mendes RO, *Arbitragem, Lex Mercatoria E Direito Estatal: Uma Análise Dos Conflitos Ortogonais No Direito Transnacional* (Quartier Latin do Brasil 2010)

Brower CN, 'Evidence Before International Tribunals: The Need for Some Standard Rules' (1994) 28 The International Lawyer 47

Caldas AR and Jobim MF, 'A Distribuição Dinâmica Do Ônus Da Prova No Sistema Processual Brasileiro E O Projeto De Novo Código De Processo Civil' (2015) 42 Revista da Associação dos Juízes do Rio Grande do Sul 32

Calliess G-P, 'Reflexive Transnational Law' (2002) 23 Zeitschrift für Rechtssoziologie 185

Calliess G-P and Renner M, 'Between Law and Social Norms: The Evolution of Global Governance' (2009) 22 Ratio Juris 260

Calliess G-P and Zumbansen P, *Rough Consensus and Running Code: A Theory of Transnational Private Law* (Hart Publishing 2010)

Carbonneau TE, 'Rendering Arbitral Awards with Reasons: The Elaboration of Common Law of International Transactions' (1985) 23 Columbia Journal of Transnational Law 579

Caron DD and Caplan L, *The UNCITRAL Arbitration Rules: A Commentary: (With an Integrated and Comparative Discussion of the 2010 and 1976 UNCITRAL Arbitration Rules)* (2nd edn, Oxford University Press 2013)

Casey B and others, 'Abuse of Document Production in International Arbitration: Remedies When the Adverse Inference Falls Short' (2020) 86 Arbitration: The International Journal of Arbitration, Mediation and Dispute Management 394

Choo AL-T and Nash S, 'Improperly Obtained Evidence in the Commonwealth: Lessons for England and Wales?' (2007) 11 The International Journal of Evidence & Proof 75

CIArb, *Guidelines for Witness Conferencing in International Arbitration* (2019)

Coester-Waltjen D, *Internationales Beweisrecht: Das Auf Den Beweis Anwendbare Recht in Rechtsstreitigkeiten Mit Auslandsbezug* (R Gremer 1983)

Cohen M, 'When Judges Have Reasons Not to Give Reasons: A Comparative Law Approach' (2015) 72 Washington and Lee Law Review 483

'Commentary to Trans-Lex Principle No. XII.1 - Distribution of Burden of Proof, < https://Www.Trans-Lex.Org/966000 > '

Competence Centre Arbitration and Crime (Basel Institute on Governance) (ed.), *Corruption and Money Laundering in International Arbitration. A Toolkit for Arbitrators.* (2019)

Cook J, 'Factual and Expert Evidence in Arbitration' (2014) 16 Asian Dispute Review 30

Cooper EH, 'Transnational Civil Procedure: Fact Pleading or Notice Pleading - A Viewpoint from the USA Harmonising Transnational Civil Procedure: The ALI/UNIDROIT Principles and Rules: II - Stages and Problem Areas in Transnational Litigation' [2001] Uniform Law Review 857

Cotterrell R, 'What Is Transnational Law?' (2012) 37 Law & Social Inquiry 500

Damrau J and Weinland A, 'ZPO § 396' in Thomas Rauscher and Wolfgang Krüger (eds), *Münchener Kommentar zur ZPO* (6th edn, C.H. Beck 2020)

Das Gupta N, 'Kurzkommentare Zu Den Änderungen in Der 2018 DIS-Schiedsgerichtsordnung' (2018) 1 SchiedsVZ-Beilage 44

David M, 'The Correspondence Theory of Truth' in Edward N Zalta (ed.), *The Stanford Encyclopedia of Philosophy* (2020th edn, Metaphysics Research Lab, Stanford University)

Demeyere L, 'An Essay on Differing Approaches to Procedures Under Common Law and Civil Law' [2008] SchiedsVZ 279

Demeyere L and Hanotiau B (eds), 'The Search for the Truth in Arbitration: Is It Possible to Start from a Definition of "Truth"?', *Do Arbitral Awards Reveal the Truth?: Reports from the Third Joint Cepani-Nai Colloquium Held on March 21, 2019* (2019)

Derains Y, 'Towards Greater Efficiency in Document Production before Arbitral Tribunals' (2006) Special Supplement ICC International Court of Arbitration Bulletin 83

Djordjević, 'CISG Article 74' in Kröll, Mistelis and Perales Viscasillas (eds), *UN Convention on Contracts for the International Sales of Goods (CISG)* (2nd edn, 2018)

DLA Piper, *DLA Piper's Legal Professional Privilege Global Guide* (2019)

Draetta U, 'The Transnational Procedural Rules for Arbitration and the Risks of Overregulation and Bureaucratization' (2015) 33 ASA Bulletin 327

Duggal K and Rangachari R, 'A Challenger Approaches: An Assessment of the Prague Rules on the Efficient Conduct of Proceedings in International Arbitration' (2020) 37 Journal of International Arbitration 27

Duggal KAN and Cai WW, *Principles of Evidence in Public International Law as Applied by Investor-State Tribunals: Burden and Standards of Proof* (Brill 2018)

Dundas H, 'Challenge to Arbitral Award and Survey of Scottish Arbitral Jurisprudence' (2017) 83 The International Journal of Arbitration, Mediation and Dispute Management 368

Ehle B and Furner C, 'Eyeopeners – The Enlightening Effect of Site Visits in Construction Disputes' (2018) 12 Dispute Resolution International 176

Ehrlich E, *Grundlegung Der Sociologie Des Rechts* (1913)

Ehrlich E, *Fundamental Principles of the Sociology of Law* (Walter L Moll tr, Routledge 2017)

Fellas J, 'Cross-Examination in International Arbitration' (2015) 254 New York Law Journal

Fellas J, 'Arbitrators' Questions: Can They Cross a Line?' [2019] New York Law Journal 8

Fernandez-Ballester MA and Arias Lozano D (eds), 'Interviewing and Preparing Witnesses for Testimony in International Arbitration Proceedings: The Quest for Developing Transnational Standards of Lawyers' Conduct', *Liber Amicorum Bernardo Cremades* (Wolters Kluwer España; La Ley 2010)

Ferrari F (ed.), 'The Rome I and Rome II Regulations in International Commercial Arbitration', *The Impact of EU Law on International Commercial Arbitration* (Juris 2017)

Ferrari F, Rosenfeld F and Czernich D (eds), *Due Process as a Limit to Discretion in International Commercial Arbitration* (Kluwer Law International 2020)

Fischer-Zernin V and Junker A, 'Between Scylla and Charybdis: Fact Gathering in German Arbitration' (1987) 4 Journal of International Arbitration 9

Flynn T, 'On "Borrowed Wits": A Proposed Rule for Attorney Depositions' (1993) 93 Columbia Law Review 1956

Foerste U, 'ZPO § 254' in Hans-Joachim Musielak and Wolfgang Voit (eds), *Zivilprozessordnung* (17th edn, Franz Vahlen 2020)

Franck TM and Cherkis LD, 'The Problem of Fact-Finding in International Disputes' 18 Case Western Reserve Law Review 1483

Freedman MH, 'Our Constitutionalized Adversary System' (1998) 1 Chapman Law Review 57

Frisch M, *Mein Name sei Gantenbein* (Fischer Taschenbuch Verlag 1964)

Gabriel S, 'Dealing With "Challenged Documents"' [2011] ASA Bulletin 823

Gaillard E, 'Transnational Law: A Legal System or a Method of Decision Making?' (2001) 17 Arbitration International 59

Gaillard E, *Legal Theory of International Arbitration* (Martinus Nijhoff Publishers 2010)

Gaillard E, 'International Arbitration as a Transnational System of Justice' in AJ van den Berg (ed.), *Arbitration: The Next Fifty Years* (Kluwer Law International 2012)

Galgano F, 'The New Lex Mercatoria' (1995) 2 Annual Survey of International & Comparative Law 99

Gidi A, 'Transnational Rules of Civil Procedure - Study LXXVI – Doc 3 - Report on the First Session, Rome, 22 to 26 May 2000'

Gidi A, 'Transnational Rules of Civil Procedure - Study LXXVI – Doc 6 - Report on the Second Session, Rome, 2 to 6 July 2001'

Gillies P and Selvadurai N, 'Reasoned Awards: How Extensive Must the Reasoning Be?' (2008) 74 Arbitration 125

Giovannini T, 'Chapter 8: Ex Officio Powers to Investigate: When Do Arbitrators Cross the Line?' in Michael E Schneider, Bernd Ehle and Domitille Baizeau (eds), *Stories from the Hearing Room: Experience from Arbitral Practice: Essays in Honour of Michael E. Schneider* (Kluwer Law International 2015)

Glenn HP, 'Comparative Legal Families and Comparative Legal Traditions' in Mathias Reimann and Reinhard Zimmermann (eds), *The Oxford Handbook of Comparative Law* (2nd edn, Oxford University Press 2019)

Goldman B, 'The Applicable Law: General Principles of Law - the Lex Mercatoria' in Julian Lew (ed.), *Contemporary Problems in International Arbitration* (Springer Netherlands 1987)

Goldstein AK, 'A Short History of Discovery' (1981) 10 Anglo-American Law Review 257

Gomille C, *Informationsproblem Und Wahrheitspflicht: Ein Aufklärungsmodell Für Den Zivilprozess* (Mohr Siebeck 2016)

Goode RM, McKendrick E and Kronke H, *Transnational Commercial Law: Text, Cases, and Materials* (2nd edn, Oxford University Press 2015)

Greger R, *Beweis Und Wahrscheinlichkeit: D. Beweiskriterium Im Allgemeinen u. Bei d. Sogen. Beweiserleichterungen* (Heymann 1978)

Greineder D, 'The Limitations of Soft Law Instruments and Good Practice Protocols in International Commercial Arbitration' (2018) 36 ASA Bulletin 907

Groz P, 'Chapter 16, Part II: Commentary on the WIPO Arbitration and WIPO Expedited Arbitration Rules, WIPO Arbitration Rules, Article 56 / WIPO Expedited Arbitration Rules, Article 50 [Witnesses]' in Manuel Arroyo (ed.), *Arbitration in Switzerland: The Practitioner's Guide* (2nd edn, Kluwer Law International 2018)

Halbfass W and Held K, 'Historisches Wörterbuch Der Philosophie, Evidenz' (Schwabe Verlag 2017)

Harbst R, *A Counsel's Guide to Examining and Preparing Witnesses in International Arbitration* (Kluwer Law International 2015)

Harbst R, 'Die (Un-)Verlässlichkeit Der Zeugenerinnerung' 2021 SchiedsVZ 49

Hart HLA, 'Positivism and the Separation of Law and Morals' (1958) 71 Harvard Law Review 593

Hart HLA, *The Concept of Law* (3rd edn, Oxford University Press 2012)

Hazard G, *Ethics in the Practice of Law* (Yale University Press 1978)

Hazard G and Taruffo M, *Transnational Rules of Civil Procedure - Study LXXVI – Doc 2 - Preliminary Draft Rules and Comments* (Joint American Law Institute / UNIDROIT Working Group 2000)

Hendricks VF and Vestergaard M, *Reality Lost: Markets of Attention, Misinformation and Manipulation* (Springer International Publishing 2019)

Henninger M, *Die Frage der Beweislast im Rahmen des UN-Kaufrechts: zugleich eine rechtsvergleichende Grundlagenstudie zur Beweislast* (utzverlag 1995)

Herlitz GN, 'The Meaning of the Term "Prima Facie"' (1994) 55 Louisiana Law Review 391

Ho HL, 'The Judicial Duty to Give Reasons' (2000) 20 Legal Studies 42

Hoffmann H and Maurer F, 'Voraussetzungen Und Grenzen Anwaltlicher Zeugenvorbereitung' [2018] NJW 257

Hulbert RW, 'When the Theory Doesn't Fit the Facts' (2009) 25 Arbitration International 157

Hunter R, 'Arbitration in Germany - A Common Law Perspective' [2003] SchiedsVZ 155

ICC Commission on Arbitration and ADR, *Report on the Accuracy of Fact Witness Memory in International Arbitration* (2020)

ICC Commission on Arbitration and ADR Task Force, *Report on Reducing Time and Costs in Arbitration* (2nd edn, ICC 2012)

ICDR, *Practice Notes for Respondents* (2015)

ICSID, 'Production of Documents - ICSID Convention Arbitration' <https://icsid.worldbank.org/en/Pages/process/Production-of-Documents.aspx>

Imbrechts L, 'Truth in Arbitration. What Instruments Do Parties Have in Search for the Truth?' in Luc Demeyere (ed.), *Do Arbitral Awards Reveal the Truth?: Reports from the Third Joint Cepani-Nai Colloquium Held on March 21, 2019* (2019)

Jackson RM, *Review of Civil Litigation Costs: Preliminary Report* (The Stationary Office 2010)

Jaffe ME, Dulani JT and Stute DJ, 'Burden of Proof as a Prerequisite to Document Production Under the 2010 IBA Rules: An Obituary' (2017) 1 Transnational Dispute Management

James F, 'Burdens of Proof' (1961) 47 Virginia Law Review 51

Jessup P, *Transnational Law* (Yale University Press 1956)

Jeuland E, 'Standard of Proof in France' in Luboš Tichý (ed.), *Standard of Proof in Europe* (Mohr Siebeck 2019)

Jolowicz JA, 'The Woolf Report and the Adversary System' (1996) 15 Civil Justice Quarterly 198

Jolowicz JA, 'Adversarial and Inquisitorial Models of Civil Procedure' [2003] International & Comparative Law Quarterly 281

Kagan RA, *Adversarial Legalism: The American Way of Law* (Harvard University Press 2001)

Kant I, *Kritik Der Urtheilskraft, Akademieausgabe Band 5* (1781)

Kant I, *Critique of Judgement* (Nicholas Walker tr, Oxford University Press 2007)

Karton J, 'International Arbitration as Comparative Law in Action' (2020) 2020 Journal of Dispute Resolution 293

Kaufmann-Kohler G, 'The Arbitrator and the Law: Does He/She Know It? Apply It? How? And a Few More Questions' 21 Arbitration International 2005

Kaufmann-Kohler G and Bärtsch P, 'Discovery in International Arbitration: How Much Is Too Much?' [2004] SchiedsVZ 13

Kazazi M, *Burden of Proof and Related Issues: A Study on Evidence Before International Tribunals* (Kluwer Law International 1996)

Keane A and McKeown P, *The Modern Law of Evidence* (13th edn, Oxford University Press 2020)

Kelsen H, *Introduction to the Problems of Legal Theory: A Translation of the First Edition of the Reine Rechtslehre or Pure Theory of Law* (Bonnie Litschewski Paulson and Stanley L Paulson trs, Clarendon Press; Oxford University Press 1992)

Kelsen H, *Reine Rechtslehre: Einleitung in Die Rechtswissenschaftliche Problematik (Studienausgabe Der 1. Auflage 1934)* (Matthias Jestaedt ed, Mohr Siebeck GmbH & Co KG 2008)

Khodykin R, Mulcahy C and Fletcher N, *A Guide to the IBA Rules on the Taking of Evidence in International Arbitration* (Oxford University Press 2019)

Kim HC, 'Burden of Proof and the Prima Facie Case: The Evolving History and Its Applications in the WTO Jurisprudence' (2007) 6 Richmond Journal of Global Law & Business 245

Kläsener AC and Dolgorukow A, 'Die Überarbeitung Der IBA-Regeln Zur Beweisaufnahme in Der Internationalen Schiedsgerichtsbarkeit' [2010] SchiedsVZ 302

Kotuby CT and Sobota LA, *General Principles of Law and International Due Process: Principles and Norms Applicable in Transnational Disputes*, vol 6 (Oxford University Press 2017)

Kröll S, 'Kröll: Die Schiedsrechtliche Rechtsprechung 2016 Und 2017' [2018] SchiedsVZ 201

Kühn W and Walter K, 'The Burden of Substantiation and Proof in Continental European Civil Procedure and the Taking of Evidence in International Arbitration' (*Best Lawyers Legal Insights*, 31 August 2017)

Kuitkowski D, 'The Law Applicable to Privilege Claims in International Arbitration' (2015) 32 Journal of International Arbitration 65

Lacy JW and Stark CEL, 'The Neuroscience of Memory: Implications for the Courtroom' (2013) 14 Nature Reviews Neuroscience 649

Landolt P, 'Arbitrators' Initiatives to Obtain Factual and Legal Evidence' (2012) 28 Arbitration International 173

Laumen H-W, 'Die "Beweiserleichterung Bis Zur Beweislastumkehr" - Ein Beweisrechtliches Phänomen' [2002] NJW 3739

Lemes SMF, 'Arbitragem. Princípios Jurídicos Fundamentais. Direito Brasileiro E Comparado' (1991) VII Revista de la Corte Espanhola de Arbitraje 31

Lugani, 'BGB § 1666' in Franz Jürgen Säcker and others (eds), *Münchener Kommentar zum BGB* (8th edn, Beck 2020)

Luhmann N, *Das Recht der Gesellschaft* (1st (reprint), Suhrkamp 2002)

Luhmann N, *Introduction to Systems Theory* (Dirk Baecker ed, Peter Gilgen tr, Polity 2013)

Mackie D, 'Discovery in Commercial Litigation' in AAS Zuckerman and Ross Cranston (eds), *Reform of Civil Procedure: Essays on 'Access to Justice'* (Clarendon Press; Oxford University Press 1995)

Marcoux J-M, 'Transnational Public Policy as an International Practice in Investment Arbitration' (2019) 10 Journal of International Dispute Settlement 496

Martínez-Fraga PJ, *The American Influence on International Commercial Arbitration: Doctrinal Developments and Discovery Methods* (Cambridge University Press 2009)

Mavromati C, 'The Laws Applicable to the Taking and Evaluation of Evidence in International Arbitration' in Franco Ferrari, Stefan Kröll and Chrysoula Mavromati (eds), *Conflict of Laws in International Arbitration* (2019)

McAlpine A, 'Hot-Tubbing in International Arbitration: Do We Need a Protocol?' (*Practical Law Arbitration Blog*, 1 May 2018)

Meier P and Jocham F, 'Die Rentabilitätsvermutung – Aufwendung Als Schaden?' [2018] JuS 1168

Meyer O, 'Time to Take a Closer Look: Privilege in International Arbitration' (2007) 24 Journal of International Arbitration 365

Miller AR, 'Confidentiality, Protective Orders, and Public Access to the Courts' (1991) Vol. 105 Harvard Law Review 427

Moses ML, *The Principles and Practice of International Commercial Arbitration* (2nd edn, Cambridge University Press 2012)

Mubiala M, 'The ICC's Interplay with UN Fact-Finding Commissions in Preliminary Examinations' in Morten Bergsmo and Carsten Stahn (eds), *Quality Control in Preliminary Examination: Volume 2*

Münch, 'ZPO § 1042' in Thomas Rauscher and Wolfgang Krüger (eds), *Münchener Kommentar zur ZPO* (5th edn, C.H. Beck 2017)

Münch, 'ZPO § 1049' in Thomas Rauscher and Wolfgang Krüger (eds), *Münchener Kommentar zur ZPO* (5th edn, C.H. Beck 2017)

Murphy JB, *Philosophy of Positive Law - Foundations of Juris: Foundations of Jurisprudence* (Yale University Press 2012)

Musielak H-J and Stadler M, *Grundfragen Des Beweisrechts: Beweisaufnahme, Beweiswürdigung, Beweislast* (C.H. Beck 1984)

Nairn K, Nelson TG and Henin P, 'Evidentiary Inferences: Do Choice of Law and Seat Make a Difference?' in Neil Kaplan and Michael J Moser (eds), *Jurisdiction, Admissibility and Choice of Law in International Arbitration: Liber Amicorum Michael Pryles* (Wolters Kluwer 2018)

New Developments in International Commercial Arbitration and Nessi S, 'Expert Witness: Role and Independence' in Christoph Müller, Sébastien Besson and Antonio Rigozzi (eds), *New Developments in International Commercial Arbitration 2016* (Schulthess 2016)

Ng I, 'Rethinking Counsel Ethics in International Arbitration' (*Kluwer Arbitration Blog*, 12 December 2019)

Nicolson D, 'Truth, Reason and Justice: Epistemology and Politics in Evidence Disclosure' (1994) 57 The Modern Law Review 726

Nicolson D, 'Taking Epistemology Seriously: "Truth, Reason and Justice" Revisited' (2013) 17 The International Journal of Evidence & Proof 1

Nottage LR, 'The Procedural Lex Mercatoria: The Past, Present and Future of International Commercial Arbitration' [2006] Sydney Law School Research Paper No. 06/51

Oetiker C, 'Witnesses before the International Arbitral Tribunal' (2007) 25 ASA Bulletin 253

'Official Records of Parliament (Bundestag Drucksache) 13/5274'

Oldham D, 'Case Management - a Judge's Perspective' (2009) 3 Journal of Personal Injury Law 212

O'Malley ND, *Rules of Evidence in International Arbitration: An Annotated Guide* (Informa 2012)

O'Malley ND, *Rules of Evidence in International Arbitration: An Annotated Guide* (2nd edn, Informa law from Routledge 2019)

Oswal A, 'Limiting Judicial Intervention (Another Pro International Arbitration Step)' (*Young ICCA Blog*, 19 November 2014)

Pargendler M, 'The Rise and Decline of Legal Families' (2012) 60 American Journal of Comparative Law 1043

Pattenden R, 'The Risk of Non-Persuasion in Civil Trials: The Case Against a Floating Standard of Proof' (1988) Civil Justice Quarterly 220

Pauker SA, 'Substance and Procedure in International Arbitration' (2020) 36 Arbitration International 1

Paulsson J, *The Idea of Arbitration* (Oxford University Press 2013)

Paulsson J and Petrochilos G, *Revision of the UNCITRAL Arbitration Rules* (2006)

Paulsson J and Petrochilos G, *UNCITRAL Arbitration* (Wolters Kluwer 2018)

Paulus CG, 'Die Beweisvereitelung in der Struktur des deutschen Zivilprozesses - rechtsgeschichtliche und rechtsvergleichende Betrachtungen' (1997) 197 Archiv für die civilistische Praxis 136

Pereira de Souza Fleury R, 'Do Arbitrators Have an Ex Officio Duty/Right to Self-Investigate Corruption?' (25 November 2015)

Pilkov K, 'Evidence in International Arbitration: Criteria for Admission and Evaluation' (2014) 80 Arbitration. The International Journal of Arbitration, Mediation and Dispute Management 147

Pinsolle P, 'The Status of Vacated Awards in France: The Cour de Cassation Decision in Putrabali' (2008) 24 Arbitration International 277

Poli R, 'Standard of Proof in Italy' in Luboš Tichý (ed.), *Standard of Proof in Europe* (Mohr Siebeck 2019)

Polkinghorne M and Rosenberg CB, 'The Adverse Inference in ICSID Practice' (2015) 30 ICSID Review 741

Pound R, 'Law in Books and Law in Action' (1910) 44 American Law Review 12

'Prague Rules Draft: Inquisitorial Rules on the Taking of Evidence in International Arbitration (The Prague Rules)'

Priestley LJ, 'Transnational Civil Procedure - Fact Pleading v. Notice Pleading: Its Significance in the Development of Evidence Harmonising Transnational Civil Procedure: The ALI/UNIDROIT Principles and Rules: II - Stages and Problem Areas in Transnational Litigation' [2001] Uniform Law Review 841

Prütting H, *Gegenwartsprobleme Der Beweislast: Eine Untersuchung Moderner Beweislasttheorien Und Ihrer Anwendung Insbesondere Im Arbeitsrecht* (C.H. Beck 1983)

Prütting H, 'ZPO § 284' in Thomas Rauscher and Wolfgang Krüger (eds), *Münchener Kommentar zur ZPO* (6th edn, C.H. Beck 2020)

Prütting H, 'ZPO § 286' in Thomas Rauscher and Wolfgang Krüger (eds), *Münchener Kommentar zur ZPO* (6th edn, C.H. Beck 2020)

Prütting H, 'ZPO § 287' in Thomas Rauscher and Wolfgang Krüger (eds), *Münchener Kommentar zur ZPO* (6th edn, C.H. Beck 2020)

Prütting H, 'ZPO § 294' in Thomas Rauscher and Wolfgang Krüger (eds), *Münchener Kommentar zur ZPO* (6th edn, C.H. Beck 2020)

Queen Mary University of London, 'International Arbitration Survey 2008: Corporate Attitudes: Recognition and Enforcement of Foreign Awards'

Queen Mary University of London, 'International Arbitration Survey 2015: Improvements and Innovations in International Arbitration'

Rajah VK, 'W(h)Ither Adversarial Commercial Dispute Resolution?' (2017) 33 Arbitration International 17

Ramina de Lucca R, 'Iura Novit Curia Nas Arbitragens' (2016) XIII Revista Brasileira de Arbitragem 54

Rauscher T, 'Einleitung' in Wolfgang Krüger and Thomas Rauscher (eds), *Münchener Kommentar zur Zivilprozessordnung* (6th edn, C.H. Beck 2020)

Redfern A and others, 'Special Section: The Standards and Burden of Proof in International Arbitration' (1994) 10 Arbitration International 317

Redish MH, 'The Allocation of Discovery Costs and the Foundations of Modern Procedure' in FH Buckley (ed.), *The American Illness: Essays on the Rule of Law* (Yale University Press 2013)

Redmayne M, 'Objective Probability and the Assessment of Evidence' (2003) 2 Law, Probability and Risk 275

Reimer N, 'Anscheinsbeweis Und Parteivernehmung Im Verkehrszivilprozess' [2018] NZV 258

Rieder MS, 'Sekundäre Darlegungs- Und Beweislast Im Schiedsverfahren?' in Rolf A Schütze and Reinhold Geimer (eds), *Fairness, Justice, Equity: Festschrift Für Reinhold Geimer Zum 80. Geburtstag* (C.H. Beck 2017)

Riofrio Piché M and de Sampaio Jalles S, 'The Armesto Schedule: A Step Further to a More Efficient Document Production' (*Kluwer Arbitration Blog*, 4 April 2020)

Riofrio Piché M and de Sampaio Jalles S, 'Model Procedural Order - Armesto Schedule' < http://arbitrationblog.kluwerarbitration.com/wp-content/uploads/sites/48/2020/04/Procedural-Order-Model.pdf >

Rosenberg L, *Die Beweislast: auf der Grundlage des Bürgerlichen Gesetzbuchs und der Zivilprozessordnung* (5th edn, Beck 1965)

Sachs K, 'Use of Documents and Document Discovery: „Fishing Expeditions" versus Transparency and Burden of Proof' [2003] SchiedsVZ 193

Sachs K and Niedermaier T, 'Die Rechtsfigur Der "Adverse Inferences" in Der Internationalen Schiedsgerichtsbarkeit' in Walter Eberl (ed.), *Beweis im Schiedsverfahren* (Nomos 2015)

Sachs K and Schmidt-Ahrendts N, 'Protocol on Expert Teaming: A New Approach to Expert Evidence' [2011] ICCA Congress Series No 15 135

Scheffer T, *Adversarial Case-Making: An Ethnography of English Crown Court Procedure* (Brill 2010)

Schlaepfer AV, 'The Burden of Proof in International Arbitration' (2015) 18 Legitimacy: Myths, Realities, Challenges, ICCA Congress Series 127

Schmidt-Ahrendts N and de Jong A, 'The "Right" Place of Arbitration: How Germany Might Profit from Brexit' [2018] SchiedsVZ 281

Schreiber K, 'ZPO § 415' in Thomas Rauscher and Wolfgang Krüger (eds), *Münchener Kommentar zur ZPO* (6th edn, C.H. Beck 2020)

Schroeder H-P, *Die Lex Mercatoria Arbitralis: Strukturelle Transnationalität Und Transnationale Rechtsstrukturen Im Recht Der Internationalen Schiedsgerichtsbarkeit* (Sellier European Law Publishers 2007)

Schütze RA, Brödermann E and Theune U (eds), *Institutionelle Schiedsgerichtsbarkeit: Kommentar* (3rd edn, Carl Heymanns Verlag 2018)

Schwab, 'BGB § 812' in Franz Jürgen Säcker and others (eds), *Münchener Kommentar zum BGB* (8th edn, C.H. Beck 2020)

Schweizer M, *Beweiswürdigung und Beweismaß: Rationalität und Intuition* (Mohr Siebeck 2015)

Seitz E, *Fact-Gathering in Patent Infringement Cases: Rule 34 Discovery and the Saisie-Contrefaçon* (Nomos 2009)

Shafir E and LeBoeuf RA, 'Rationality' [2002] Annual Review of Psychology 491

Sharpe JK, 'Drawing Adverse Inferences from the Non-Production of Evidence' (2006) 22 Arbitration International 549

Sindler M and Wüstemann T, 'Privilege Across Borders in Arbitration: Multi- Jurisdictional Nightmare or Storm in a Teacup' (2005) 23 ASA Bulletin 610

Sklansky DA, 'Anti-Inquisitorialism' 122 Harvard Law Review 1637

Skontzos AV, 'The Burden and Standard of Proof in Model International Procedural Law: Dealing with the Burden and Standard of Proof in International Disputes' (2018) 23 Uniform Law Review 569

Smith JM and Nadeau-Séguin S, 'The Illusive Standard of Proof in International Commercial Arbitration' (2015) Volume 18 Legitimacy: Myths, Realities, Challenges, ICCA Congress Series 134

Solis MJ, 'Adverse Inferences in Investor–State Arbitration' (2018) 34 Arbitration International 79

Sourgens FG, Duggal KAN and Laird IA, *Evidence in International Investment Arbitration* (Oxford University Press 2018)

Spellenberg, 'Rom I-VO Art. 18' in Franz Jürgen Säcker and others (eds), *Münchener Kommentar zum BGB* (8th edn, C.H. Beck 2021)

Spigelman JJ, 'Judicial Accountability and Performance Indicators' (2002) 21(Jan) Civil Justice Quarterly 18

Statistisches Bundesamt (Federal Statistical Office), 'Publikation: Justiz & Rechtspflege; Zivilgerichte (2019)'

'Status: UNCITRAL Model Law on International Commercial Arbitration (1985), with Amendments as Adopted in 2006' <https://uncitral.un.org/en/texts/arbitration/modellaw/commercial_arbitration/status>

Steffen R, 'The Prima Facie Case in Non-Jury Trials' (1959) 27 The University of Chicago Law Review 94

Stephen JF, *Digest of the Law of Evidence* (12th edn, Macmillan & Co 1936)

Strong SI, 'Reasoned Awards in International Commercial Arbitration' (*Kluwer Arbitration Blog*, 19 February 2016)

Stürner R, 'Transnational Rules of Civil Procedure - Study LXXVI – Doc 1 - Feasibility Study'

Stürner R, 'The Principles of Transnational Civil Procedure, An Introduction to Their Basic Conceptions' (2005) 69 Rabels Zeitschrift für ausländisches und internationales Privatrecht 201

Taslitz AE, 'Temporal Adversarialism, Criminal Justice, and the Rehnquist Court: The Sluggish Life of Political Factfinding' (2005) 94 The Georgetown Law Review 1589

Terrell T, *Terrell on the Law of Patents* (19th edn, Sweet & Maxwell 2019)

Teubner G, 'Introduction to Autopoietic Law', *Autopoietic Law: A New Approach to Law and Society* (de Gruyter 1988)

Teubner G, 'Globale Bukowina' (1996) 15 Rechtshistorisches Journal 255

Teubner G, 'Global Bukowina' in Gunther Teubner (ed.), *Global Law Without a State* (Dartmouth 1997)

Teubner G, 'Global Private Regimes: Neo-Spontaneous Law and Dual Constitution of Autonomous Sectors in World Society?' Paper prepared for the Workshop on 'Globalisation and Public Governance' 17/18 March 2000 European University Institute, Florence

Thibaut J, Walker L and Lind EA, 'Adversary Presentation and Bias in Legal Decision-making' (1972) 86 Harvard Law Review 386

Thöne M, 'Delocalisation in International Commercial Arbitration' [2016] SchiedsVZ 257

Tichý L, 'Standard of Proof' in Luboš Tichý (ed.), *Standard of Proof in Europe* (Mohr Siebeck 2019)

'Trans-Lex Principle XIII.3.2 - Determination of Rules of Procedure, < https://Www.Trans-Lex.Org/969030 > '

Trittmann R, 'The Interplay Between Procedural and Substantive Law in International Arbitration' [2016] SchiedsVZ 7

Trittmann R and Schardt R, '§2.05' in Gustav Flecke-Giammarco (ed.), *The DIS Arbitration Rules - an Article-by-Article Commentary.* (Kluwer Law International 2020)

Tsatsos DA, 'Burden of Proof in Investment Treaty Arbitration: Shifting?' [2009] Humboldt Forum Recht 91

Turner JM, 'Prague Rules… or Does It?' (*Practical Law Arbitration Blog*, 23 April 2019)

Twining W, 'Some Scepticism about Some Scepticisms' (1984) 11 Journal of Law and Society 137

Twining W, *Rethinking Evidence: Exploratory Essays* (2nd ed, Cambridge University Press 2006)

UNCITRAL, 'A/Cn.9/669 - Report of Working Group II (Arbitration and Conciliation) on the Work of Its Fiftieth Session'

'UNCITRAL Notes on Organizing Arbitral Proceedings'

Underwood RH, 'The Limits of Cross-Examination' (1997) 21 American Journal of Trial Advocacy 113

Varga I, *Beweiserhebung in transatlantischen Schiedsverfahren: eine Suche nach Kompromissen zwischen deutscher und US-amerikanischer Beweisrechtstradition* (Nomos 2006)

Vienna International Arbitral Centre of the Austrian Federal Economic Chamber (ed.), 'Article 29 [Establishing the Facts of the Case]', *Handbook Vienna Rules: A Practitioner's Guide* (2014)

Vos G (ed.), *Civil Procedure ('White Book')* (Sweet & Maxwell; Thomson Reuters 2019)

Wagoner DE, 'U.S. Court Demonstrates Pro-Enforcement Bias in a Comprehensive Review of a Cietac Award Under the New York Convention' (1998) 16 ASA Bulletin 289

Waincymer J, *Procedure and Evidence in International Arbitration* (Kluwer Law International 2012)

Walter MJ, 'Controlling the Witness on Cross-Examination' in John G Koeltl and John Kiernan (eds), *The Litigation Manual - Trial* (American Bar Association (Section of Litigation) 1999)

Weinberger O, *Rechtslogik* (2nd edn, Duncker & Humblot 1989)

Wexler S and Effron J, 'Burden of Proof and Cause of Action' (1983) 29 McGill Law Journal 468
Wietzorek M, 'Luxembourg's Rejection of the French Approach to the Recognition and Enforcement of Annulled Arbitral Awards' (2019) 37 ASA Bulletin 316
Wigmore JH, 'The History of the Hearsay Rule' (1904) 17 Harvard Law Review 437
Wigmore JH, *A Treatise on the System of Evidence in Trials at Common Law* (3rd edn, Little, Brown 1940)
Windau B, 'Das Googelnde Gericht – Ist Der Beibringungsgrundsatz Noch Zeitgemäß?' [2018] NJOZ 761
Wong D, 'Summary of Young-OGEMID Symposium No. 3: "Prove It! Evidence in International Arbitration (6–15 June 2016)"' (2017) 14 Transnational Dispute Management 20
Woolf H and Campbell-Holt C, *The Pursuit of Justice* (Oxford University Press 2008)
Yuen P and Townsend M, 'New CIArb Guidelines on Witness Conferencing' (*Kluwer Arbitration Blog*, 25 April 2019)
Zaki AG, 'Adversarial or Inquisitorial: Which Approach Is Closer to Arbitration?' [2006] Thesis Submitted to the The American University in Cairo
Zimmermann W, 'ZPO § 402' in Thomas Rauscher and Wolfgang Krüger (eds), *Münchener Kommentar zur ZPO* (6th edn, C.H. Beck 2020)
Zimmermann W, 'ZPO § 412' in Thomas Rauscher and Wolfgang Krüger (eds), *Münchener Kommentar zur ZPO* (6th edn, C.H. Beck 2020)
Zumbansen P, 'Transnational Legal Pluralism' (2010) 1 Transnational Legal Theory 141

Table of Cases

Australia

Bremer Handelsgesellschaft mbH v Westzucker GmbH (No 2) [1981] 2 Lloyd's Rep 130, 172

Austria

OGH, Judgment of 6 February 2018 18 ONc 4/17h, 49

Finland

FinnHEMS Oy v Skärgårdshavets Helikoptertjänst AB, Court of Appeal of Helsinki, Case No S 18/854, Decision No 626 of 23 May 2019 ITA Arbitration Report, 55

England and Wales

Bank Mellat v Helliniki Techniki SA [1984] QB 291, 26
Bond v Dunster Properties Ltd & Ors [2011] EWCA Civ 455, 100
BPE Solicitors & Anor v Hughes-Holland (in substitution for Gabriel) (Rev 1) [2017] UKSC 21, 51
Compagnie Financiere du Pacifique v Peruvian Guano Co [1882] 11 QBD 55, 73
Dallah Real Estate and Tourism Holding Company v The Ministry of Religious Affairs, Government of Pakistan [2010] 3 WLR 1472, 23
Fiona Trust & Holding Corporation Ors v Privalov Ors [2010] EWHC (Comm) 3199, 108, 149, 150, 155, 156
H & Ors (minors), Re [2000] UKHL 16, 155
Holcombe v Hewson [1810] 2 Camp, KB 391, 74
In re B (Children) (FC) [2008] UKHL 35, 155
Jafari-Fini v Skillglass Ltd [2007] EWCA Civ 261, 156
Miller v Minister of Pensions [1947] 62 All ER 372, 154
Post Office Counters Ltd v Mahida [2003] EWCA Civ 1583, 146, 169
Pyrrho Investments Limited, MWB Business Exchange Limited v MWB Property Limited, Rick Aspland-Robinson, Keval Pankhania, Richard Balfour-Lynn, Jagtar Singh [2016] EWHC 256 (Ch), 68, 76

France

Germany

Federal Constitutional Court

Federal Court of Justice

Courts of Appeal

International Court of Justice

Lebanon

Poland

Scotland

Singapore

Switzerland

United States

Table of Arbitral Awards and Decisions

Ad hoc arbitrations

Continental Transfert Technique Ltd v Federal Government of Nigeria, Ad Hoc Final Award of 14 August 2008 Arbitrator Intelligence Materials, 168
Glamis Gold Ltd v United States, UNCITRAL, Ad Hoc Final Award of 8 June 2009 ITA Board of Reporters, 78
Government of the State of Kuwait v The American Independent Oil Company (AMINOIL), Ad-Hoc Award of 24 May 1982 [1984] IX Ybk Comm Arb 71, 23
Himpurna California Energy Ltd v PT (Persero) Perusahaan Listruik Negara, Ad-Hoc Award of 4 May 1999 [2000] XXV Ybk Comm Arb 13, 162
Texaco Overseas Petroleum Company v The Government of the Libyan Arab Republic, Ad-Hoc Award of 19 January 1977 https://www.trans-lex.org/261700, 27

Arbitration Institute of the Stockholm Chamber of Commerce (SCC)

SCC Case No 2018/072, Final Award of 29 October 2019 [2020] XLV Ybk Comm Arb 1, 179

Court of Arbitration for Sport (CAS)

CAS Case No 1999/A/246, Award of 11 May 2000 2 Digest of CAS Awards II 1998-2000, Digest of CAS Awards Series Set 505, 145
CAS Case No 2000/A/274, Award of 19 October 2000 2 Digest of CAS Awards II 1998-2000, 105

International Centre for Settlement of Investment Disputes (ICSID)

Abaclat and Others v Argentine Republic, ICSID ARB/07/5 (formerly Giovanna a Beccara and Others v The Argentine Republic) Dissenting Opinion to Procedural Order No 15 of 20 November 2012, 136
Abaclat and Others v Argentine Republic, ICSID ARB/07/5 (formerly Giovanna a Beccara and Others v The Argentine Republic) Consent Award of 29 December 2016, 136

International Chamber of Commerce (ICC)

International Center for Dispute Resolution (ICDR)

Iran-United States Claims Tribunal (IUSCT)

Permanent Court of Arbitration (PCA)

Vienna International Arbitral Centre (VIAC)

Waren-Verein der Hamburger Börse (WVHB)

Index

INTERNATIONAL ARBITRATION LAW LIBRARY

1. Moshe Hirsch, *The Arbitration Mechanism of the International Center for the Settlement of Investment Disputes*, 1993 (ISBN 07-923-1993-1).
2. Aida B. Avanessian, *Iran-United States Claims Tribunal in Action*, 1993 (ISBN 18-533-3902-4).
3. Isaak I. Dore, *The UNCITRAL Framework for Arbitration in Contemporary Perspective*, 1993 (ISBN 18-533-3573-8).
4. Vesna Lazić, *Insolvency Proceedings and Commercial Arbitration*, 1998 (ISBN 90-411-1115-8).
5. Joachim Frick, *Arbitration in Complex International Contracts*, 2001 (ISBN 90-411-1662-1).
6. Katherine Lynch, *The Forces of Economic Globalization: Challenges to the Regime of International Commercial Arbitration*, 2003 (ISBN 90-411-1994-9).
7. Christoph Liebscher, *The Healthy Award: Challenge in International Commercial Arbitration*, 2003 (ISBN 90-411-2011-4).
8. Hamid G. Gharavi, *The International Effectiveness of the Annulment of an Arbitral Award*, 2003 (ISBN 90-411-1717-2).
9. Abdulhay Sayed, *Corruption in International Trade and Commercial Arbitration*, 2004 (ISBN 90-411-2236-2).
10. Gabrielle Kaufmann-Kohler & Thomas Schultz, *Online Dispute Resolution: Challenges for Contemporary Justice*, 2004 (ISBN 90-411-2318-0).
11. Christopher R. Drahozal & Richard W. Naimark (eds), *Towards a Science of International Arbitration: Collected Empirical Research*, 2005 (ISBN 90-411-2322-9).
12. Ali Yeşilirmak, *Provisional Measures in International Commercial Arbitration*, 2005 (ISBN 90-411-2353-9).
13. Christian Bühring-Uhle, *Arbitration and Mediation in International Business*, second revised edition, 2006 (ISBN 978-9-041-12256-8).
14. Bernard Hanotiau, *Complex Arbitrations: Multi-party, Multi-contract and Multi-issue – A Comparative Study*, Second Edition, 2020 (ISBN 978-94-035-1261-7).
15. Loukas A. Mistelis & Julian D.M. Lew (eds), *Pervasive Problems in International Arbitration*, 2006 (ISBN 978-9-041-12450-0).
16. Julian D.M. Lew & Loukas A. Mistelis (eds), *Arbitration Insights – Twenty Years of the Annual Lecture of the School of International Arbitration, Sponsored by Freshfields Bruckhaus Deringer*, 2006 (ISBN 978-9-041-12606-1).
17. Mark Kantor, *Valuation for Arbitration: Compensation Standards, Valuation Methods and Expert Evidence*, 2008 (ISBN 978-9-041-12735-8).
18. Christoph Brunner, *Force Majeure and Hardship under General Contract Principles: Exemption for Non-Performance in International Arbitration*, 2009 (ISBN 978-90-411-2792-1).

19. Loukas A. Mistelis & Stavros L. Brekoulakis (eds), *Arbitrability: International & Comparative Perspectives*, 2009 (ISBN 978-90-411-2730-3).
20. Sam Luttrell, *Bias Challenges in International Commercial Arbitration: The Need for a 'Real Danger' Test*, 2009 (ISBN 978-90-411-3191-1).
21. Monique Sasson, *Substantive Law in Investment Treaty Arbitration: The Unsettled Relationship Between International Law and Municipal Law*, Second Edition, 2017 (ISBN 978-90-411-6103-1).
22. Ileana M. Smeureanu, *Confidentiality in International Commercial Arbitration*, 2011 (ISBN 978-90-411-3226-0).
23. Won Kidane, *China-Africa Dispute Settlement: The Law, Economics and Culture of Arbitration*, 2011 (ISBN 978-90-411-3674-9).
24. Karel Daele, *Challenge and Disqualification of Arbitrators in International Arbitration*, 2012 (ISBN 978-90-411-3799-9).
25. Crina Baltag, *The Energy Charter Treaty: The Notion of Investor*, 2012 (ISBN 978-90-411-3428-8).
26. Alexandra Diehl, *The Core Standard of International Investment Protection: Fair and Equitable Treatment*, 2012 (ISBN 978-90-411-3869-9).
27. Manuel Indlekofer, *International Arbitration and the Permanent Court of Arbitration*, 2013 (ISBN 978-90-411-4766-0).
28. Günther J. Horvath & Stephan Wilske (eds), *Guerrilla Tactics in International Arbitration*, 2013 (ISBN 978-90-411-4002-9).
29. Albert Badia, *Piercing the Veil of State Enterprises in International Arbitration*, 2014 (ISBN 978-90-411-5162-9).
30. Nadja Erk, *Parallel Proceedings in International Arbitration: A Comparative European Perspective*, 2014 (ISBN 978-90-411-5264-0).
31. Simon Vorburger, *International Arbitration and Cross-Border Insolvency: Comparative Perspectives*, 2014 (ISBN 978-90-411-5419-4).
32. Ahmad Ali Ghouri, *Interaction and Conflict of Treaties in Investment Arbitration*, 2015 (ISBN 978-90-411-5417-0).
33. Reto Marghitola, *Document Production in International Arbitration*, 2015 (ISBN 978-90-411-5159-9).
34. Alfonso Gómez-Acebo, *Party-Appointed Arbitrators in International Commercial Arbitration*, 2016 (ISBN 978-90-411-6671-5).
35. Jonas von Goeler, *Third-Party Funding in International Arbitration and Its Impact on Procedure*, 2016 (ISBN 978-90-411-5015-8).
36. Dean Lewis, *The Interpretation and Uniformity of the UNCITRAL Model Law on International Commercial Arbitration: Focusing on Australia, Hong Kong and Singapore*, 2016 (ISBN 978-90-411-6700-2).
37. Stavros Brekoulakis, Julian D.M. Lew & Loukas Mistelis (eds), *The Evolution and Future of International Arbitration*, 2016 (ISBN 978-90-411-7004-0).
38. Rémy Gerbay, *The Functions of Arbitral Institutions*, 2016 (ISBN 978-90-411-6217-5).

39. Maximilian Clasmeier, *Arbitral Awards as Investments: Treaty Interpretation and the Dynamics of International Investment Law*, 2017 (ISBN 978-90-411-8357-6).
40. Tony Cole (ed.), *The Roles of Psychology in International Arbitration*, 2017 (ISBN 978-90-411-5921-2).
41. Pietro Ferrario, *The Adaptation of Long-Term Gas Sale Agreements by Arbitrators*, 2017 (ISBN 978-90-411-8232-6).
42. Jacob B. van de Velden, *Finality in Litigation: The Law and Practice of Preclusion – Res Judicata (Merger and Estoppel), Abuse of Process and Recognition of Foreign Judgments*, 2017 (ISBN 978-90-411-8342-2).
43. Dolores Bentolila, *Arbitrators as Lawmakers*, 2017 (ISBN 978-90-411-8354-5).
44. Giacomo Marchisio, *The Notion of Award in International Commercial Arbitration: A Comparative Analysis of French Law, English Law, and the UNCITRAL Model Law*, 2017 (ISBN 978-90-411-8391-0).
45. Csaba Kovács, *Attribution in International Investment Law*, 2018 (ISBN 978-90-411-9675-0).
46. Mary Mitsi, *The Decision-Making Process of Investor-State Arbitration Tribunals*, 2019 (ISBN 978-90-411-9600-2).
47. Ahmet Cemil Yıldırım, *Interpretation of Contracts in Comparative and Uniform Law*, 2019 (ISBN 978-94-035-1130-6).
48. Beata Gessel-Kalinowska vel Kalisz, *The Legal, Real and Converged Interest in Declaratory Relief*, 2019 (ISBN 978-94-035-1244-0).
49. Maximilian Pika, *Third-Party Effects of Arbitral Awards: Res Judicata Against Privies, Non-mutual Preclusion and Factual Effects*, 2019 (ISBN 978-94-035-1273-0).
50. Yulia Levashova, *The Right of States to Regulate in International Investment Law: The Search for Balance Between Public Interest and Fair and Equitable Treatment*, 2019 (ISBN 978-94-035-0931-0).
51. Flavia Marisi, *Environmental Interests in Investment Arbitration: Challenges and Directions*, 2020 (ISBN 978-94-035-1723-0).
52. Martina Magnarelli, *Privity of Contract in International Investment Arbitration: Original Sin or Useful Tool?*, 2020 (ISBN 978-94-035-2020-9).
53. Xu Qian, *Water Services Disputes in International Arbitration: Reconsidering the Nexus of Investment Protection, Environment, and Human Rights*, 2020 (ISBN 978-94-035-2203-6).
54. Nobumichi Teramura, Ex Aequo et Bono *as a Response to the 'Over-Judicialisation' of International Commercial Arbitration*, 2020 (ISBN 978-94-035-2073-5).
55. Bruno Guandalini, *Economic Analysis of the Arbitrator's Function*, 2020 (ISBN 978-94-035-2265-4).
56. Zena Prodromou, *The Public Order Exception in International Trade, Investment, Human Rights and Commercial Disputes*, 2020 (ISBN 978-94-035-2031-5).
57. Jürg Künzle, *Multiple Contracts and Coordination in International Construction Projects: A Swiss Law Analysis*, 2020 (ISBN 978-94-035-2024-7).

58. Cornel Marian, *The State's Power to Tax in the Investment Arbitration of Energy Disputes: Outer Limits and the Energy Charter Treaty*, 2020 (ISBN 978-94-035-1752-0).
59. Luke Nottage, Shahla Ali, Bruno Jetin & Nobumichi Teramura (eds.), *New Frontiers in Asia-Pacific International Arbitration and Dispute Resolution*, 2021 (ISBN 978-94-035-2855-7).
60. Eva Litina, *Theory, Law and Practice of Maritime Arbitration: The Case of International Contracts for the Carriage of Goods by Sea*, 2021 (ISBN 978-94-035-3035-2).
61. Franco Ferrari & Friedrich Rosenfeld (eds), *Autonomous Versus Domestic Concepts under the New York Convention*, 2021 (ISBN 978-94-035-3173-1).
62. Doğan Gültutan, *Moral Damages under International Investment Law: The Path Towards Convergence*, 2022 (ISBN 978-94-035-4025-2).
63. Simon Foote QC, *The Bona Fide Investor: Corporate Nationality and Treaty Shopping in Investment Treaty Law*, 2022 (ISBN 978-94-035-4185-3).
64. George A. Bermann, *Twilight Issues in International Arbitration*, 2023 (ISBN 978-94-035-1746-9).
65. Emmanuel O. Igbokwe, *Dealing with Bribery and Corruption in International Commercial Arbitration: To Probe or Not to Probe*, 2023 (ISBN 978-94-035-2066-7).
66. Peter Sester, *Contract Law in International Commercial Arbitration*, 2023 (ISBN 978-94-035-1036-1).
67. Julian Bickmann, *Fact-Finding in International Arbitration: The Emergence of a Transnational* Lex Evidentiae, 2023 (ISBN 978-94-035-1886-2).